HURON COUNTY LIBRARY

Date Due

D0931012

CANADIAN
SQUADRONS
IN
COASTAL COMMAND

Andrew Hendrie

Vanwell Publishing Limited

St. Catharines, Ontario

CANADIAN SQUADRONS IN COASTAL COMMAND

Andrew Hendrie

Vanwell Publishing Limited

St. Catharines, Ontario

Vanwell Publishing Limited
P.O.Box 2131
St. Catharines, ON L2R 7S2

Printed in Canada
99 98 97   1 2 3
Design Susan Nicholson

Canadian Cataloguing in Publication Data

Hendrie, Andrew
  Canadian Squadrons in Coastal Command

Includes bibliographical references and index.
ISBN 1-55125-038-1

1. Canada. Royal Canadian Air Force - History- World
War, 1939-1945. 2. World War, 1939-1945 - Aerial
operations, Canadian. I. Title.

D792.C2H45 1997   940.54'4971   C97-930356-7

Contents

Acknowledgements

In preparing this work I gained help from the Canadian High Commission, London, England and the National Archives of Canada.
Editors of the following publications kindly included requests on my behalf:
Intercom (Aircrew Association); *Air Force* (Canadian Air Force Association); *Maritime Patrol Aviation* (VP International); *The Calgary Herald, The Edmonton Journal, The Vancouver Sun, The Winnipeg Free Press, Telegraph-Journal* of New Brunswick, *The Telegram* in St. John's, Newfoundland; *The Chronicle-Herald* of Halifax, NS; *The Globe and Mail* of Toronto, *The Toronto Star, Ottawa Citizen, The Gazette* of Montreal; and in Saskatchewan, *The Leader Post.*
Many British and Canadian personnel, both aircrew and groundstaff who had served in Coastal Command, were kind enough to write to me. May I now thank for their help all those listed hereunder:
Adamson A.C. 10 sqdrn RCAF; Anderson E.J. 172 sqdrn RAF; Capt Ken Ashfield, DFC, FRMetS 415 sqdrn and 524 sqdrn; Attrill, Phil.J. 404 sqdrn.
Barcham, F/Lt L.J. DFC, RAF, 404 sqdrn; W/Cmdr G.C.C. Bartlett, AFC, RAF, 224 and 59 sqdrns; Bassett, F/Lt Peter RAF, 404 sqdrn; Bathgate, Roy, 407 sqdrn; Bayly, T. 413 sqdrn; Beaton, R. 407 sqdrn; Bennett, G. 413 sqdrn; Benton, R.J.; Birchall, A/Cmdre L.J. OBE, 413 sqdrn; Bishop, S/Ldr A.A. DFC, 423 sqdrn; Botham, A. 407 sqdrn; Burns F/O H.A. 162 sqdrn; Butler, S.DFC, 422 sqdrn.
Callaway, F/O B.C. 413 sqdrn; Campbell, F/O G.DFC, 162 sqdrn; Campbell, J.M. 413 sqdrn; Chadwick, F/Lt N.415 sqdrn; Cleaver, F/Lt W.C. 53 sqdrn; Clubb,G.W. 415 sqdrn; Cunningham, S/Ldr C.A. 202 and 423 sqdrns. Eadie, J.S. 422 sqdrn.
Flynn, F/Lt P. DFC, 404 sqdrn; Frizzle, J.R. G/Capt 422 and 423 sqdrns; Gatward, G/Capt K.DSO, DFC,* 404 sqdrn; Gavlas, Capt J. 407 sqdrn; Giles, L. 422 sqdrn; Gowans, S/Ldr J. DFC, 413 sqdrn; Graham, W/Cdr J.DFC 269 and 228 sqdrns; Greva, P. 423 sqdrn.
Hagley, J.H. 162 sqdrn; Harper, F/Lt C.M. 10 sqdrn; Harper, S. 407 sqdrn; Harvey, G/Capt N.T. 201 sqdrn; Hawkins, T. 407 and 500 sqdrns; Henderson, E. 407 sqdrn; Hennigar, M. 413 sqdrn; Hill, Mrs. Anne (407 sqdrn); Hiscox, E. 422 sqdrn.
Jamieson, F/Lt J. 10 sqdrn; Jamieson, L. 413 sqdrn; Jamieson, R. 162 sqdrn; Jewett, R. 407 sqdrn; Johansen, E. L/Col. 333 sqdrn; Johnson, D. 162 sqdrn;
Kendell, L/Col P.J. 407 sqdrn; Kitchen,W.C. 422 sqdrn; Labreque, Capt M. 404, 407, and 423 sqdrns;
Laughlin, F. 423 sqdrn; Lee, F/Lt M.D. 423 sqdrn; Logan, A.E. 407 and 422 sqdrns; Logan, J. 422 sqdrn; Logan N.J. 423 sqdrn; McBratney, G/Capt V.H.A. AFC, 413 sqdrn; McKeachie, J.G. 10 sqdrn; McRae, F/Lt J. DFC*, 162 sqdrn;
Maier, G.F. 422 sqdrn; Matheson, F/Lt S.E., DFC*, 162 sqdrn; Melatini, J.C. (407 sqdrn); Middlemiss,W. AFC, 407 sqdrn; Morton, W/O F. 422 sqdrn; Moyles, J. 422 sqdrn; Murray, L.R. 407 sqdrn;
Nespor, J.E. 422 sqdrn; Norquay, Dr. J.S. 415 and 423 sqdrns;
Page, F/Lt C. 404 sqdrn; Park, D.A.F. 422 sqdrn; Parrott,W.C. 407 sqdrn; Passmore, L. 407 sqdrn; Pettem, D.G. 10 sqdrn; Plant,Rev.R.C. 413 sqdrn; Pocknell, D. 423 sqdrn; Prest,J.(404 sqdrn);
Queau,H. 404 sqdrn;
Randall, G/Capt L.H. 413 sqdrn; Rankin, F/Lt J.P. 413 sqdrn; Reed, R.H. 10 and 162 sqdrns; Rump, A./Cmdre, F.J.W. CBE, 423 sqdrn; Scannell,J. 413 sqdrn; Sheardown, S/Ldr H. 423 sqdrn; Shulemson, F/Lt S. DSO,DFC, 404 sqdrn; Smith,W/O H. 413 sqdrn; Steed, R. 422 sqdrn; Stewart, J.C. 404 sqdrn; Stokes,R. 407 sqdrn; Symons, F/Lt J. DFC 404 sqdrn;
Taylor, S/Ldr C. DFC, 407 sqdrn;
Wales, F/O R. 162 sqdrn; Walker C.E. 162 sqdrn; Wells, F/O D. 413,422 sqdrns; White,G. 407 sqdrn; Williams, D. 10 sqdrn; Willis, G/Capt C.A. DFC, 404 sqdrn; Witney,B. 423 sqdrn; Woodnutt,E.C. 407 sqdrn; Wright, J.H. 423 sqdrn.

Introduction

A number of Canadians joined the Royal Air Force (RAF) before World War II to serve with RAF squadrons, some rising to take command of either RAF or RCAF squadrons.

During the war more Canadians joined the Allied services, and some RAF squadrons had as much as a third of their aircrew from Canada. The Canadian government, however, wished to have its own units, and the whole of its squadrons "Canadianized"; this was hardly achieved, and typically in Coastal Command, aircrews tended to be of mixed nationalities.

Six Royal Canadian Air Force (RCAF) squadrons were formed within Coastal Command during World War II while another Canadian squadron, No. 162, served on loan to the Command. For a brief, but notable, period, No. 10 Squadron RCAF came within the jurisdiction of the Command.

The Canadians successfully operated many types of aircraft allocated to them, including Blenheims, Beaufighters, Hudsons, Hampdens, Wellingtons, Cansos, Catalinas, Sunderlands, and Albacores. Operations were flown over the North Atlantic, the English Channel, the North Sea and the Bay of Biscay. A detachment was made from No. 422 Squadron to Russia, and following the Japanese advance in the Far East, one of the Coastal squadrons, No. 413, was posted to Ceylon where it served with distinction.

The squadrons remaining with Coastal Command operated along the coast controlled by the enemy from Norway to France. Such operations included not only reconnaissance (recce), but also many shipping strikes to Norway, The Netherlands, and the French coast. In such strikes, two of the Canadian squadrons in only two raids, suffered some of the highest losses of the war, 54%. Those losses were incurred by 404's Beaufighters in a Norge strike, and 407's Hudsons off the Dutch coast. The Canadians rightly gained many awards, including a VC to F/Lt David Hornell of No. 162 Squadron.

In this project I have endeavoured to cover every recorded success achieved by the Canadian squadrons listed in Coastal Command's record for World War II. That record includes attacks on U-boats and on enemy-controlled ships. I am aware that some are still controversial despite checking against other published sources. In addition to references in the script, I have listed these successes in the appendices.

There were many variations in marks of aircraft, their armament, and ultimate range; the representative data given in the appendices for the machines operated by the Canadians should thus be considered only as a guide.

Andrew Hendrie
Storrington, 1995

Chapter 1

Early History

On 25 August 1914 following the outbreak of war in Europe, a Canadian Cabinet Minister (Col. Sam Hughes) cabled the British Secretary of War, Lord Kitchener, to ask if the service of aviators was required. The British War Office replied that six expert aviators could be taken immediately and possibly more later.

The first Canadian military aviator casualty was Lt W.F. Sharpe, who was killed at Shoreham, West Sussex, on 4 February 1915 while on a training flight.

In April 1915 the British Admiralty arranged with the Canadian Naval Service in Ottawa to enrol applicants for the Royal Naval Air Service (RNAS), which effectively became the precursor of the RAF's Coastal Command. At that time, candidates for both the RNAS and the Royal Flying Corps (RFC), needed to obtain a pilot's certificate at their own expense before being commissioned.

One of the first U-boat successes was achieved by Flight Sub-Lieutenants N.A. Magor and C.E.S. Lusk in a flying-boat escorted by a Sopwith Camel fighter on 22 September 1917, when they released two 230 pound bombs scoring direct hits on UC-72, which sank.[1]

The RNAS was amalgamated with the RFC to form the Royal Air Force on 1 April 1918, and an agreement was reached the following month for a nucleus of Canadian squadrons to be formed within the RAF. A detachment of the Canadian Air Force (CAF) was initially made at Halton for the training of mechanics to serve with the two intended "all Canadian" squadrons within the RAF.

By the time of the Armistice on 11 November 1918, about 22,000 Canadians had served in the RNAS, RFC, and RAF, with a loss of 1,563 lives. The first CAF units formed in the United Kingdom were Numbers 81 and 123 Squadrons RAF. Formed at Upper Heyford (Northamptonshire, England) with all Canadian personnel on 20 November 1918, they became the nucleus of a Canadian Air Force as Numbers 1 and 2 Squadrons CAF. An Order in Council on 18 February 1920 authorized the formation. A further Order in Council followed on 30 June for a provisional establishment of 5,245 officers and men.

The King approved the CAF being designated "The Royal Canadian Air Force" on 15 February 1923, and the RCAF came to adopt the RAF-style pattern uniform, badges, and ensign. The former CAF's motto, *Sic Itur ad Astra* was replaced by *Per Ardua ad Astra* (through travail to the stars) and on 1 April 1924, the King's Regulations and Orders for the RCAF came into effect.

The date 1 April 1924 is considered the birthday of the RCAF, and its Silver

Jubilee was commemorated by the publication of an RCAF Logbook.[2] By 31 August 1939, the RCAF had a total strength of 4,061 officers and airmen and 270 aircraft, including 19 Hurricane fighters. Following the British Prime Minister's declaration of war against Germany on 3 September 1939, Canada declared war on 10 September.

The British Commonwealth Air Training Program

On 17 December 1939 the United Kingdom, Canada, Australia, and New Zealand signed an agreement in Ottawa to produce 520 pilots in Elementary Flying Training (EFT); 544 pilots in service training, plus 340 observers and 580 wireless operator/air gunners every four weeks.[3]

By the end of 1939, the total strength of the RCAF had doubled, to 8,287 officers and men with fourteen operational squadrons in Canada.

An overseas headquarters for the RCAF was formed in London at Lincoln's Inn on 1 January 1940. The RCAF's first overseas unit—No. 110 Squadron, augmented by No. 2 Squadron personnel, and the first of forty-eight RCAF squadrons to serve overseas in World War II—disembarked at Liverpool, England on 25 February 1940.

In June, the King approved the RCAF ensign, an adaptation of the RAF ensign where the maple leaf replaced the red circle roundel.

The following year, on 7 January, a supplementary agreement was signed in London to provide for twenty-five RCAF squadrons to be formed in the United Kingdom in the next eighteen months in addition to the three squadrons which had already arrived in the United Kingdom.

To avoid confusion with RAF units, RCAF overseas squadrons were re-numbered in the 400 series, No. 110 thus became 400, No. 1 became 401, etc.

The RCAF squadrons in 1941 which came under Coastal Command control were numbered 404, 407, 413, and 415. All these RCAF Coastal squadrons were formed within a period of four months from April to August.

Canada declared war on Japan on 7 December 1941 and by the end of that year there were twenty-five RCAF squadrons in the UK, with fourteen operational; and sixteen in Canada.

During 1942, two more RCAF squadrons were formed within Coastal Command: RAF No. 422 Squadron in April, and No. 423 in May. They completed the RCAF squadrons in the 400 series to operate with Coastal Command. Later, No. 162 Squadron RCAF became attached to Coastal Command on loan, and No. 10 Squadron RCAF came under Coastal Command control in a brief but notable episode.

Coastal Command: Early History

A naval wing of the Royal Flying Corps was established in 1912. On the outbreak of war with Germany in 1914, it came under the administration of the Admiralty. By August 1915 the RNAS in a directive from the Admiralty was to be considered in all respects an integral part of the Royal Navy.[4]

With the formation of the Royal Air Force in 1918, 2500 aircraft and 55,000 men were transferred from the Royal Navy to the newly formed service. The Portsmouth Group of the RNAS became

No. 10 Group RAF under Wing Commander A.W. Bigsworth, CMG, DSO, AFC. No. 10 Group RAF, consisted, by 1920, of one operational and one cadre squadron at Lee-on-Solent with headquarters in London and a designated "Coastal Area".[5]

In 1924 the Air Ministry became responsible for the provision of aircraft for the Royal Navy, but the Admiralty was to specify the types and numbers of aircraft for its Fleet Air Arm (FAA).[6]

A radical change in organisation of the Royal Air Force occurred in 1936 when units were formed according to function rather than area.[7] Thus was Coastal Command formed in July 1936 with Air Marshal Sir Arthur Longmore, KCB, DSO, as Air Officer Commanding-in-Chief.

Sir Arthur had served as Air Officer Commanding Coastal Area since October 1934. He was a true pioneer in maritime aviation, having been one of four Naval officers, who in 1911, took up flying at Short Bros, Eastchurch, initially with land aircraft and then with seaplanes.[8]

In December 1937 there was a directive since the Air Ministry that the primary role of Coastal Command in the event of war would be trade protection, reconnaissance and co-operation with the Royal Navy. The Joint Staff decided that since there would probably be unrestricted submarine and air attacks, convoys should be introduced. However, the navy considered surface warship raiders to be the major threat, and thus it was decided that the main task of Coastal Command would be to cover the North Sea exit routes.

Coastal Command's estimated aircraft requirements for these tasks were:

In home waters
  convoy escorts, 165;
  North Sea recces, 84;
  North Sea area, 24;
  northern patrols, 18;
Abroad:
  at Atlantic convoy assembly points, 48.

Thus a total of 339 aircraft were required, but by 1 April 1939 only 194 were available.[9]

Area Combined Headquarters (ACHQ) were to be formed within the Coastal Command at Plymouth (No. 15 Group), Chatham (No. 16 Group), and Rosyth (No. 18 Group). At the time of the Munich crisis in 1938 however only No. 16 had been organised, and at the outbreak of war in September 1939 only Rosyth was considered "properly installed".[10]

Air Marshal Philip B. Joubert de la Ferté succeeded Sir Arthur Longmore in August 1936, and in turn relinquished command the following August when Air Marshal Sir Frederick Bowhill became AOCinC Coastal Command. Sir Frederick moved his headquarters to Northwood in the summer of 1939.

With the British having naval superiority and Coastal Command looked upon as an adjunct to the Navy, the Command came third after Fighter and Bomber Command in respect of priorities.

By 3 September 1939, of the eleven general reconnaissance squadrons equipped with the short-range Anson, only No. 224 had converted to Hudsons. The Ansons were unable to cover the North Sea from Britain to Norway, so these patrols were undertaken by the Hudsons and the two Sunderland flying-boat squadrons, Nos. 204 and 228.

In 1939 No. 15 Group was responsible for the Western Approaches from Devonport to Belfast; No. 16 Group, the sea area from Portland to the Humber; and No. 18 Group, the northern areas around the Hebrides, Orkneys, and Shetlands plus the potential exits for surface raiders in the North Sea. This latter duty required patrols from the United Kingdom to the Norwegian coast.[11]

Winston Churchill had asked the Admiralty to move control of the Western Approaches from Plymouth to the Clyde in August 1940 and on 7 February 1941 a move was made from Plymouth to Liverpool.[12] A new RAF Coastal Command group was formed at Plymouth, No. 19, initially under Air Vice Marshal Geoffrey R. Bromet.

At Liverpool the ACHQ were located in Derby House which, despite its unostentatious frontage, became virtually the nerve centre for what came to be known as The Battle of the Atlantic.

It was manned by both Navy and Air Force officers and had a direct link to Churchill himself. Some business was undertaken at the nearby Royal Liver Building, including convoy conferences where masters of the merchant ships were briefed and had the opportunity to voice their views, such as in this writer's brief experience, requesting more aircraft escorts.

While the initial prime duty for Coastal Command was considered by the Admiralty to be covering exit routes of surface raiders; the role of Coastal Command extended to shipping strikes, air-sea rescue, meteorological flights, photo-reconnaissance, and special operations, i.e "cloak and dagger trips." The prime duties, however, were to be anti-submarine warfare involving convoy escorts, sweeps, searches, and strikes.

In addition to bases in mainland Britain, Coastal Command had others in Northern Ireland, the Hebrides, the Shetland Isles, Iceland, Gibraltar, and the Azores. Detachments were also sent to Russia and West Africa; at the latter a new headquarters was ultimately set up outside Coastal Command's control.

There was flexibility in the deployment of squadrons, and not infrequently, units were posted from one group to another; thus Bomber Command "borrowed" Coastal Command units for such as the second "thousand bomber raid" while, on occasions, a Bomber Command squadron was loaned to Coastal. There were further interchanges of Coastal squadrons, when, for example, No. 413 was sent to the Far East or conversely, when maritime squadron No. 230 was recalled from the Far East.

Other countries besides Canada provided units for the Coastal Command, including Australia, the United States of America, (USN and USAF), The Netherlands, Czechoslovakia, Norway and Poland. The RAF's own squadrons included personnel from many countries also.

Armament in Coastal Command

The 100 pound anti-submarine bomb dating back to 1925 came into service in 1931 but proved to be virtually useless against U-boats. There was also a 250 pound anti-submarine bomb which needed to detonate within 6 feet of a pressure hull to cause any serious damage.[13]

The first depth charge, a 450 pound Mark VII became available to the Command in July 1940. The Mark VII was effectively a modified naval depth charges, and could only be carried by the flying boats.[14] In the spring of 1941 a 250 pound depth charge was introduced, the amatol-filled Mark VIII.[15]

By the end of April 1942 the Mark XI torpex-filled, 250 pound depth charge, considered to be 30-50% more powerful than the amatol-filled charge was coming into service. A further improvement was the introduction of a pistol which could cause detonation from 20-25 feet compared with the earlier one of 34 feet. A number of figures are given for the lethal range of a 250 pound depth charge and they vary from 10-11 feet,[16] to 33 feet.[17] A more likely figure is perhaps 19 feet.[18]

The number of depth charges carried by aircraft varied according to the type of aircraft and its intended endurance, but typical loads would have been four DCs for Hudsons and eight DCs for Sunderlands.

A crucial factor for aircraft attacking U-boats was the forward firing guns, and initially, the Command's aircraft were sadly lacking; as late as 1942-43, some squadrons were endeavouring to improve such armament on their own initiative; for example No. 500 adding a .5 Browning to Hudsons.[19] Hudsons had just two fixed .303 Brownings in the nose, and Sunderlands only one, out of its initial total of seven machine guns. Later, Sunderlands had four fixed guns in the nose in addition to those in the front turret plus possibly some additional manual ones fitted in some squadrons. With the emphasis given by the Command to machine guns rather than cannon, its aircraft were generally at a disadvantage in terms of range against both enemy aircraft and U-boats. The enemy, both German and Italian, were using cannon in their

aircraft and submarines. Letters from former air gunners to the author indicate that at least one Hudson had a cannon fitted, albeit firing aft; the record number of machine guns fitted to a Hudson was eleven or twelve, while for the Sunderland, up to twenty-one! These figures, however, were for aircraft in the Far East and Pacific areas, although by June 1944, some Sunderlands were operating over the Bay of Biscay with eighteen guns, including some 0.5s.

By 1943 Hudsons with Nos. 48 and 608 Squadrons were being fitted with rockets, and in the summer of 1943 those two squadrons claimed U-boats sunk by rocket projectiles. Beaufighters and other types of aircraft were also being fitted with rockets and were to prove an effective weapon against surface vessels in addition to U-boats.[20] Retro-fired rockets were fitted to some Catalinas operated by the USN within Coastal Command control in conjunction with MAD gear (Magnetic Anomaly Detection) which proved effective in the conditions prevailing in the Straits of Gibraltar.[21]

It is noteworthy that the two aircraft to gain a special mention and with respect, in the German U-boat diaries are the Sunderland and Beaufighter when they were operating over the Bay of Biscay.[22]

The First Canadian Squadron Formed within Coastal Command

In World War II the first Canadian maritime squadron to be formed within RAF Coastal Command was No. 404, and designated "Coastal Fighter" with initially Bristol Blenheim aircraft. Authority for the formation was given by HQ Coastal Command on 15 April 1941, and subsequently eighteen Blenheims were delivered to Thorney Island from Nos. 38, 272, and 603 Squadrons on 4 May. S/Ldr Patrick H. Woodruff arrived to command No. 404 (RCAF) Squadron. S/Ldr Woodruff flew to Catfoss in Z6181 to obtain the syllabus of his aircrew; the strength of the squadron was to be sixty-six including ten pilots, two observers, six wireless operator-air gunners, and ground staff.

The unit was posted to Castletown, Caithness, in Scotland, in June and thirteen of their aircraft, Mark I and Mark IV Blenheims were flown there on the 20th. Essential service equipment was ferried in Handley-Page Harrows. An experienced Blenheim pilot, ex-248 Squadron, L/Lt E.H. McHardy, DFC, RAF, a New Zealander, joined the squadron in July as 'B' Flight Commander.

No. 404 became operational on 22 September 1941 when four convoy escorts were flown. In the same month, 2-gun turrets were being installed in their Blenheims.

A prelude to impending Norwegian patrols was a lecture given by Capt Lund of the Norwegian section of the Air Ministry on 3 October to the pilots and observers; later that month B Flight was detached to Sumburgh, in the Shetlands, with the remainder of the squadron going to Dyce, near Aberdeen. The prospect of No. 404 taking long-range fighter patrols was discussed by the CO with W/Cmdr Devitt.

The first action against the enemy occurred on 16 October 1941, when an enemy convoy of merchant vessels escorted by a destroyer was sighted near Haugesund, Norway by Z6313. The Blenheim was crewed by Sgts Bell, Matkin, and Mullen, who machine-gunned two merchant vessels, but there was return fire from the destroyer and the shore.

The squadron's first casualties were Sgts Barber, Shaw, and Gillam, who were believed to have crashed in the sea off Lerwick while returning from a convoy patrol on 19 October in Z5753. Further losses were suffered on 1 November when two aircraft collided, resulting in three crew being killed and two injured, and on the 5th, L9337 was missing from a recce being flown off the Norwegian coast.

Possibly the first success against the enemy shipping was by S/Ldr McHardy who, while on patrol south of Stadtlandet on 19 November, attacked two ships and a D/F station. No. 404 Squadron was credited with damaging the merchant vessel *Mars*, of 699 tons.[23]

No. 404 (RCAF) Squadron in the Shetland Isles

A month later No. 404 Squadron moved from Dyce to Sumburgh and on 11-12 December took part in a combined operation escorting commando and naval vessels to Vaagso Island, south of Stadtlandet, Norway. This operation was aborted when the Navy was unable to locate the objective, but a further attempt was to follow. On 18 December W/Cmdr Woodruff while flying T/404 Z5753 fifty miles east of Sumburgh, intercepted a JU88. The enemy aircraft was then 200 yards away and at 200 feet altitude. W/Cmdr Woodruff made a diving quarter attack from 700 ft. The JU88 turned sharply to starboard and was climbing for cloud cover, but a 3-second burst from the Blenheim's guns resulted in thick, white smoke from both the JU88's engines. There was continuous return fire from the enemy, and Sgt Sims the observer, was wounded in the leg by bullet splinters. The only damage to the Blenheim was caused by bullets through the starboard wing, the nose, and a tire. P/O Matthews was the Blenheim's air gunner.

Vaagso and Lofoten Islands Operations

The Vaagso raid which had earlier been aborted was arranged as a diversion from what was to be a major assault on the Lofoten Islands, the latter commanded by R/Admiral Hamilton in the cruiser HMS *Arethusa* supported by destroyers, corvettes, minesweepers, and auxiliary vessels sailing on 21 December from Scapa Flow. The major force lacked fighter cover, and the Admiral decided to withdraw, but not before some landings had been made, and prisoners captured, and also some small enemy craft. The Vaagso task force commanded by R/Admiral Burrough in HMS Kenya was successful, with landing parties achieving their objectives and with about 16,000 tons of enemy-controlled shipping sunk.

The naval historian Capt Roskill states that the enemy air attacks were beaten off by Coastal Command long-range fighters, and this is endorsed by 404's record.[24] Eleven aircrews were at Wick on the 24th in preparation for the raid, but extended servicing aid to two other squadrons, Nos. 236 and 248.

As part of the Vaagso operation, B/404 Blenheim Z6181 was airborne at 0640 hrs on 27 December 1941, crewed by Sgts McCutcheon, Cleaver and Cruickshanks. During their six-hour flight they successfully engaged three ME109 fighters and claimed one probable and one possible.

This engagement was apparently with another 404 squadron Blenheim flown by P/O Pierce.

The Formation of No. 407 (Demon) Squadron

Thirty-three men, an adjutant, and a commanding officer were allocated a hangar partially wrecked by enemy action but with some of the roof remaining and some offices usable. Such were the beginnings of one of the most successful Coastal Command squadrons. Its aircrew proved to be some of the most courageous, and they were supported by a dedicated ground staff.

No. 407 (RCAF) Squadron was officially formed on 8 May 1941 at RAF Thorney Island, although the CO, S/Ldr H.M. Styles, an Englishman and commissioned in the RAF, did not arrive until the 20th. Until electric light and telephones were installed in the hangar offices, two offices in Station HQ were used.

Initially, the squadron was to receive Blenheims, but at the end of May was informed that Lockheed Hudsons were to be allocated. Thus on 1 June, twenty key maintenance personnel were attached to No. 206 Squadron RAF to gain experience with Hudsons; meanwhile, wireless operator-air gunners (Wop/AGs) arrived from another Hudson-equipped squadron, No. 500 RAF. They included Sgts Lees, Herbert, Wallis, Hawkins, and Lewis.

Of this period, one of those Wop/AGs, Trevor Hawkins, writes:

> I was a pre-war regular RAF having served variously on Ansons and Blenheims. I was posted on to 500 squadron at Detling and Bircham Newton about July/August 1940 to

serve on Ansons. Early in 1941 they started to convert to Blenheims but half of us were sent to Thorney Island in May 1941 to help form 407 on Blenheims.

By 11 June, No. 407 had on charge a dual Blenheim Mark I plus a solo Hudson and three Blenheim Mark IVs. Hudson Vs had been intended and three of these were delivered by the Air Transport Auxiliary (ATA) on 13 June.

The first "operational" trip was to escort a captured Heinkel 115 to Lizard Point, Cornwall and was undertaken by Sgt Ross with Sgt Moss as navigator and F/Sgt Ainley as wireless operator.

Two engineers from the company which produced engines for Mark V Hudson aircraft, Pratt & Whitney, arrived on 1 July at Thorney Island, but the same day, No. 407 received orders to move to North Coates on the east coast by 11 June.

No. 407 Squadron's First Shipping Strikes

Four Hudsons were flown to North Coates on 2 July, where W/Cmdr Styles reported to the Station CO G/Capt Mason. Coastal Command was adept in moving its squadrons, often at quite short notice; No. 407 was to experience a number of moves but always with good grace.

At North Coates on 1 September 1941, the unit became operational, and on 6 September undertook one of the many shipping strikes which were to become a feature of 407's record. In this strike Hudsons "L" and "E" were on a Rover patrol from Terschelling to Borkum. A merchant vessel of 1000-1500 tons was attacked with four 250 pound SAP bombs from 50 feet altitude with an 11-second delay, and in Terschelling harbour another

small ship in a similar manner; a true precursor of 407's "mast height" shipping strikes.

Their CO, W/Cmdr Styles, (one of many Coastal Command squadron commanders who "led from the front") while on a similar Rover patrol from Terschelling to Borkum, bombed a merchant vessel from a Hudson AM556 when six miles north of Borkum on 7 September.

There were further strikes on shipping by 407's Hudsons in September concluding with F/Lt Anderson on the 30th claiming a direct hit on a 1000 ton merchant vessel, between the funnel and bridge, which started a fire. The ship was one of a convoy of twelve sailing seven miles NW of Ameland with five escort vessels. Anderson was flying in K/407 AM626, which returned at 2330 hrs.

The squadron's first anti-shipping success recognised in the Command's post-war record was the sinking of a 100 ton dredger, *Hamm* 109, off Terschelling on 13 October.[25] This was followed by damage to *Braheholm*, a merchant vessel of 5,676 tons off the Dutch coast on 1 November during a Rover patrol, of which Trevor Hawkins gives this account:

> Four crews including Monty Styles were out in our respective sectors of the Dutch coast from Ijmuiden to the Heligoland Bight. The other three crews saw nothing, but I had the good fortune to find on ASV a stationary convoy just off Borkum. We attacked what we estimated to be a 6000 tonner from below mast height. There was a lot of flak, principally light stuff; we had caught them sleeping. We cleared the convoy, climbed to about 2-3000 feet to allow me to get off a sighting report and weather state, also

convoy details; then back to deck to return about 2140 hrs at Donna Nook, our satellite airfield, and were transported back to North Coates in the inevitable little Hillman 5cwt pick-up truck. Meanwhile Peter Lewis who was acting squadron CO in the absence of Monty who was still out, is reputed to have called his own and seven other crews to the ops room for briefing, after which he climbed onto a table and said, "You know what to do, do it," and marched off to the crew room and away. That was typical of the man.

Monty was driving back from Donna Nook just as Red Frazer was taking off for "our" convoy. Red was followed by Don Moss, Peter Lewis, Jimmy Codville, Roly Dann, Dale Cowperthwaite, Lucky Cooper and Bill Shankland in that order. Don Moss was first at the convoy, attacking a 7000 ton tanker, unfortunately he had to belly-land at base but without casualties. Peter Lewis attacked a 4000 tonner a few minutes later; but by this time the convoy had woken up and the flak was getting thick. Jimmy Codville was next into an 800 tonner followed closely by Dale Cowperthwaite taking on a 5000 ton merchantman. Lucky Cooper followed with a 3000 tonner and last came Bill Shankland who took on a 6500 ton merchantman. All the ships were seen to have suffered hits by the attacking crews or the crews going in or coming out. Bill lost his port engine through cannon fire, but was unable to feather the prop but was able to fly back to Donna Nook.

As soon as Monty got back to North Coates he decided to lay on another strike. We were given another aircraft and were airborne again at 0120 hrs on 2 November. Peter Lewis landed at about 0120 hrs, refuelled, rearmed and was off again at about 0320 hrs. The second strike was away before all the first were back. This time we took on a 7000 tonner from deck level, and she was seen to be hit close to the aft mast and steam bursting from amidships. About 45 minutes later, Peter attacked another 6000 tonner from deck level and a red glow was seen just after the bombs were released. Wally Creedon, who had not been out before, attacked the same convoy from sea level and two direct hits were seen and it was believed his blew up as the whole sky was lit up. Eight ships were attacked that night.

The following evening of 2 November, two aircraft were out on a Rover. Jimmy Codville attacked a 1500 ton ship in a seven-ship convoy; Red Frazer took on a 7000 ton tanker and in both attacks hits were seen.

It was as a result of these attacks that Lional Shapiro of the *Montreal Gazette* gave us the name "The Demon Squadron." For all this effort the only award was a DSO to Monty, which being the gentleman he was, said that it was not his but the Squadron's.

A Joint Operation With No. 86 Squadron Beauforts

On 11 November there was a joint operation for No. 407 Squadron Hudsons with Beauforts of No. 86 Squadron. W/Cmdr Styles reported attacking a 900 ton tanker; another Hudson captain in M/407, F/Lt Davy, claimed no result. Nevertheless, an auxiliary vessel of 190 tons, the Vios IV, which was sunk off Ijmuiden, was credited to 407.[26]

Some Canadians had sailed from Halifax in the Louis Pasteur for Gourock, Scotland, arriving there on 13 November. They included Stan Harper, an airframe mechanic who joined the squadron at North Coates on the 19th. Of the Atlantic crossing he recorded:

> The night of November 8th was very, very rough. Just as we settled in our bunks, there was a loud bang and the lights went out. Everyone jumped to the conclusion that we were hit by a torpedo but it was only a beer barrel that had broken through a wooden wall...the next morning we went on deck and found sand boxes, rafts and lifeboats all smashed.

On arriving at North Coates he recorded:

> This is a very wet and miserable place. The food is terrible and we are staying in an old wireless station called Tetney Beam. We are about 13 miles from Grimsby and as there are a lot of RAF ground crew, Bob and I usually spend our time in Grimsby. Every night now around seven, Jerry comes over and bombs Hull which is across the river.

On 9 December all of 407's aircraft were recalled due to poor weather conditions, but the following evening undertook a Rover patrol. Attacks on enemy shipping were made by W/Cmdr Styles, P/O Cooper, and P/O McCulloch. Credited to 407 and No. 217 Squadrons in a post-war list was the 8,777 ton merchant ship *Madrid* sunk off Ijmuiden.[27]

On 5 December Hudson AM556 was shot down over the North Sea, the crew including the twins Sgts Gerald and James Drennan. The squadron suffered another loss on the 22nd, when V/407 with Sgts Moss, Cluff, McDonald, and Herbert failed to return to base from a Rover patrol.

W/Cmdr Styles led a force of eleven Hudsons for a strike with take-off at 1630 hrs on 28 December. During the attack on a merchant vessel estimated to be of 5-6000 tons, L/407 AM838, crewed by P/O Cowperthwaite, F/Sgt Thesiger, and Sgts Middlemiss and Jones, the gunner, Sgt Middlemiss, was wounded in both feet. Bomb bursts were seen amidships of the vessel, and one on its port side.

This was 407's last major strike in 1941. Meanwhile, two other Canadian squadrons had been formed within Coastal Command.

Formation of the "Tusker" Squadron

No. 413 (RCAF) Squadron was officially formed on 1 July 1941 at Stranraer on Loch Ryan in Scotland. The unit's first CO, an Irishman commissioned in the RAF, was W/Cmdr V.H.A. McBratney. G/Capt McBratney in a letter to the author recalls:

> I reported to a dismal RAF camp at Stranraer on 1 July 1941, having come straight off flying Beaufighters in Yorkshire. I was a young acting Wing Commander and very keen!
> My first reaction to the posting was one of anger and was—"Who wants to fly a damn Catalina? Who wants to face the enemy in a Catalina? Why should an RAF officer be charged with forming an RCAF squadron?"
> In fact the whole project was an experimental "first." I was given eight

experienced operational aircrew, mainly from Coastal Command Blenheim squadrons, all ex land-plane trained to learn the web-foot art, and I believe, all volunteers. I was, for the record, an ex boat pilot (201 and 230 squadrons) and an ex Central Flying School instructor.

With regard to Stranraer as a base: There was nothing except a row of mooring buoys and a very small marine craft unit; no RAF quarters; we lived in requisitioned civil hotels and/or houses; no slipway for bringing boats ashore; no technical services of any kind and no personnel except myself; I was No.1!

There was a Station Commander; Wing Commander Laddie Cliff, an older guy and Coastal Command character and boat pilot who was established in a requisitioned building with a small administrative staff. He was a nice guy and very easy to get on with.

At my first briefing by Cliff on 1st July 1941, he advised me that three U.S. Naval Officer pilots were due to arrive on attachment to 413 squadron to assist in the training programme, also three USN technical staff of Flight Sergeant or Warrant Officer rank to accompany them. All these Americans were on the strength of the American embassy in London and were given the status Neutral Observer was the United States was not then at war. They wore their service uniforms and functioned exactly like members of the squadron. The arrangements worked very well and remained harmonious throughout.

The Americans arrived on 2nd July and our pupils, days later. The USN trio were headed by one Lieut. George Hughes and included two ensigns called Smith and...?

Hughes and I collected the first ever No. 413 squadron Catalina from RAF Maintenance Unit at Greenock on 4 July 1941. He flew as captain as I had never been in a Catalina prior to that date.

This flight in Catalina Z2141 on American Independence Day represented a series of "firsts." For W/Cmdr McBratney, his first wedding anniversary; for Hughes, the first time he had flown in the UK, the first time a neutral observer had flown as captain; and for 413, its first flight in its first aircraft.

What disturbed him was that the Catalinas supplied to 413 were without the standard RAF blind-flying panel, and thus had no artificial horizon. W/Cmdr McBratney corrected this omission by driving to the RAF maintenance depot at Carlisle and obtaining two of the required panels, together with a number of other items which 413 Squadron lacked.

On 5 July Catalinas W8428 and AH566 arrived from Greenock, and three days later W8419 was received from Bowmore. F/O Frazer, F/O Hirst, and P/O Baldry arrived on 9 July, together with F/Lt Gordon, who was attached to 413. Flying training commenced immediately, but of this G/Capt McBratney adds:

This was not "flying training" as such; these boys were experienced pilots, it was simply concerned with the handling of a flying-boat on water, and how to cope with the varying water surface conditions such as *glassy calm, rough seas, swell conditions, cross winds*; then the aerodynamic reactions by the aircraft to any of these varying conditions.

I thought the whole project was fallacious... the one thing a pilot requires to cope with the above is experience, and we could not endow him with this. It had been traditional for pilots to "serve their time" as 2nd pilots beside an old hand who knew it all, and who passed on his "art" over a period of time which could be as long as one or two years.

The Blenheim navigators accustomed to trips of up to five hours, were now on Catalinas, that were likely to be out of sight of land on trips of seldom less than 14-16 hours and requiring astro-navigation in which Blenheim navigators had not been trained. The Canadian F/Lt Gordon proved to be for W/Cmdr McBratney "an excellent specialist officer" who gave lectures to the pupils on VLR navigation.

By 16 July, two pilots, F/O Fowler and P/O Baldry, were able to fly "solo" on Catalinas, and two Wop/AGs, P/O Hoover and F/O Little, had reported for duty. Two days later S/Ldr Ware, DFC, and F/Lt Thomas. DFC, joined the squadron, S/Ldr Ware apparently as a Flight Commander.

With S/Ldr Ware, W/Cmdr McBratney; "drew up a flying training programme for the pilots, which he (S/Ldr Ware) supervised. The USA pilots did most of the conversion instruction up to solo flight, and the Flight Commander did the final pilot's flying tests."

W/Cmdr McBratney found the Catalina:

A simple unexciting aircraft to fly with no odd characteristics. It was the only boat I had ever flown that could be landed in a "full stall" attitude with nose up and tail down. It could also be landed in the flat, "skimming on"

attitude, semi-stalled, like the Sunderland. We taught both but did not recommend the former especially with any kind of load on. Towards the end of July, we had six of our "pupil" officer squadron members fully converted to 1st pilot (or captain) by day but had not started night flying.

On 28 July S/Ldr Ware, DFC was posted to special duties; another Catalina, AH556, arrived; and by the end of the month, No. 413 had five Catalinas serviceable.

Two officers from No. 5 Squadron RCAF were posted to 413 on 18 August, F/Lt Scott and F/Lt Randall. Both were later to take command of 413, in 1942 and 1943, respectively. W/Cmdr McBratney handed over to W/Cmdr Briese the following day. Of this occasion, G/Capt McBratney remarks:

W/Cmdr Briese—much older than myself, built on the large and heavy side, a quiet, pleasant type. Shortly after that I left with the job half done! I was posted to command No. 120 Liberator B.24 Squadron, on formation at Nutts Corner....while at Nutts Corner I learned two items of sad news re No. 413 Squadron.

First they had a fatal accident during night-flying practice at Stranraer in which an American Lieut Eldred (instructor) and Flying Officer Fowler were killed. Then later I learned that Wing Commander Briese and crew were lost on the squadron's very first operational trip—I believe a survey of some sort in the region of the Norwegian coast. This brought to mind a remark made by me to Briese that, in my opinion, the Norwegian coast was a graveyard for RAF aircraft as the Huns had a ME 109 wing at Bergen and that aircraft should enter that area in conditions of heavy cloud cover or darkness. With regard to the two night-flying casualties; Lieut Eldred was a specially nice officer [who] came later as No. 4 USN officer. Flying Officer Fowler, DFC, was a very experienced flyer on Blenheims.

Of the crash involving F/O Fowler it was at about 2250 hrs on 23 August when the weather was considered fit for local flying. Catalina AM556 crashed during a night take-off. Killed were F/O Hirst, F/O Fowler, Sgt Cody, RCAF wireless operator, and AC O'Brien, a fitter IIE. Missing were Ensign D.A. Eldred, USN, and injured, A.C. Muir, F/Mechanic, and Sgt Scroggs, Wop/AG. The body of F/O Fowler was recovered the following day. A funeral was conducted at Stranraer cemetery on 27 August for the four men killed in the crash: the American Ens Eldred, F/O Fowler from New Zealand, the Canadian Sgt Cody, and AC O'Brien, although Eldred's body was not recovered until 10 September from Loch Ryan. On 5 September F/O Frazer flew to Bowmore in W8426 with F/O Hill to install an ASV beacon. Later in the war, Bowmore, Isle of Islay, became a base for another RCAF squadron, No. 422.[28] A USN XPB2Y flyingboat which had arrived from Argentia on 15 September, was inspected by officers from Coastal Command HQ the following day. It left for Argentia on the 28th. About this time, Coastal Command was investigating various areas as potential bases for flyingboats, and on 19 September F/Lt Furman flew Catalina 8434 to Queensferry prior to taking W/Cmdr Briese to Sullom Voe in the Shetlands (he returned the following day). F/Lt Thomas took the CinC Western

Approaches with G/Capt Revington to Reykjavik in AM561 on the 26th.

F/Lt Hunter (perhaps the one later to serve with 422 Squadron), flew the Crown Film Unit to Lough Foyle, Northern Ireland, on 28 September. Although not stated in 413's record, this was possibly in connection with the production of the official film Coastal Command which was to involve squadrons, OTUs, and many types of aircraft, including Sunderlands, Catalinas, Beaufighters, Beauforts and Hudsons, plus, it is understood, the cruiser HMS Jamaica standing in as a "pocket battleship."

One of 413's Catalinas, AH569, co-operated with Beaufighters from 143 Squadron on 10 October, perhaps as part of the filming.

No. 413 Squadron Moves to Sullom Voe.

On 2 October two Sunderlands from 201 Squadron took on an advance party of twenty men of 413 Squadron to Sullom Voe. The CO, W/Cmdr Briese, flew with three Catalinas captained by F/Lt Thomas, F/Lt Meikle, and F/O Naish. All the crews were ordered to fly round the Shetland Isles and undertake practice firing and release DCs. Three days later, S/Ldr Gibbs arrived with three more Catalinas W8428, AH566, and W8419 from Stranraer; the main party left by rail and boat from Stranraer to reach Sullom Voe on 9 October.

What appears to have been 413's first operational sortie was undertaken by F/Lt Thomas, who flew Catalina AH561 on 6 October to escort a tanker. The ship did not sail, and F/Lt Thomas was recalled. The following day, however, he had a trip of eight hours in the same aircraft to escort

Olaf Fostenes, a ship which was sunk a year later by U-380 when in convoy ON129.[29]

There were a series of convoy escorts, including HX153 from Halifax, Nova Scotia, by F/O Frazer in W8428 on 16 October and F/O Naish in AH569 with convoy ON26.

As conditions for night landings were unsuitable, the Catalinas had to be recalled. On 21 October, F/Lt Thomas was airborne at 0405 hrs to escort another Halifax convoy, HX154, which was met at 0810 hrs in position 5814N 1154W. It comprised 46 merchantmen and five escort vessels, including three destroyers, and was heading east at 9 knots. The Catalina received a message from the Senior Naval Officer (SNO) to give to the Commander-in-Chief of the Western Approaches and to the Naval Officer in charge at Oban on returning to base. On that same day the AOC of No. 18 Group RAF arrived at Sullom Voe. He was AVM Marix, an AOC who quite exceptionally flew on a shipping strike later that month in Hudson G/220 to Alesund.[30]

The loss of his successor, W/Cmdr Briese, as recalled by G/Capt McBratney, occurred on 22 October in Catalina AH566 when captained by a Canadian, P/O C.C. Proby, on a recce of the Tromso area. In the crew were P/O W.J. Hoover, Sgts. K.C. Lowry, W.H. Martin, L.J. Harris, R.E. Austin, and airmen A.H. Agus, T.H. Atkins, and W. Benson.

On 31 October F/Lt Meikle and P/O Rumbald escorted convoy SN83A but met a mine-laying force of three merchantmen with four destroyers and a cruiser. A large area of floating mines which appeared to be German was marked out with flame floats.

F/O Baldry in Catalina W8422 was on an A/S patrol on 3 November co-operating with "Force RA". He was airborne from Sullom Voe at 0627 hrs and met the battleship HMS *King George V* with its three-destroyer escort in position 5909N 0432W when the ships were steaming south-west at 25 knots. At 0830 hrs they were joined by a fighter escort. F/O Baldry left the ships at 1500 hrs after signalling HMS *King George V* and, due to bad weather at Sullom Voe, touched down at Invergordon on the Cromarty Firth.

Icing Conditions and Catalina AH569

On 7 November P/O Naish was detailed for a "Sentry 2" patrol and was airborne at 1700 hrs in Catalina AH569. At 1730 hrs he set course for position 6343N 0007W but just over an hour later there was severe icing. Windows were frozen up and he was unable to see ahead, and the elevators were affected. At position 6218N 0003W, course was altered westwards to avoid icing from cloud seen northwards. More cloud was encountered and a further southwards alteration was made. At 1910 hrs P/O Naish signalled base that he was returning due to icing-up of his aircraft and headed for the Butt of Lewis. Having failed to contact base, a bearing was obtained from Stranraer. A signal was received from No. 15 Group for the Catalina to land at Invergordon. At 2250 hrs a bearing was obtained from Dyce near Aberdeen when Naish thought he might be over the Orkneys, and he altered course for Invergordon. On failing to identify the coast, a W/T fix was obtained and course was altered to Stranraer which had proved to be one of only two stations from which bearings could be obtained.

Naish's position was pin-pointed over Lough Neagh at 0025 hrs and a bearing was obtained from Stranraer. Twenty-five minutes later a gap in the clouds enabled Naish to descend, after flying at altitudes between 9000 and 13,000 feet with both elevators and windscreen iced-up. The temperature in the Catalina was so low that hot tea froze in seconds, and the second pilot was suffering from badly frozen fingers, though he was wearing gloves. The weather improved enough for P/O Naish to go down to 2000 feet. The elevator became easier and funtioned normally at 4000 feet. The Catalina was waterborne at Stranraer on 8 November at 0118 hrs. The auto-pilot had been used throughout to control the rudder and elevators, and when icing occurred on the elevators, the servo mechanism was turned up to maximum pressure, enough to overcome the icing. There had been 10/10ths cloud at 1000 feet and icing from sea level to 1500 feet plus heavy hail and snow until 2253 hrs.

P/O Naish from the outset after take-off had flown through hail and snow. On finding a section where the height of the cloud was 3000 feet, he had climbed up it, only to find that the height of the cloud increased as he headed towards the patrol area. Ultimately he climbed to 13,600 feet with full throttle and maximum revs and an airspeed of 70 knots but could not get above the cloud, which could well have been up to 15,000 feet. With the elevators iced-up, it needed the efforts of two pilots to control the Catalina. The crystals in the radio, controlling the operational frequencies proved to be unserviceable. When there was a "hole" in the clouds, the navigator attempted to obtain an astro fix, but his breath froze on the sextant.

Although manufacturers designed heating systems, they were removed from some aircraft. In the writer's limited experience of Catalinas in northern latitudes, the one scrap of comfort for him was a Spam sandwich.

On 13 December an officer from RCAF Overseas HQ, F/Lt Johnson, came with two members of the Canadian Broadcasting Corporation, Mr. M.C. Peach and Mr. Wadsorth, to record messages from Canadian personnel on the squadron for friends and relatives in Canada.

S/Ldr Randall undertook a recce of the Faeroe Islands on 29 December. By that time, No. 413 Squadron's total strength was 281 personnel including three RCAF officer aircrew, six RCAF officer groundstaff, fifteen non-commissioned aircrew and forty-five airmen.

Two of the last sorties for 413 Squadron while still with Coastal Command were flown by S/Ldr Birchall and F/Lt Thomas in February 1942.

F/Lt Thomas was airborne in "Y" on 24 November from Sullom Voe at 2042 hrs for a recce of the Norge coast in the Stadlandet and Utvaer areas. At 0450 hrs the following morning, he was at position 6303N 0650E but was waterborne at base at 0854 hrs, making this a trip of over twelve hours.

S/Ldr Birchall was airborne at 1620 hrs for a cross-over patrol off the Norge coast and early the following morning was in position 6508N 1040E and suffered heavy snow showers. He was back at base after flying for just eighteen hours.

Japan's Advance in the Far East

Following the fall of France in 1940 the Vichy government in France had permitted the Japanese to send a military mission to French Indo-China. The former

French colonies were to be a useful "back door" for the Japanese to enter the Malayan Peninsula. On 7 December 1941 the Japanese attacked the American fleet at Pearl Harbor, temporarily putting much of the American fleet out of action.

Winston Churchill despatched the battleship HMS *Prince of Wales* with the battlecruiser HMS *Repulse* to the Far East intended as a "vague menace," but they were attacked by Japanese aircraft and sunk.

The way was open for the Japanese to extend their influence; Hong Kong surrendered to them on 25 December, Kuala Lumpur was entered on 11 January, Burma and Siam were invaded on 16 January and on 30 January, British forces withdrew to Singapore, which fell to the enemy on 15 February 1942.[31]

The posting of No. 413 Squadron was just one of the belated measures to give support in the Far East; and as was to be shown, was of great significance.

No. 413 Squadron is Posted to Ceylon

The unit was informed of its overseas posting on 27 February 1942, and the following day was preparing to leave Sullom Voe. Two aircraft left for Pembroke Dock on 1 March, with the remaining aircraft following the next day.

By 5 March, No. 413 Squadron was being issued with tropical kit at West Kirby, a transit camp for those proceeding to or from overseas. All ranks were granted embarkation leave. All aircrew were to proceed by air, and with a few exceptions, all ground personnel were to be RCAF. Original RAF personnel were to remain at West Kirby for other postings.

The CO who had succeeded W/Cmdr Briese in November, W/Cmdr C.J.D. Twigg, visited West Kirby with S/Ldr Birchall on 11 March to obtain information about the squadron. By 15 March all personnel had returned from leave and were awaiting embarkation orders. They were visited by the Canadian AOC A/Cmdre Curtiss at West Kirby, who gave a farewell speech. On 17 March eight officers and 327 other ranks under the command of A/S/Ldr Emond embarked on HMT *Nieuw Holland* at Liverpool. The troopship sailed three days later, arriving at Glasgow on 21 March. W/Cmdr J.L. Plant had assumed command of the squadron on 20 March, succeeding W/Cmdr Twigg. F/Lt Thomas was one of the first in the squadron to fly out from the United Kingdom to Ceylon and left Lough Erne on 18 March following the route; Gibraltar, Cairo, Aboukir, Basra, Karachi to arrive on 28 March. After reporting enemy ships on 9 April, F/Lt Thomas, DFC was shot down.[32] He was highly respected and as the squadron records "one of our best pilots and his loss will be keenly felt by the squadron."

While based at Koggala on 4 April, S/Ldr Birchall was on a search for enemy shipping when a large enemy force was sighted. Its position, course, and speed were reported before he also was shot down, but to become a POW. The report was considered the means of saving Ceylon from a Japanese invasion. Now as A/Cmdre Birchall he is remembered as "The Saviour of Ceylon."

No. 413 Squadron's ground crews who had sailed in the troopship *Nieuw Holland* reached Cape Town on 23 April and continued their voyage eastwards on 27 April. Post war, No. 413 was officially in being again on 1 April 1947 at Rockcliffe,

Ontario. With its badge depicting an elephant's head it is nicknamed "The Tusker Squadron," and circa 1995 has an active Squadron Association, including many veterans.

Torpedo Strike Aircraft

At the outbreak of World War II, Coastal Command had only two strike squadrons, and they were equipped with outdated Vildebeest aircraft.

Possible bombing sorties were considered the prerogative of Bomber Command and attacks on merchant vessels were not contemplated. Coastal Command lacked a properly equipped and trained striking force.[33] Following the occupation by the Germans of The Netherlands, Denmark and Norway, the RAF was permitted in July 1940 to "sink on sight" ships in the North Sea from approximately Tromso to The Hook of Holland. Later in September, the area permitted for attacks was extended to the English Channel and the Bay of Biscay.[34]

It was to be early 1940 before two Coastal Command squadrons were equipped with Beauforts to replace Vildebeests. Just how successful torpedo aircraft could be was demonstrated by the Fleet Air Arm at Taranto and by the Japanese at Pearl Harbor and their subsequent attacks on HMS *Prince of Wales* and HMS *Repulse*.

A Canadian Torpedo Squadron is Formed

No. 415 (RCAF) Squadron was formed at RAF Thorney Island on 20 August 1941 as a torpedo-bomber unit within RAF Coastal Command. By 26 August it had a strength of four officers and 129 other ranks commanded by S/Ldr E.L. Wurtele.

The following day, No. 5 hangar at Thorney Island was occupied and temporary offices set up pending the arrival of equipment.

The squadron's first aircraft, a Mark I Bristol Beaufort N1082 coded GX-A, arrived on 2 September. It was followed by two more the next day—L9893 and L9819. An officer commissioned in the RCAF, F/Lt M.E. Jones, succeeded P/O E.M.B. Fermoy as adjutant on 18 September. One of the squadron's first Wop/AGs was Gordon Club, who refers to his operational training being with No. 415 rather than at an OTU, and adds "I had 22 hours 20 mins on Norseman, Tiger Moths and Fairey Battles."

Gordon Club joined the squadron in October and found that the other aircrew were in various stages of training.

An officer from an RAF Beaufort squadron, No. 86, F/Lt T.I. Mathewson, arrived on 24 November to become attached and assist in training. Due to the RAF's committments in the Middle East, there was a lack of Beaufort aircraft, but by the end of 1941, 415 Squadron had six Mark I Beauforts and two Mark IV Blenheims. As was the case for the other two squadrons, 404 and 407, No. 415 was to be deployed on shipping strikes which covered the sea lanes from Norway down to the Bay of Biscay.

References to: Chapter 1

1. HAJ IV p.73
2. AHS p.19
3. AHS p.61
4. WR p.485
5. PJ p.73
6. SWR I p.29
7. RAF I p.26

8. WR p.26
9. SWR I p35
10. SWR I p.36
11. SWR I p.37 chart
12. WSC III p.103
13. RAF I p.6
14. SWR p.135-136
15. RCAF III p.378
16. SEM I p.211
17. JH p.426
18. RCAF II p.474
19. AH 'S&S' p.123
20. AH 'S&S' p.263
21. AH 'FC' p.65
22. JuH para.296, 315, 360
23. CCWR p.24
24. SWR I p.514
25. CCWR p.20
26. Ibid
27. Ibid
28. Ibid
29. JR p. 124
30. AH 'S&S' p.56
31. JK pp. 19-20
32. AH 'FC' p.106
33. SWR I p.509; RAF I p.56; RCAF III p.417
34. RCAF III p.417

Chapter 2

The Strike Squadrons: January– December 1942

At the beginning of 1942, No. 404 Squadron was at Sumburgh in the Shetlands but with a detachment at Dyce near Aberdeen equipped with Blenheims; No. 407 squadron was based at North Coates operating Hudsons; while No. 415 at Thorney Island, and with a detachment at Detling near Maidstone, was not operational.

The enemy still had a powerful surface fleet, including the battleship *Tirpitz* and the battlecruisers *Scharnhorst* and *Gneisenau*, plus the *heavy cruisers Admiral Hipper* and *Prinz Eugen* with the pocket battleship *Admiral Scheer*.[1]

For German U-boats there was operation *Paukenschlag* which began on 2 January with Admiral Dönitz ordering U-boats to the Newfoundland banks and others westwards to the American coast from French ports, as well as U-boats which had been en route to the Azores.[2]

Convoys were now sailing to Russia in addition to the vital Atlantic convoys and others to various parts of the world with the whole of the west European coastline from North Cape to the French ports potentially hostile; both the Royal Navy and Coastal Command were fully stretched.

The Germans were running their own convoys southwards from Norwegian ports such as Narvik carrying, notably, high-grade iron ore, and Coastal Command's strike squadrons had the duty of attacking those convoys throughout the war, as the records of 404 Squadron, for example, were to show.

The Heink

While the Command's aircraft were flying eastwards across the enemy coast, Luftwaffe aircraft were frequently encountered heading westwards. Such encounters were to prevail throughout the war.

Air-to-Air Combats

There were two air-to-air combats on 15 January by Blenheims of 404 Squadron; P/O Inglis captained Q/404 Z5736 on a South Stab patrol of the Norwegian coast, when his observer sighted a Heinkel III flying at 50 feet. "Q" closed to 50 yards on the Heinkel's tail and fired from dead astern, developing into a quarter attack with a five-second burst. Inglis saw tracer hit the enemy's rear gun position all along the fuselage to the Heinkel's starboard engine. Inglis turned sharply to port for his rear gunner to get a six-second burst. The Heinkel's starboard engine was now smoking and there was a definite lag in the propeller. The Blenheim's gunner saw bombs jettisoned by the enemy. Inglis now turned away in a steep diving turn to port and attacked from the port quarter. The Heinkel took evasive action down to sea level making slow "S" turns towards the Norwegian coast. Inglis gave a ten-second burst from 300 ft before pulling out at 100 ft. Tracer was seen entering the Heinkel's port wing root and the fuselage.

S/Ldr McHardy in X/404 6279 was flying at 1000 feet when a Heinkel 115 was sighted at sea level three miles away to port. He climbed to 2000 ft to stalk the enemy aircraft before diving to attack on the starboard quarter with the Heinkel crossing from port to starboard. McHardy gave one long burst from 500 yards, closing to 100 yards, as the enemy turned to port. For a second attack he broke away this time giving a short burst while diving from 250 to 150 yards range.

The Blenheim's gunner gave a short burst as they broke away. As the Heinkel climbed steeply, McHardy attacked from below and astern at point-blank range until his ammunition was exhausted. Just before the Heinkel disappeared into cloud, smoke was seen from between its port engine and fuselage and it was lurching with its nose dropping sharply.

By 31 January 1942, No. 404 (RCAF) Squadron was equipped with eighteen Blenheim IVs and one Mark I. Personnel were of mixed nationality, including both British and Canadians, with some of the latter such as W/Cmdr Woodruff, and F/Lt Foster commissioned in the RAF.

Sumburgh was raided on 1 February with a JU88, releasing a 500 pound and a 250 pound bomb, which exploded beyond the hangar area. Six airmen were wounded and two died of their wounds later. Seven aircraft were made temporarily unserviceable.

An SOS was received by flying control, 18 Group, on 21 February, forty minutes after Blenheim V5433 was due to return from the Norge coast. At 0840 hrs, Sumburgh also received an SOS. Bearings were taken, but at 0930 hrs the Blenheim crashed on Grunay Island, Outer Skerries. A coast guard had seen it approaching on one engine and in obvious difficulties. F/Sgt Lacy flew Blenheim A/404 4847 on an attempted ASR but at 0955 hrs saw smoke from the Outer Skerries. Flying to investigate, he signalled a merchant vessel if an aircraft had crashed?—Yes. The crashed aircraft was then seen on the rocks south of the island, but it was impossible for the ASR launch to reach it due to high cliffs.

It was largely burnt out, but bullet holes were seen in the tail section. Of the crew, F/Sgts Brown and Oliver were buried at Lerwick on the 28th and Sgt Coy's body went to his parents' home.

An Attack on the Heavy Cruiser Prinz Eugen

On 17 May 1942 No. 404 Squadron took part in a major operation against the German heavy cruiser *Prinz Eugen*. A No. 608 Squadron Hudson had reported the cruiser north of Lister while it was en route from Trondheim to the Baltic. Beauforts were used as strike aircraft while 404 Squadron Blenheims served as a fighter escort, in addition to Beaufighters. Hudsons were used as diversionary bombers. W/Cmdr Woodruff was airborne from Leuchars at 1800 hrs in Z6035, followed by F/Sgt Butler, F/Lt McCutcheon, S/Ldr McHardy, W/Cmdr Bellis, and W/O Bell. W/Cmdr Woodruff, on sighting the enemy, made a dummy attack on a destroyer astern of *Prinz Eugen* and was himself attacked by ME109s from 100 yards range. The Blenheim was hit and his navigator, F/Lt Fletcher, was wounded. Woodruff broke away and followed the Beauforts taking evasive action from AA fire. Sgt Saunders gave first-aid to the navigator and Woodruff, short of fuel, set course for base.

A Beaufort was seen in the water and there was fire on the sea near the cruiser. F/Sgt Butler had been airborne a minute after W/Cmdr Woodruff and had sighted the enemy force consisting of a cruiser and four destroyers 8-10 miles on his starboard beam. He made a run against a second destroyer ahead of and to starboard of *Prinz Eugen*. An ME109 was then seen attacking a Beaufort flying at 1000 ft and 2000 yards to port. While Butler was attacking the ME109, the Beaufort was hit by AA fire and crashed in flames. Another Beaufort was apparently jettisoning some ammunition, and Butler escorted it back to base.

S/Ldr McHardy in Z5747 made a dummy run over a destroyer before turning steeply to port onto the tail of an ME109 and at 400yards opened fire. The enemy fighter then turned to attack another Blenheim.

A Beaufighter coded LA-A (235 Squadron) was seen in difficulty flying on its port engine with the starboard engine smoking and lacking its cowling. It force-landed, and a dinghy was dropped from the Blenheim 30 yards from the Beaufighter crew then in the water. They were able to swim to the dinghy and

clamber in. McHardy then formated on a Beaufort J/42 which was heading west.

W/O Bell in Z5729 saw an ME109 circling to attack M/404, then dead ahead of R/404. R/404 then attacked an ME109, which turned and broke away.

Bell's crew had seen black smoke, followed by an explosion and then two men in the water; this astern of *Prinz Eugen* and, most likely, the demise of a Beaufighter.

From an Australian account of this action against the *Prinz Eugen*, the second wave of Beaufort torpedo aircraft had been attacked by twenty ME109 fighters, and four of the Beauforts were lost.[3]

No. 404 Squadron lost three more of their aircrew on 23 May when Z6181 crashed soon after taking off for an intended ASR mission. They crashed at Newmachar, a few miles north of Dyce near Aberdeen. The dead were F/Sgt Morrow, Sgt.White and P/O Thomas.

Before the end of the month, 404 Squadron was to be credited with damaging another merchant vessel; this was the 1876-ton *Uranus*, on the 26th.[4]

Conversion of No. 404 Squadron to Beaufighters

A prelude to the conversion of 404 Squadron from Blenheims to Beaufighters occurred on 2 June when W/Cmdr Woodruff tested Beaufighter T3292. He was awarded the DFC on the 4th and a week later was posted to No. 9 OTU at Aldergrove. He was succeeded by W/Cmdr J.A. Dixon, who became CO of 404 on the 18th. The new CO crashed at 1215 hrs on 13 July while flying aerobatics from Sumburgh. His funeral was attended by Mrs. Dixon two days later.

There were two more crashes in June; on the 12th, Blenheim Z6179 struck a balloon cable when over South Shields and two of the crew, Sgts Brockington and Mellor, were killed. Z6175 crashed at Leuchars on 16 June with three killed and one seriously injured.

No. 404 Squadron received a signal on 27 July to move to Sumburgh in the Shetlands, and the main party departed by ship from Invergordon on 4 August.

The conversion of the squadron to Beaufighters began in early September. The first two Beaufighter Mark IIs out of the initial ten aircraft, arrived at Dyce on 9 July, with F/Lt McCutcheon flying down from Sumbrugh to Dyce for conversion.

By the end of September, fifteen Mark IIF Beaufighters were on 404's charge, but their Mark IV Blenheims were to be returned to a maintenance unit.

The Beaufighter

Although No. 404 Squadron operated Blenheim and later Mosquito aircraft, much of the unit's World War II record was with Beaufighters. The following account of the Beaufighter is given by F/Lt John Symons, DFC from Vancouver:

I first met the Beaufighter at No.132 OTU East Fortune, near Edinburgh in February 1943. The Beaufighters at East Fortune were Mark IIs with Rolls Royce Merlin engines. Firstly, however, we did most of our training on various versions of Blenheims. The Beaus were painted all black which tended to make them look rather formidable. It was more than rumour that advised us that it was a rather sensitive (some said unstable) aircraft, especially in the fore and aft plane. Apparently in a steep turn the control

column developed pressure towards the pilot requiring a push to maintain a proper turn. Otherwise the aircraft could stall and spin out, very embarrassing, if not fatal. It also swung on take-off. So most of us had a little trepidation towards our first flight in a Beaufighter.

There were no dual Beaus so the first take-off was solo. Whenever I had some spare time at the flights, I climbed up into a Beau and went over the cockpit check.

Towards the end of our course my turn to take up the Beaufighter came along. I concluded that I would get airborne alright but I had a little concern about the landing. Once airborne I found the aircraft to be very light on the control requiring a soft touch on the controls. After experimenting with modest manoeuvres it was time to try a steep turn.

Sure enough, the control column wanted to continue towards me but by pushing away I soon was managing a controlled turn with little effort, although it did feel odd pushing rather than pulling as on other aircraft. I then started having some fun with this powerful and responsive plane, diving, climbing and twisting among the large white clouds. After a while I heard my call sign and a dry voice "Are you happy?"

I had not expected that they would be watching me but apparently it was their practice to keep an eye on first-timers.

I replied that this was a great aircraft and I was having a good time. The bemused voice suggested that maybe I should take it a little easier for the first time. This I did and soon afterwards made a perfect approach and landing. I only flew the Mark II once more before being posted to Catfoss where we flew the radial Hercules-engined Beaufighter, a much more stable aircraft.

For most of our tour we flew the Beaufighter X which had the dyhedral tailplanes. The Beaufighter turned out to be a very stable aircraft. Because we did so much low flying, on approaching enemy coastlines, this was a positive characteristic. I particularly liked the excellent forward visibility from the cockpit.

It also had an excellent heating system which could easily be adjusted to any temperature. Because especially in winter, one could not survive in the sea for, it was said, more than a few minutes, most of us flew in our shirt sleeves. It was pleasant sitting in our cosy office while tearing up the Norwegian coast through scattered snow flurries and to look over at a squadron mate similarly with his sleeves rolled up.

We came to rely on our Hercules engines, which seldom let us down and would fly comfortably on one engine, if necessary, especially after we obtained feathering propellers.

But the Beau's stability did have one minor drawback in that, at very high speeds, such as in a dive, the controls got very heavy. On a couple of occasions, I had to trim my way out of a dive, otherwise the aircraft was entirely manageable.

Like the rest of our pilots, I was impressed with the firepower of the Beau, with its four 20 mm Hispano cannons and six Browning machine guns. At first we used these to strafe enemy ships just ahead of 144 Squadron's Beaus with their torpedoes, as they went in at low altitude and steady speed to drop their fish.

In August 1943 the squadron went in rotationo Tain, Scotland to learn to fire rockets, with which we were to be armed... They were armed with armour-piercing heads and could pass straight through a ship. They were harmonized so that a pair of rockets arrived with a spread of twenty feet between each pair. When entering the water they levelled out and thereby struck a ship underwater. Aiming was relatively easy; we fired them when we reached a point in our twenty degree dive from 1200 feet where our cannon and machine guns harmonized. This could be determined by the splashes we observed in the water. Early in our dive the splashes were all around the ship. As we got closer the splashes converged until they all met at 700 ft, the point of harmonisation. At that point we pressed the button on the left of the control column and off went the rockets. They would then automatically straddle the ship.

Only if our aim of the cannons and machine guns was off or the aircraft was skidding, were we likely to miss. So in our own right, we did damage to ships and we still cleared the way for the torpedo carrying Beaufighters to sneak in under. We found that our strafing efforts almost silenced anti-aircraft fire altogether. We consequently developed confidence in our prowess and felt that we usually held the upper hand.

Admittedly in my first and early

attacks I was semi-petrified, not knowing what to expect; but with success we attacked with only a mild level of anxiety.

Finally, the Beaufighter was a very strong aircraft. It could sustain a lot of damage in the air and still get home.

From time to time we saw remarkable sights of pranged aircraft, such as one in Scotland that went through a thick stone wall leaving both wings, engine and stern frame behind but, from what was left, both crew members walked away unhurt.

A Change of Squadron Command

Following the loss of W/Cmdr Dixon, the New Zealander commissioned in the RAF, S/Ldr McHardy had assumed command of No. 404 (RCAF) Squadron on 14 July 1942.

With the rank of Wing Commander, he attended a conference on board the battleship *King George V* regarding the method of escorting the Fleet during operations. On 8 October he received a telegram from Coastal Command HQ to attend the premier of the official film *Coastal Command* on the 10th since with others from 404 Squadron he had portrayed German aircraft in some battle scenes.

W/Cmdr G.G. Truscott succeeded as CO of the squadron on 17 October, no doubt as part of the Canadian wish to "Canadianise" their units. No. 404 Squadron was visited by 18 Group's Senior Staff Officer, G/Capt Hopps, who had earlier been a highly respected CO of RAF station, Wick.

On 28 October, HRH the Duchess of Gloucester visited the base to inspect the WAAFs (Womens' Auxiliary Air Force).

Before the end of 1942, two of the Beaufighters were lost in crashes: V8157 in a high-speed stall from Dyce on 5 December with F/Sgt N.Taylor and Sgt S.E. Pike killed and WO1 Ensom with Sgt J.B. Elder crashed on 7 December in V8211.

No. 407 Squadron at North Coates

The first success for No. 407 Squadron in 1942 was on 5 January. At first light four of their Hudsons, captained by S/Ldr Anderson, P/O Cowperthwaite, Sgt Ross, and Sgt Creeden were on a Rover patrol from Borkum to Den Helder. While S/Ldr Anderson sighted a convoy of four vessels leaving Ijmuiden harbour, Cowperthwaite's crew noted three or four ships within the harbour. The leading vessel in the convoy was attacked, and two direct hits were scored on the aft hatch, resulting in clouds of black smoke and debris.

Sgt. Ross, while flying round the Dutch coast near The Hague, sighted a JU88.

He jettisoned his bombs and endeavoured to close the range with both fixed front guns and rear guns in action. Tracer was seen all around the enemy aircraft, but no definite damage was noted. The Hudson's ammunition was now low and the JU88 was heading for the town, and Ross broke off the action.

All available aircraft from 407 were later detailed to operate from The Hook of Holland along the coast eastwards in conjunction with three aircraft from No. 217 Squadron. At 2320 hrs Hudson E/407 sighted two merchant vessels of 5-6000 tons with three escort ships. The largest merchantman was attacked from mast height and a small explosion was seen, followed two minutes later by a large red explosion. Post-war, the *Cornelia Maersk* of 1,892 tons was credited as being sunk by 407 Squadron off Ijmuiden.[5]

On 7 January, W/Cmdr Styles, DSO was succeeded by W/Cmdr Alan Coatsworth Brown as CO when the squadron was still based at North Coates. Of his former CO, Trevor Hawkins writes:

> Monty Styles was a man apart. We would all, without exception, follow Monty to hell and back; it is a pity that like all good leaders he was not destined to make it all the way, but he lost his life as I firmly believe he would have wished, doing what he most loved, flying.

Visits to the squadron followed the change of command; a reporter for the *Toronto Star*, Miss Norah Eastwood, visited the unit ten days later, and the following month, HRH the Duke of Kent visited the station.

There was a tragic accident on 22 January. F/O Dann, the captain of M/407 AM602, had taken off on a strike at 1930 hrs but on return at 2245 hrs attempted to land at Donna Nook, the satellite field. Initially he overshot and while attempting another circuit, he crashed and the bombs in the Hudson exploded. All the crew were killed: F/O Dann, and Sgts Wilkins, Gaudet, Duval and Romain. Thirteen ground staff had gone to help and they were also killed. One of the ground staff, Stan Harper, wrote in his diary:

> "I was in Grimsby at the time which is 18 miles away and I heard the explosion."

Another crew was lost on 31 January; Sgt Jaggard captained Hudson AM R/407 taking off on a Rover patrol at 1050 hrs from North Coates. He failed to return.

With him were P/O Parker, and Sgts Sykes and Palmer.

The Channel Dash

In January 1942 Hitler gave orders for the battlecruisers *Scharnhorst* and *Gneisenau* with the heavy cruiser *Prinz Eugen* to leave the French port of Brest for Germany. The move from Brest was to be under cover of darkness and the shortest route through the English Channel would be covered by the Luftwaffe during daylight. Moon phases and tides indicated early February as a suitable time to sail. Such a move had been anticipated by the British in "Operation Fuller" and the Admiralty's appreciation giving 2 February as a likely date closely agreed with the German intentions.

Sir Philip Joubert of Coastal Command had correctly forecast a breakout of the vessels taking place between 10 and 15 February and in fact Admiral Ciliax sailed in *Scharnhorst* on 11 February.

At 1615 hrs, six hours before the departure of the German forces, a Spitfire over Brest confirmed the presence of the two battlecruisers with the heavy cruiser and destroyers. The presence of minesweepers and E-boats was indicative of an imminent departure.

Air patrols had included those by No. 224 Squadron Hudsons from St. Eval, but their success was dependent on ASV, which proved unreliable. The Royal Navy had deployed a lone submarine, HMS *Sealion*, which at a crucial stage withdrew from the Brest area.

Although the Admiralty had anticipated the breakout, they had not expected the German forces to risk reaching the Dover Straits in daylight following a night exit from Brest, and thus was an initial surprise achieved by Vice-Admiral Ciliax.

The Royal Navy's Home Fleet remained in Scapa Flow, ostensibly covering a possible breakout of the battleship *Tirpitz* from Norway, but many RAF Squadrons had been placed on stand-by. By 0830 hrs on 12 February radar stations had detected the enemy aircraft covering the German warships, but it was about 1020 hrs before a Spitfire pilot fortuitously sighted the warships. The Navy deployed such as six destroyers from Harwich plus torpedo boats; the RAF operated torpedo aircraft, bombers and fighters but there was a lack of co-ordination. Shore batteries in the Dover Straits were effectively neutralised by radar jamming, and low cloud precluded accurate bombing by aircraft.

For 11 February, No. 407 Squadron has recorded: "Unfavourable weather prevented operations" but for the 12th a strike was laid on following a report of twenty-five to thirty ships with five escorts of large sloops or destroyers, and the force included "three battleships."

Eight of 407's Hudsons were detailed for the strike, captained by F/Sgts Foley, Majeau, Abbott, Wallace, Creeden, S/Ldr Anderson, P/O Race, and F/O Cowperthwaite. They flew in two formations; one led by S/Ldr Anderson, the other by F/O Cowperthwaite, with the latter's flight including one aircraft from No. 59 Squadron. They took off from North Coates at about 1330 hrs for Manston in East Kent, ostensibly to rendezvous with torpedo and fighter aircraft, only to find utter confusion at Manston due to lack of briefing for some units or changed instructions.

From 407's operational record both of their flights reached the target area and

S/Ldr Anderson's flight released their bombs from 900-400 ft through a break in the clouds, while F/O Cowperthwaite's flight released bombs from 1500 ft. F/Sgt J.W. Creeden dived through intense flak to make a low-level attack on a destroyer; he, together with his two RAF Wop/AGs Sgts G. Hancox and H.G. Everett, was awarded the DFM for that feat. S/Ldr Anderson with his crew, F/Sgts Jordan, and Walker and Sgt Spicer, did not return and were posted missing. F/O Cowperthwaite with his crew P/O Lister, F/Sgt Jones, and Sgt. Lenover, similarly. Kim Abbott, who was a pilot on the squadron at that time is able to give a more personal account in his book and suggests that F/Sgt Creedon may have attacked the destroyer Z29.[6] He rightly pays tribute to the characters of S/Ldr Anderson and F/O Cowperthwaite, and from reference to the terse squadron record alone, this writer concurs.

No. 407's Hudsons were intended as a diversion for a torpedo squadron such as No. 42 RAF to release their torpedoes. From the official RAF history by Denis Richards, the Hudsons attacked through heavy flak with the loss of two out of six aircraft.[7]

Fleet Air Arm Swordfish biplanes of No. 825 Squadron armed with torpedoes, were airborne from Manston led by L/Cmdr Eugene Esmonde, RN, without effective fighter cover. All the Swordfish were lost; there were five survivors. L/Cmdr Esmonde was awarded a posthumous VC. F/O Cowperthwaite gained a mention in despatches.

The most effective weapon against the movement of the enemy ships proved to be mines laid by the RAF. At 1431 hrs the *Scharnhorst* struck a mine off the Scheldt and at 1955 hrs the *Gneisenau* was mined off Terschelling. *Scharnhorst* hit another mine about $1\frac{1}{2}$ hrs later. Despite some damage, *Scharnhorst* reached Wilhelmshaven on 13 February and *Gneisenau* and *Prinz Eugen* sailed to Brunsbuttel.

The official naval historian Capt Roskill suggests that the main cause for failure to damage the enemy ships was the failure of the RAF to give adequate warning.[8]

It may be questioned how much damage a few destroyers ex-Harwich, not knowing what armament to use, would have done to battlecruisers, assuming they breached the E-boat and destroyer screen.[9]

There was a subsequent enquiry headed by Mr. Justice Bucknill following public outrage that enemy forces could sail up the English Channel virtually unscathed. The episode was perhaps best summed up by the German Naval Staff as "a tactical victory, but a strategic defeat."

Their warships' intention then became to defend Norway against a possible Allied invasion instead of posing an immediate threat of breaking out into the Atlantic on raiding sorties.[10]

Coastal Command's Hudson Squadrons

No. 407 (The Demons), was one of a number of squadrons within No. 18 or No. 16 Group RAF Coastal Command such as Nos. 48, 608, 53, 59, and 320, equipped with Hudsons, whose tasks included shipping strikes. While Nos. 48 and 608 covered the northern areas towards Norway; No. 407 wih 53, 59 and 320 operated off the Dutch coast. In early 1942 while squadrons such as No. 48 were on Norge trips, No. 407 was covering the

enemy-controlled coastline from the Elbe to the Hook of Holland.[11]

Following the "Channel Dash" a number of Coastal Command Squadrons were re-deployed; thus No. 224 moved from St. Eval in Cornwall to Limavady in Northern Ireland, while 407 changed its base from North Coates to Thorney Island, with the main party leaving by train on 18 February.

No. 407 Squadron at Thorney Island

Of this move, Stan Harper, stated in his diary for 17 February:

We are moving to Thorney Island tomorrow so the kites are leaving today. The purpose of going there is to train new aircrew. The kites took off one after the other. "R" was the sixth off but no sooner got airborne than F/Sgt Goulding made a tight bank and the wind caught the underside of the starboard mainplane and she crashed. It caught fire immediately about a 100 yards away from me. I couldn't get near it for a large dyke and the heat. The whole crew burnt... All the other kites landed at Thorney island alright except "K" which crashed but none of the crew was hurt and the kite is repairable.

For March this diarist records:

Four kites smashed up today on the drome or at least three here and one at another drome. "V" went over the sea wall here but all the crew got out OK—it was written off. "P" for some reason landed with the undercarriage up—none hurt. "E" piled up also and none hurt. "O" was the kite that landed at the other drome and was shot up from an ops trip but the crew were unhurt.

While based at Thorney Island, 407 was visited by the CinC, Coastal Command, Air Chief Marshal Sir Philip Joubert de la Ferté, who spent some time with the squadron giving two talks, one to the officers and one to other aircrew and ground crews. No. 407 received the accolade of the Air Ministry with [in the Squadron diary for 22 March]: "The Council has learned with much satisfaction of the records of certain units of Coastal Command, which reflects greatly on all concerned and wish to convey an expression of the Council's pleasure to the COs of the units concerned with special reference to No. 407 (RCAF) Hudson Squadron which has maintained the excellent record reported."

No. 407 Squadron at Bircham Newton

After little more than a month at Thorney Island, 407 moved to Bircham Newton with the main party arriving there by 31 March, when they had two Mark IIIs and seven Mark V Hudsons on charge. Of Bircham Newton the squadron scribe records:

"The Station itself is very creditable but difficulty is encountered in trotting into the odd pub for a 'quick one.'" He reported inadequate transport as the only trouble and records an excellent station cinema, with films screened six out of seven nights plus an ENSA or other show on the seventh night. He concludes with the many facilities available for sports.

On 2 April two of 407's Hudsons operated off the Dutch coast; one, captained by P/O Majeau from Edmonton,

failed to return. In his crew were Sgt Wheadon, F/Sgt Richard, and Sgt Hancock. They lost another Hudson three days later when the aircraft captained by Sgt Murphy failed to return. He had been in one of the four Hudsons operating off the Danish coast. The other three had encounted a JU88 which they attacked but experienced no return fire. It was thought that Sgt Murphy's aircraft had been shot down by an enemy fighter. Operations off the Dutch coast were to remain hazardous right up to the end of the war; coastal batteries, enemy fighters, flak ships, all took their toll.

April concluded for 407 with three Hudsons on a shipping strike off Borkum. Two were unsuccessful, but the third, captained by P/O Paige, sighted sixteen merchant vessels and attacked one of 3-4000 tons. His gunner saw the ship enveloped in dense smoke and it appeared to be listing.

May 1942 began for 407 with five aircraft on a night operation on the 3rd, but only the Hudson captained by F/Sgt Howey from Exeter, Ontario, made any attack. This was on a 2000-ton merchantman which was left burning.

There were no operations the following day, but on the 5th two aircraft from 407 were on a recce off the Dutch coast. They were flown by W/Cmdr Brown and P/O Mosier, who were airborne at 2200 hrs. Off Terschelling, a convoy of twelve ships was sighted. There was intense flak, but P/O Mosier bombed from low level, and he believed that his bombs caused some damage. W/Cmdr Brown sent a sighting report and then dive-bombed from 1000 to 400 ft and claimed hits. Within fifteen minutes of base receiving his sighting report, four more aircraft were airborne. Of these, only two found the convoy and attacked. P/O Paige was first in, but his aircraft was hit and he was severely wounded. He was forced to break off but managed to return to bring his Hudson back to base, where he was rushed to hospital. F/Lt Christie bombed a large merchantman despite intense flak but his starboard engine was hit, caught fire, and stopped. He also managed to bring his aircraft back. It is not clear who might claim the lethal hits with his bombs, but the merchantman of 4,647 tons, the *Sizilien,* was sunk off Terschelling and credited to 407.[12]

These operations the squadron apparently considered "routine" as 407's record refers to no opportunity for a "big do" against enemy shipping until 7 May when the unit was "on the mark" with twelve serviceable aircraft. Two Beaufighters from No. 236 Squadron had reported enemy shipping off the Dutch coast and within thirty minutes of them landing, W/Cmdr Brown led a formation from 407 to their datum at Terschelling. All twelve Hudson captains picked their targets and released their loads. Seven ships were considered to have been definitely bombed, with one probable. Some aircraft were damaged but all returned safely.

For the night of 7-8 May the Command's record gives the merchant vessels *Ruth* (3,726 tons) as sunk, and *Namdo* (2,860 tons) as damaged by 407 Squadron off Texel. The Dutch Squadron No. 320, which had close liaison with 407, was credited with damaging the ship *Burgundia* (1,668 tons) off Emden.[13]

54% Losses by The Demons

A week later twelve aircraft from 407 were again detailed for a strike off the Dutch coast that was to show what a "dicey do" in aircrew jargon, a shipping strike could be. Due to the CO's wife being seriously injured in a car accident, F/Lt Christie led nine aircraft, while F/O Kay led eight from 320 Squadron and two from 407. The first attack was led by F/O Kay on what another pilot, Cam Taylor, recorded at the time as "a heavily defended convoy off the east Frisian Islands." Kay's aircraft was seriously damaged and he was wounded, while one of 320's Hudsons in his flight was lost.

After that first attack, the convoy was fully aroused and "turned on the heat" against Christie's flight which followed, with "everything they had...directed against our lads." One or two ships were seen to be on fire but one of 407's Hudsons exploded in mid-air and several others were shot down. Of those returning, one, captained by P/O Creedon, crashed at Conningsby and all the crew were killed instantly. Two others, those flown by F/L Christie and F/O Kay, were badly shot up and crash-landed at Docking. P/O Kippen, from Toronto, Kay's navigator, died of his injuries; the others were taken to the RAF hospital at Ely, Sgt Thorneloe with spinal injuries and Sgt Sadesky with a fractured clavicle. P/O Kay had gunshot wounds and a fractured ankle. F/Lt Christie had been forced to crash-land with his instruments shot away and undercarriage unserviceable. Hudsons of 407 which failed to return were captained by P/O Haliburton, F/Sgt Doern, F/Sgt Daubner, and Sgt Alger; five out of the original eleven returned safely. Another Canadian Squadron—No. 404,

The Buffaloes—was to suffer similar terrible losses (54%) in February 1945.[14]

Cam Taylor, who was on leave at the time, wrote in his diary that Wally Creeden had been killed over the target and his Hudson flown back by his navigator; all the crew were buried in Bircham Newton churchyard. It was a high price for sinking two ships—*Selje* of 6,698 tons and *Madeleine Louise* of 464 tons, the auxiliary VP. 2002, off Terschelling. Coastal Command operations were not always a doddle as some suggest.[15]

In the last two months, 407 had attacked thirty-eight enemy-controlled merchant vessels, scoring hits on the majority, but had lost twelve aircrews on operations.

No. 407's first year of service was commemorated on 22 May by a dance in the Officers' Mess. The airmen's party was organised the following evening when a number could not attend due to the exceptional operations.

About that time, a DSO was awarded to F/Lt Christie and DFCs to P/O E.F. Paige and P/O Kay. These made up the squadron's awards to two DSOs, two DFCs, and three DFMs. The brother of E.F. Paige, B.C. Paige, also serving with 407, earned his DFM while with No. 500 Squadron RAF.

Successes and Losses for the Demons

May 1942 concluded notably for 407, with successes shared with No. 320 (Dutch) Squadron and No. 59 RAF.

F/Lt R.M. Christie, DSO, led the eight Hudsons from 407 with his other captains, P/O O'Connell, P/O Patterson, P/O Marland, P/O Arnett, W/O Bryan, F/Sgt Howey and Sgt Santy.

P/O O'Connell earned the rare distinction of being mentioned in the RAF's official history.[16] The Canadian record gives: "For the second time in two nights P/O O'Connell successfully bombed enemy shipping. He went in so low to attack that he struck a mast and hung one of the bomb doors thereon." O'Connell's Hudson was seriously damaged in a number of places and his rear gunner, P/O White, had a bullet sear through his trousers. F/Sgt Howey's aircraft was also considerably damaged, but he managed to attack what was his third ship. P/O Marland made his second shipping attack despite damage to his Hudson and his navigator being wounded in the leg by shrapnel.

Out of the total strike force, six crews failed to return.[17] They included F/O C.F. Race from Edmonton, Alberta, with the other three in his crew, F/Sgt Clarke, Sgt Summers, and P/O Robinson. Their aircraft was last seen going through intense flak to attack a merchant ship. According to the squadron record, P/O Race was one of only two original members of 407, the other apparently surviving by being off flying for 1½ months.

From the Command's and 407's records it appears that O'Connell and Howey sank the merchantman ship *Varmdo* (2,956 tons), and off Ameland, the *Niels R. Finsen* (1,850 tons), Sperrbrecher No. 150, *Veriato* (750 tons) was sunk by 320 Squadron, and *Nordcap*, an auxiliary VP1103 of 285 tons, was sunk by No. 59 Squadron.

According to 407's ops record:

In May 1942 the squadron attacked 83,000 tons shipping with several crews attacking three ships each in the period, and with the exception of new crews, all made claims. The previous record in Coastal Command was also held by 407 when from 1 September to 1 December 1941, 407 was credited with damaging 150,000 tons. Since the squadron became operational again on 1 April 1942, twelve crews were lost with fifty personnel either killed or missing on operations.

Six crews were killed or missing with the loss of twenty-seven lives in May 1942. This does not take into consideration that after every major operation, at least two-three aircraft are so badly damaged that they are of no use to any squadron.

In 1980 this writer saw for the first time Coastal Command's terse résumé of the shipping strikes covering, notably, 407 and 220 Squadrons, operating Hudsons. It prompted him to begin writing, but unlike the Coastal record, to include the names of those men who flew Hudsons. The Coastal Command record gives only one VC for the RCAF, and even his name is omitted; there were many more no less worthy of that honour.

Losses suffered by 407 were compensated when seven new crews reported to the squadron from Silloth OTU on 8 June at Bircham Newton. By then 407 had twenty-five complete crews, but only nine aircraft, half of them unserviceable. One of the nine was lost on 13 June when P/O W.S. Patterson, on a training flight from Thorney Island, crashed into the sea two miles off Selsea Bill. Only his body was recovered. With Patterson in the Hudson were his crew, Sgts A.R. Thomson, C.J. Pearson, A.N. Urquhart, and two ground staff, F/Lt Grant and LAC E.R. Watson. It was thought that Patterson crashed into the mast of the ship being used for practice bombing.

P/O Taylor was one of four captains on a recce off the Dutch coast on 12 June from Bircham Newton. His crew sighted an enemy convoy and attacked a ship of 1,500 tons. His gunner saw at least three direct hits on the ship followed by an orange glow, and debris was thrown into the air. Taylor circled the ship and saw that it was on fire. It was a merchantman, *Senta* of 1,497 tons and later credited as sunk off Borkum.[18]

According to P/O Taylor's own account of his success:

> Self and crew briefed for Frisian Nomad patrol. Airborne from Docking at 0008 hrs; set course for DR position, then to Heligoland—flew at deck level; enemy aircraft above apparently did not see us—flew into Elbe estuary—hot reception. In position off Wanggerooe sighted convoy attacked large tanker from mast height—three direct hits, caught fire—later blew up—came home on the deck—landed Docking 0430 hrs. Target attacked in position 5355N 0734E.

On 19 June 1942 a news report from Stockholm reported also in English newspapers that Swedish shipping owners had protested to Germany that Swedish ships were being used to transport iron ore to Rotterdam.

Only ten percent of the ships were German, and in view of the high casualty rate and continued sinkings, Swedish ships would not in future sail to Rotterdam.

Of the squadron's aircraft and their shipping strikes, S/Ldr Cameron Taylor wrote to the author:

407's Hudsons were equipped with two fixed .303 Brownings firing forward; one each side of the aircraft, and two mounted in a Boulton & Paul turret. This armament was never modified. Our bomb load generally consisted of four 250 pound AP or HE bombs; the load was however adjusted to suit the target. No. 407 perfected the science of skip bombing against enemy shipping with a marked degree of success. This required that the attack be pressed home at close range and from zero height, generally lifting just over the target ship and flying between the masts. As enemy ships increased their defensive armament our losses mounted and eventually skip bombing was replaced by bombing from heights up to 4000 ft with limited success.

Change of Bombing Tactics

The official histories for both the RAF and RCAF, refer to this change in tactics.19 Earlier, even Beaufighters of No. 2 Group had been withdrawn from shipping strikes because of the high casualty rate. For the Hudsons, as much as 25% losses were suffered despite using the cover of darkness. From the RCAF account, the enemy convoys were being warned by radar and their ships were being more heavily armed.[20] While still based at Bircham Newton in June, 407's Hudson aircrews were detailed for high level bombing practice at North Coates. However the AOCinC Coastal Command, Sir Philip Joubert, on 1 July, gave orders for mast height bombing to be discontinued in favour of high-level bombing.

The Thousand Bomber Raid: Millenium II

On the morning of 25 June in 407 Squadron "all expected something big but efforts to get the story from Wingco were fruitless." Eleven crews were to go on a bombing raid, not a shipping strike, target unknown until briefing. As the squadron record gives, "our target was to be Bremen and there were shouts of glee when the Group Captain announced [it]. There was disappointment seen on faces of those crews who were told they were to stay at home."

The object of the raid was to attack enemy installations that would have a direct effect on the Battle of the Atlantic. Such installations included the docks at Bremen, the Focke-Wulfe works which produced "Kondors" and the Deschimag U-boat building yards.

Memos from Churchill to both the Admiralty and Coastal Command made it clear that he expected 250 Coastal Command aircraft to take part in what was ostensibly a Bomber Command operation.[21]

A moonlight night with clear skies was considered essential, although such conditions would favour the enemy's night fighters. Coastal Command provided Wellingtons and Hudsons, the latter including crews from two OTUs and 59, 206, and 224 Squadrons; and 407 found that some squadrons joined them at their base. It appears very likely that the adjuntant, F/Lt Walley, who flew with P/O O'Connell on this raid, wrote the following account:

Taking off shortly before midnight, 407 in company with about 1000 aircraft of Bomber Command proceeded to Bremen. Our route took us over one well known to 407. All along the Dutch coast from Terschelling to south of Heligoland and then the scenery changed and we turned south towards our target. Flying at 12,000 feet above a white mass of clouds which obliterated everything below, flak was encountered from Terschelling to Bremen. One hardly needed a navigator to take ourselves there as the path of other aircraft was quite visible. Unfortunately although the night was magnificent, at that height the only thing that could be seen of the target itself was the ring of flak around the city. Of the eleven aircraft from 407, six crews reached Bremen and dropped bombs on the city.

No. 407, as for the other Coastal aircraft, had been allotted a definite target, the Deschimag U-boat yards, but only one crew managed to locate it through a break in the cloud. Due to shortage of fuel, two of 407's pilots, P/O Watson and F/Sgt Howey, attacked Wilhelmshaven despite heavy flak.

S/Ldr Cooper with P/O Paige's crew was attacked by two enemy fighters when within about thirty-five miles of Bremen. His rear gunner fired at the second enemy, the first having disappeared, and it was believed the fighter was damaged as it broke off the engagement. P/O Bryan was also attacked by enemy aircraft but after four minutes the enemy disappeared.

One of 407's captains on the raid, Cameron Taylor, recorded his own account:

June 25/42; All available aircraft ... helluva flap ... oxygen equipment to be placed in service-most aircraft it is unserviceable as it is never used on our low-level operations. At 1845 hrs all crews briefed in station cinema ...target Bremen in conjunction with Bomber Command ... our specific target to be the large naval shipyards. Further briefing at 2215. Airborne 2320 ... oxygen on at 8000 feet but doesn't work...climbed to 13,000 feet s/c Bremen, dodging heavy flak around Wilhelmshaven ... over Bremen at 0151 dropped bombs ... three immense fires burning ... sky full of flak ... can't get over it so must dodge around it. Returned to base very short of fuel ... landed Docking 0500 hrs/June 26.

All our aircraft returned but five or six did not reach the target because of shortage of fuel. Most aircraft including our "R" had some flak damage.

According to the Bomber Command war diaries, five out of the 102 aircraft deployed by Coastal Command were lost in this Bremen raid, in contrast with the six out of eleven lost on a shipping strike by 407 and by 404 Squadron (54% losses). Of the Bremen bomber raid, total losses were 4.9% and of the 102 aircraft from Coastal Command, five were lost.[22]

Added to 407's account is the note "without exception squadron personnel were elated with the success of the recent venture and it is hoped that further opportunities to bomb Germany will occur."

HRH Air Commodore The Duke of Kent inspected all aircrews at Bircham Newton on 27 July. The Duke spoke to many of them and was introduced to the squadron commander and flight commanders. He paid tribute to No. 407 Squadron and remarked on its general efficiency and appearance. The Duke himself was lost in the following month while en route from the Cromarty Firth to Iceland in a Sunderland flying-boat.

High-Level Bombing Strike

On 30 July a strike was laid on which must have been the first for the 407 Squadron Hudsons to adopt high-level bombing instead of their earlier "mast height" tactics. It was to be in conjunction with Nos. 59 RAF and 415 (RCAF) Squadrons. No. 407 was briefed at 2030 hrs and all their aircraft were airborne by 2238 hrs. W/Cmdr Brown led eleven from 407 and he elected to find the convoy and shadow it for an hour while homing other aircraft, including those from 59 and 415 by S.E. (Special Equipment). Satisfied that part of his procedure was complete, W/Cmdr Brown climbed from sea level to 4000 ft and dropped a flare to illuminate the target before making his own attack and claiming two definite hits on a ship. The others from 407 acted similarly, releasing flares and then attacking with bombs, although some cloud obscured the ships. As the Canadians left, the RAF Squadron No. 59 dropped their flares and released bombs on the convoy.

No. 415 (RCAF) Squadron used the light from 59's flares to release their torpedoes.

Cameron Taylor from 407 was airborne at 2235 hrs in:

> bright moonlight...good for night fighters so went on the deck...found target (a convoy of eight merchantmen with four escorts).
> Attacked at 0106 hrs right on time scored hits on large MV. Took photographs...flak hot and heavy. Returned to find Docking under fog...vis zero down to deck. Diverted

to Manston, still zero vis. Diverted to Donna Nook, no vis then Cranwell. Still closed in...no fuel, flying at 150 ft flashed SOS on downward recognition lights. Searchlights came up and directed me to Hibaldstow. Landed in very low cloud and poor vis. Good old terra firma. Fuel remaining 10 gallons. Target strike at 5333N 0535E.

P/O Watson was also diverted to Manston and like Taylor had limited fuel. He was unable to find the airfield and crash-landed in a field. His fuel gauge indicated 15 gallons. The other aircraft landed at various aerodromes.

By 1 August 1942 units at Bircham Newton included No. 320 Squadron (RDNAS) (Royal Dutch Naval Air Service), 407, an ASR Squadron, a Met flight, and Nos. 811 and 819 Squadrons of the FAA, the latter equipped with Swordfish. As 407 recorded: "quite cosmopolitan."

No. 407 were informed that they were to transfer all their Mark III and Mark IIIa Hudsons to No. 48 Squadron then at Wick, while No. 407 was to receive Mark Vs. No. 407 rated the Mark IIIs higher than Mark Vs and were nonplussed to hear that No. 59 Squadron was to receive Mark VI Hudsons. This was later modified to 407 expecting to receive Mark VI Hudsons while No. 59 converted to Liberators.

Some of the equipment in the old Hudsons included the out-dated radio "1082/1083", which required a manual change of coils for changes in frequency. This was in sharp contrast to the American Bendix radio which had a crystal-controlled transmitter and was much easier to use, and with a greater range, certainly from Liverpool to

Gibraltar ground-to-air, and 200 miles ground-to-ground.

Both aircrew and ground crew were ill-used in respect of aircraft allocated to them; ultimately, the new Mark VI Hudsons went to No. 320 Squadron while 407 received "time expired" Mark Vs from OTUs and maintenance units. Three of the Mark Vs had already completed 600 hours flying, and two were almost due for complete engine changes.

W/Cmdr Brown's aircraft had struck a balloon cable in March, and on 12 August he ferried W/O Tisdale and crew down to St. Eval, Cornwall to pick it up. It had taken five months for the wing to be changed.

Many aircrews came to accept the hazards of operational flying within a squadron; at least they could attempt to counter any dangers encountered. Once that routine was broken in any way, their feelings could be very different. A 407 Squadron crew which went on a short armament course at Thorney Island was glad to get back to ops after only nine days—they found the German bombing more of a worry!

By August 1942 the intended squadron badge had been approved by the Chester Herald, and it was to go to Canada and ultimately the King for final sanction. The motto "To Hold on High" was taken from the poem by John McCrae *In Flanders Fields*. The badge comprised three objects: a red trident symbolising control over the sea and indicative of attack; golden wings representing speed and power; and a broken anchor in the form of a "V" for victory representing sunk or damaged enemy shipping.

A Strike to the Frisian Islands

Even as late as 1945, Texel, Frisian Islands was considered a dangerous area for Coastal Command aircraft, but on 20 August 1942 ten crews from 407 were briefed to attack a convoy of thirteen merchant vessels and two escort ships. Two Hudsons took off between 2030 and 2045 hrs to act as homing aircraft but subsequently only four found the convoy and attacked. Direct hits were claimed by F/O Urquhart and W/O Tisdale. F/Lt Mosier was unable to locate the convoy and searched around and over Texel. He experienced much heavy flak and while flying at 4500 feet, a shell exploded close to his Hudson, which was turned completely over. Mosier went down to 500 ft before recovering control. His bombs were released on Texel and he returned to base with his aircraft undamaged. The first three aircraft to return reported that they had been chased by enemy fighters.

The weather at Bircham Newton on 25 August was described as "poor" when a convoy of six merchantmen with four escort vessels was reported off Schiermonnikoog, The Netherlands and six of 407's Hudsons were detailed for a strike, but five took off, the first being airborne at 1955 hrs. From the squadron record the convoy was sighted off Ameland, and F/Sgt Collins flew over it at 500 feet. Other aircraft seeing the flak, turned towards the convoy to attack from 4000 feet all releasing flares. Smoke was seen from the 3000-ton ship attacked by W/Cmdr Brown. Two other ships were bombed by P/O Walsh and Witcombe when a 100 pound AS bomb was seen to burst on a ship's stern.

P/O Cameron Taylor, who was airborne at 2035 hrs recorded:

Weather improved some. Bright moonlight over Frisians—flew over convoy at 150 feet, aircraft shot up; climbed, dropped flares and bombed from 4000 feet direct hit on No. 2 ship, large column of black smoke—leaving target picked up by three JU88s gave us a bad time for about 75 miles. Flew into low cloud and heavy rain—made landfall near North Coates—followed coastline south at zero height—landed Docking in blinding rainstorm at 0110 hrs. Actual strike off Terschelling at 5335N 0513E. P/O Casey Walsh also got a ship.

A Combined Strike Force

A major force was organised for 28 August which included No. 320 (Dutch) Squadron, 407, and an FAA Squadron together with the Royal Navy's MTBs (Motor Torpedo Boats). The operation was based on a possible sighting report from three Beaufighters but two of those aircraft were shot down by enemy fighters and the third returned with nil report and the intended strike was cancelled; "much to everyone's dismay" on 407 Squadron. The intention had been for the Hudsons to bomb from high level; the FAA Swordfish would have released torpedoes, and the Navy's MTBs would have finished off the job with torpedoes and guns. One of the Beaufighter crews had sent a fix before ditching, and they were rescued by ASR launches thirty miles off the Dutch coast.

New tactics were used by 407 Squadron in conjunction with the Dutch Squadron against an enemy convoy on 9 September. The convoy was located by F/O Arnett north of Schiermonnikoog,

and forty-eight flame floats were then dropped ahead of the convoy by the Hudson marking the position. The enemy had been reported by a Beaufighter off the Frisian Islands and was thought to comprise nine merchantmen, possibly including a 4-5000-ton liner and escorted by E-boats. F/O Arnett attacked a ship releasing two 250 pound bombs, and F/O Ellam scored a hit on another vessel. P/O Taylor found the convoy off Ameland and released a stick of bombs across the bows of the largest ship. He experienced no flak, and as he records, saw "only one night fighter." Taylor had been airborne at 2145 hrs from Docking and landed again at 0045 hrs.

A Raid on Cherbourg Harbour

On 15 September all 407's available aircraft, nine Hudsons, were flown to Thorney Island. A 10,000-ton ship had been reported to be in Cherbourg Harbour which that afternoon had been attacked by Bomber Command Bostons. One of the Hudsons captained by P/O Taylor, landed at Thorney Island at 1715 hrs and was briefed at 1945 hrs. From Taylor's contemporary account, the vessel was a tanker which had suffered direct hits from the Bostons, causing fuel oil to cover the harbour. No. 407's target was changed to attack the harbour but without changing the bombload to incendiaries. P/O Taylor encountered intense flak and searchlights but bombed from 12,000 feet. He returned to Thorney Island, "only to have our own defences open up on us."

Six others from 407 released their bombs but made no claims of damage, the squadron record quotes a German statement: "Damage was caused by this attack to buildings in the dock area."

A large enemy convoy of twenty-four ships was reported off Texel on 18 September, and W/O Tisdale served as Rooster for No. 320 (Dutch) Squadron and No. 819 Squadron FAA. Tisdale released both flares and flame floats ringing the convoy for the strike force. F/O Taylor of 407 was briefed at 1815 hrs and was airborne from Docking at 1950 hrs. Although he searched for sixty miles each way along the convoy route off the Dutch coast, he sighted no shipping. He then entered Den Helder harbour and bombed both shipping and the docks reporting: "terrific explosion and fires; searchlights and flak intense. Aircraft shot up; fires could still be seen from thirty miles at sea. Returned to base on the deck, landing at Docking in heavy rainstorm at 2325 hrs."

Four days later F/O Taylor was introduced to the AOC Coastal Command, Air Marshal Sir Philip Joubert by the Station Commander, G/Capt Mason. The AOC told F/O Taylor that the Bomber boys could see the Den Helder fire from fifty miles away, and it was thought that the strike force had demolished a large factory and a torpedo dump in addition to one ship. The Texel/Den Helder area was always considered to be one of the most heavily defended sections of the Dutch coast, and Sir Philip applauded F/O Taylor's action with the comment: "bloody fine show."

No. 407's other aircraft had been detached to Thorney Island, and thus missed this strike, but they returned on 20 September in time for a farewell party for the squadron CO, W/Cmdr Brown, who was to be succeeeded by W/Cmdr C.F. King. The Station CO paid tribute to W/Cmdr Brown, and the AOC No. 18 Group RAF requested that 407 Squadron be released for a party.

The Demons to St. Eval

No. 407 Squadron was informed on 26 September 1942 that they were to proceed to St. Eval for operations. Their scribe reflects the mood in the following entry:

It would appear therefore, that our "striking" days are over and The Demons were feeling particularly gloomy over the prospect of anti-sub patrols in the Bay of Biscay....it is indeed a sorry day that a less adventurous form of sport, though none the less, if not in fact, more important employment has been found for us.

Unlike the Catalinas, the Hudson era appears to have inspired few poets, but the following was written by an English wireless operator/air gunner while serving at North Coates with 407 Squadron in 1942:

WE FLEW

We flew into the pitch black sky
Through rain and snow prepared to die,
That we could guard our islands free,
And give our country liberty.

We flew so low above the waves,
Where some of us would find our graves,
We flew to find the ships of foe,
Laden with munitions, low.

We flew that they may never reach,
The safety of their friendly beach;
We flew down low——the clouds above;
We flew to save the land we love.

Onward we flew to hostile land,
The coast we kept at our right hand;
Four young men in the prime of life,
Senses as sharp as whetted knife.

Two pilots, and two Wop/AGs,
We flew above the surging seas;
Onward we flew, bombs to employ,
To render harm to the convoy.

"Ships ten degrees to port,
Merchantmen and their escort;
The range, twelve miles I see,
Thank the Lord for A.S.V."

"To port ten," the skipper said;
"This is the night their crews will dread'
"Standby" the skipper called to crew,
Excitedly, onward we flew.

"Bomb doors open, throttle wide,
Approaching from the starboard side."
Below their mast-height on we sped,
The flak was flashing o'er our head.

Upward we flew into the night,
"Bombs gone!" the call came with delight,
Downward we flew when we were past,
The danger from the rising mast.

"Ten seconds passed," the gunner called,
"Two direct hits, she's badly mauled,
One burst near her stern,
One by her bridge that's made her burn."

We flew up to three thousand feet.
The wireless op was in his seat,
And to Headquarters off he sent,
A signal of the foe's intent.

Their course, speed and composition,
And most important—-their position,
When sure the message had been sent,
Back down low we gladly went.

We flew to West as dawn was breaking,
A welcome landfall we were making;
Over coastline on we flew,
To bring back a happy crew.

We flew towards the flare path bright,
We flew to see another night,
We flew as dawn was now expanding,
We flew to make a perfect landing.

We flew that in the coming years,
Our kinsmen should be free of fears;
That, they may have no need to fly,
Perhaps to live, perhaps to die.
We flew.

Trevor Hawkins,
RAF North Coates,
February 1942

At the time Lockheed Hudson crews of four comprised two pilots with two Wop/AGs, one of the pilots acting as navigator. With their "mast height" bombing, it was essential that the bombs should not explode on contact; hence the ten seconds delay.

At the end of September before 407 left for St. Eval, there was a Grand March led by F/O McLaurie and Sgt Macauley with his bagpipes. The procession included officers, aircrew, ground crew, NCOs, and erks. All sections of the Station were visited, and G/Capt Mason was serenaded outside his house. It was terminated with "three vociferous cheers for an extremely popular Station Commander...The majority of the lads have been happy and are very sorry to say goodbye."

Prelude to Operation Torch

After a 300-mile journey taking fifteen hours, the main party of No. 407 Squadron arrived at St. Eval on the north coast of Cornwall. "All managed to find a bed with the exception of the adjutant who thoughtfully arranged accommodation for everyone but himself and slept in a chair."

This was on 1 October, and three days later five of the Hudson crews were detached to Thorney Island for "secret ops." The other aircrews were on anti-sub training. By 5 October, 407 was considered operational; the squadron had settled down and was becoming "anti-sub minded" albeit with the aircrews "feeling gloomy because the unit had been taken off strikes." The following day, eight crews were detailed for A/S patrols over the Bay of Biscay and released leaflets on Spanish fishing vessels. Spain at that time was considered pro-German, and it was thought that Spanish fishing vessels were assisting German U-boats.

On 7 October, 407 received instructions from Coastal Command HQ to remove the squadron's code letters, "RR" from aircraft. Two Mark VI Hudsons were received the following day. Coastal Command had published a booklet giving the required radio procedure to be followed by wireless operators, although it was not issued to them, being considered too secret. Some American AAC and USN Squadrons came under Coastal Command control and on 11 October, F/O McLeod was flown to Gibraltar by a DC3 to instruct American radio operators on RAF procedure.

Anti-Submarine Patrols by No. 407 Squadron

While based at St. Eval, the Squadron's Hudsons were covering areas south of Ireland and the Bay of Biscay, but it was thought that U-boats were remaining submerged during the day due to the high coverage by aircraft over the Bay. The Hudsons were then detailed for night patrols to deter the U-boats from surfacing. One of 407's Mark VIs was lost on 20 October—EW921—crewed by F/Sgt Zumar, F/Sgt Keil, and Sgts Marchant and Grain and with Sgt Willett as a passenger.

Some of the squadron were detached to Thorney Island on 11 October and while there F/O Cameron Taylor undertook searches along the French coast for enemy shipping. On the 15th the sortie was in co-operation with the Royal Navy's destroyers from Dieppe to Cap de Fleur. All Taylor sighted, however, apart from the destroyers, was an ME110.

Three of 407's Hudsons were detailed for a night patrol on 24 October, and one of these, "K" captained by F/Sgt Collins, attacked a merchantman, with three depth charges. Collins straddled the stern of the vessel and clouds of steam were emitted. F/Sgt Ferguson sighted two E-boats which opened fire on the Hudson. The electrical circuits were made unserviceable and the bomb doors could not be opened, but his gunner estimated hits on the vessels. Post-war records for 25th and 27th October credit 407, however, with damaging two vessels—*Emma* and *La Mouette* of 150 and 303 tons respectively in the Bay of Biscay.[23]

Eleven crews were detailed for armament practice at Carew Cheriton together with ground personnel. The adjutant called the Movement Control Officer stating: "We require to move twenty-four bodies by rail." A skeptical voice repeated the number "twenty-four' and stated it would call back. Confirmation was then requested of "twenty-four corpses"! The term "bodies" at that time was part of RAF jargon for "personnel."

The crews and the six Hudsons which had been taken, returned on 30 October after training on evasive action with Beaufighters, low-level bombing, air firing, and BABS (Beam Approach) exercises.

While testing a new 100 pound A/S bomb off Newquay on 3 November, 407's CO, W/Cmdr King, crashed into the sea. His crew were Sgt Shook, F/O Worthington, and Sgt Ward. He had as passengers Sgt Valette and the Station Armament Officer, F/Lt Kellas. It was thought that the bombs were dropped while in a dive-in at 50 feet and the blast damaged the aircraft. A further loss occurred at Carew Cheriton when Sgt

Huddleston crashed into a hill. He was killed instantly with his navigator, Sgt Belac. Sgt Page died in hospital, and the fourth in the crew, Sgt A. Maier, was in critical condition. The adjutant was recalled from leave, the third time in eight months. He had enjoyed just eight days leave in 2½ years.

Due to limited accommodation at St. Eval and what was then considered the limited range of the Hudsons, 407 received a signal on 4 November to move to Bircham Newton. The dispirited comment was: "The Hudson has had its day. 407 has first been taken off shipping strikes owing to heavy casualties and to unsuitability against heavily protected convoys; now we are useless owing to insufficient range for A/S patrols."

Operation Torch

In 1942 consideration was given by the Allies to the opening of a second front, prompted partly by the wish to relieve pressure on the Russian front. The American General Marshall favoured the Brest-Cherbourg peninsula; the American Admiral King, the Pacific, but Churchill wished for a front to be opened on north-west Africa followed perhaps by one on northern Norway.

Field Marshal Sir John Dill, who was respected by President Roosevelt, became his envoy to the USA, and following a memorandum from Roosevelt to Harry Hopkins, General Marshall, and Admiral King which gave a detailed review of the world situation, the American president cabled Mr. Hopkins on 25 July 1942 that plans for an invasion of north-west Africa were to go ahead.[24]

Landings were to be made at Casablanca, Oran, and Algiers and, ultimately, the final date of Operation Torch, as it came to be known, was fixed for 8 November. The British 8th Army had been fighting against General Rommel in North Africa, and on 4 November General Alexander informed Churchill of the 8th Army's victory at El Alamein.[25]

The American General Eisenhower had been appointed C-in-C of the invasion forces on 14 August, while Admiral Sir Andrew Cunningham became Naval Commander.[26]

They were to be responsible for forces including 70,000 assault troops and about 340 British ships; all of the latter were to approach Gibraltar in sequence and then to proceed through the Straits between 1930 hrs on 5th and 0400 hrs on 7th November.[27]

Admiral Cunningham arrived at Gibraltar in the cruiser HMS *Scylla* on 1 November, and General Eisenhower on the 5th to stay in the convent with the Governor of "The Rock" L/General Macfarlane.[28]

Following the collapse of France in June 1940, their warships and aircraft, together with their bases in North Africa, had remained potentially hostile to the British as, even as late as 1943, some Coastal Command aircrew were to find.[29]

During the assault on Oran there was a fierce reaction by the French, and the Royal Navy suffered losses. A major airfield south of Oran at Tafaraouri received Spitfires from Gibraltar on 8th November, and the airfield was used by No. 500 Squadron Hudsons.[30] In addition to French fleet units at Oran, there had been others at Dakar such as the battleship *Richelieu*. The French scuttled their fleet at Toulon on 27 November. For the British naval historian Capt Roskill, the landings represented a gain of French ships and air cover for convoys from Gibraltar to Freetown, but most importantly, additional security for Atlantic shipping and the potential opening of the Mediterranean.[31]

Gibraltar

The Rock of Gibraltar is 12,1400 ft high, three miles long, and 3/4 mile wide, and in 1942 it was crucial to Operation Torch; it was to be the hub or focal point for the whole operation. For the Royal Navy it was a port for Force H; for the RAF, a base for, initially, 233 Squadron Hudsons and No. 202 Squadron Catalinas. Two more Hudson Squadrons joined 233, Nos. 500, and later, 608 to move to North Africa; while another flying-boat Squadron, 210, joined 202. The strip of land connecting the Rock to the Spanish mainland had previously served as a racecourse. The grandstand served the RAF as an operations room, and the stables provided some accommodation for messing and offices, but those buildings were supplemented by black Nissen huts.

Adjacent to the fenced Spanish border were flight offices and closely parked aircraft for servicing. This was on the north side of the runway which was being constructed in 1942 and being extended in 1943. This was undertaken by the Army blasting rock from the north face, at great risk to the Nissen huts and the spoil then deposited at the west end of the runway and extending 450 yards into the harbour.

At the east end the beach was littered with scraps of crashed aircraft. Features at the time of Torch were four-gallon petrol tins and "Spitfire boxes." The petrol tins served at more than one RAF station as building materials, even to construct a cinema; and at Gibraltar, Spaniards could

be seen using them to carry scraps of bread picked up from the road. The "boxes" were large enough to be used as additional offices, and the timber was used to construct furniture. The more serious aspect was that after assembly, Spitfires were flown off, as many as 128 in 1½ hrs if this writer recalls correctly. In addition to the RAF using the North Front base, a squadron of FAA Swordfish had the task of covering the Straits of Gibraltar. By their nature such aircraft were most suitable for such patrols. While acting as a base for both flying-boats and land aircraft, Gibraltar served as a valuable staging post, whether from the north, south, east or west.

By November 1942, additional squadrons flew in to Gibraltar to cover the convoys for Operation Torch and to counter the expected U-boats. They were the Hudsons of Nos. 500 and 608, the Wellingtons of 179, and Catalinas of 210. No. 48 Squadron followed them with Hudsons in December, and because No. 233 had suffered a number of losses at the hands of the French, 48 Squadron remained at North Front.

Although these were RAF units, the RCAF was strongly represented, with perhaps as many as one-third of the aircrew on such as 233 and 48 being Canadian. No. 233 had as an acting CO the Canadian S/Ldr Baudoux, and from 48 there were some who, for their second tour, joined No. 422 Squadron.

Deployment of the Canadian Squadron in Coastal Command

Despite the close cover necessary for Operation Torch, Coastal Command's other duties could not be neglected. The Battle of the Atlantic never ceased;

U-boats were forever entering and leaving French Biscay ports; there was the constant threat of a breakout from Norwegian fjords of such as the battleship *Tirpitz*.

Thus in November 1942, No. 404 Squadron was using Scottish bases—Dyce, Sumburgh, and Wick—to cover the Norwegian area; 422 was at Oban, 423 at Castle Archdale, Northern Ireland, but with a detachment at Pembroke Dock; No. 407 moved down to St. Eval and Thorney Island, while 415 had a detachment at St. Eval. Thus additional cover was given to the Biscay area by 407 and 415. St. Eval had been organised to take a maximum of 72 aircraft, and Chivenor, Devon, 88 aircraft.

Coastal Command was so stretched that another Canadian Squadron—405—was borrowed from Bomber Command to deploy their Halifaxes, and the USAAF sent eight B24 Liberators.[32]

No. 415 Squadron Equips with Hampdens

No. 415 Squadron was informed in January 1942 that it was to be equipped with Handley-Page Hampdens, which were to be operated as torpedo-bombers, with the first one arriving on 24 January. By the end of the month eleven Hampdens had been allocated and fitted for torpedoes but were at the factory awaiting despatch. The squadron received the last of its Hampdens from the English Electric company on 25 February, bringing the total to twenty aircraft with the unit. Drift recorders had been fitted to the Hampdens "as an experiment," and "proved satisfactory."

Due to heavy snow in the middle of January, flying had proved impossible, and personnel were involved in snow-clearing. S/Ldr W.W. Bean visited another Hampden Squadron at Balderton in Nottinghamshire, No. 408 (RCAF), to gain some information regarding the operational use of the aircraft. This was at the end of February by which time at least thirteen of 415's pilots had qualified on Hampdens.

The Commanding Officer, W/Cmdr Wurtele, visited the RCAF Overseas HQ in London and also the Chester Herald at the College of Arms, the latter concerning a badge for the squadron.

One of the ground staff to join 415 in March 1942 was Scott Norquay who, writing in retrospect, states: "My service in Coastal Command revolved around fitting and sometimes removing, guns, bombs, torpedoes, depth charges and cannons etc on quite a variety of so-called aircraft." Norquay was with 415 until January 1944 when he was posted to No. 423 (RCAF) Squadron, then at Castle Archdale in Northern Ireland.

The first recorded flying accident occurred for the squadron on 9 March when Hampden J/415 AT248 crashed during take-off, but none of the crew was injured. Three days later however, the crew of AT247 W/415 failed to return from a non-operational trip. The body of one of the crew, P/O Herbert was picked up by a trawler off the Isle of Wight on 18 March and buried the following day at Thorney Island cemetery. On 23 March another of the Hampdens AT239 crashed at Hambleton, Hampshire; the crew of four, F/Sgt C.H. Jay, Sgts P.G. O'Brien, M.F. Ramsey, and R.R. Oliver, were all killed.

No. 415 Squadron to St. Eval

The squadron's main party left Thorney Island via Emsworth station on 11 April for Padstow, Cornwall, and squadron equipment was being unloaded at St. Eval on the 13th. The move was completed on the 15th when F/O Vaughan arrived with the rear party. This was to be just one of many moves which 415 was to suffer; perhaps one of the most ill-used squadrons in the whole of Coastal Command.

P/O Stronach was airborne at 0755 hrs on 27 April in Hampden AT232 on an A/S patrol, touching down again at 1410 hrs. This appears as 415's first operational sortie. Two other aircraft that were airborne about the same time were AT244 with W/Cmdr Wurtele, and AT235 captained by F/Lt Hobbs.

A month later the CO, W/Cmdr Wurtele, led a detachment of six aircraft to North Coates on the east coast with ground crew following by rail. On 27 May two formations of the Hampdens, armed with bombs, were on a shipping strike in flights with two other squadrons. P/O Lawrence led one formation, W/Cmdr Wurtele, the other.

P/O McMillan captained Hampden N/415 AT243 in formation with two other aircraft and was airborne from North Coates at 2220 hrs. Just after midnight, the three Hampdens were in position 5337N 0545E when an enemy convoy was sighted twenty-five miles away and noted due to AA fire from the ships, a merchantman escorted by five flak vessels heading north-west.

The merchant vessel was attacked by releasing four 250 lb bombs. A shell burst close to McMillan's Hampden; and his rear gunner was thrown from his seat and ammunition pans were dismantled from his guns. P/O George Lawrence from Calgary in AT239 sighted a convoy in the same position, but given as six merchantmen with five escort vessels, heading westwards. Lawrence attacked a 3-island type merchantman just as a Beaufighter was leaving the target. There was heavy AA from the escort vessels and both port and starboard wings of the Hampden were hit.

Lawrence attacked from 600 ft, releasing four 250 pound bombs spaced at 30 ft and at 180 mph. Lawrence took evasive action but saw an explosion and a cloud of smoke near the bows of the ship. On returning to North Coates at 0255 hrs the following morning, he overshot the runway but no one was injured. Large holes were seen in both wings and fuselage resulting from AA fire.

Hampden R/415 AT236 was airborne at 2225 hrs on 29 May, captained by P/O Sargent. R/415 was one of three on a sortie about that time; it failed to return. Another crew was lost off the Frisian Islands on 4 June when three of 415's aircraft were on a Rover patrol. F/Sgt McBride's gunner saw a red flash on the water and F/Lt Sumner saw two E-boats in the area. D/415 captained by P/O F.H. Mahn failed to return. Ninety miles east of North Coates, wreckage and a pigeon container were seen, and at position 5329N 00231E, a body in a Mae West. P/O Mahn was rescued at sea on 18 June. The *Montreal Standard* 18 July 1942 reported that Mahn, who had taken off from North Coates for the Frisians, had been flying at 200-300 feet when his port engine failed. The aircraft went into a turn which he was unable to correct before he crashed into the sea in position 5334N 0231E. Mahn escaped through the cockpit hood, an air gunner left through the astro hatch, and later, the navigator surfaced but was semi-conscious. The other air gunner was not seen. The dinghy had released and the air gunner and Mahn hoisted in the navigator.

They waited until daylight before opening rations, as the dinghy was full of water, and baling was avoided in case equipment was lost. Food was contimated with petrol, but the two-quart container of water was OK. On the second and third days they were still cheerful and relieved at having survived, but on the fourth day there was a high north-west wind and a heavy swell keeping the dinghy wet. The first bottle of water was finished on the fifth day, and the sea remained rough until the eighth day, when rescue appeared hopeless. Two hours before sundown a JU88 circled for about forty-five minutes before a Beaufighter dived to attack. The JU88 escaped; the Beaufighter flew low over the dinghy before disappearing. The navigator died that evening. Four Hudsons flew near on the ninth day at 600-700 ft without apparently seeing the dinghy. The air gunner drank sea water on the tenth day, and Mahn threw the can into the sea. When it began to rain, Mahn collected some in a piece of canvas which the airgunner refused, and Mahn drank it. The air gunner became delirious and died after two hours. On the thirteenth day Mahn had his first food. A seagull alighted and Mahn grabbed it. On 18 June a ship approached; a line was thrown and one of its crew went aboard the dinghy. Mahn was taken below in the ship and given soup and fruit juices but without any stomach upset.

Torpedo Strikes by Hampdens to the Frisians

At the end of June and the beginning of July 1942, 415 Squadron's Hampdens were armed with torpedoes and undertook a series of shipping strikes off the Frisian Islands in conjunction with Hudsons from No. 59 Squadron. They encountered severe AA and suffered losses, with F/Sgt Garfin as captain of Hampden AT245 and F/Sgt McCullum in AT229 failing to return. Others which did return were badly shot up, and F/Sgt McComb crash-landed at Donna Nook with his Hampden a write-off. McComb and his crew survived this crash only to be lost on 30 July when they crashed on the shore south of North Coates.

On 4 August, No. 415 Squadron prepared to move to Wick with ground staff arriving there two days later. The CO, W/Cmdr Wurtele, was posted to Canada, and S/Ldr R.R. Dennis assumed command. F/Lt Sumner was posted to No. 423 (RCAF) Squadron which had formed at Oban and was equipped with Sunderlands.

W/Cmdr Dennis was leading a small formation of torpedo-armed Hampdens to Egero, Norway on 10 August when, eleven minutes after take-off, his starboard engine cut. After ditching, the aircraft's dinghy broke loose but was recovered by Sgt Stallard. Although it was inverted, all the crew climbed aboard. The other Hampdens circled, and obtained a fix, and an ASR launch picked up the crew at 0530 hrs the following morning to take them to Aberdeen. One of the formation had seen the Hampden go down two miles off Bell Rock, another reported the Hampden sinking in less than thirty seconds.

The following month, 415 was taken off operations for rest and training but suffered another crash when a Hampden broke off from a formation during training and all the crew were killed.

A No. 415 Squadron Hampden Crashes at St.Eval

On 1 November 1942, a shipping strike was flown from Thorney Island, but on returning, one of the Hampdens crashed at St. Eval. F/O J.H. Godfrey and F/O R.G. Frederick were killed, Sgts D.M. Coates and R.A. Clarke were taken to Truro hospital suffering from burns. A subsequent report by F/Sgt Coates to his CO included the following:

I was sitting on the floor of the aircraft with my back to the wing root when we crashed. The inboard fuel tank in the starboard wing exploded through the gas cock and the fire flared up just in front of my face. I was dazed for a few seconds and tried to paw the fire away from my face with my right hand. Recovering from the daze, I pulled myself up, turned round and prepared to escape through the observer's escape hatch. F/O Frederick was trying to get out but seemed to be in difficulty so I gave him a push. When he was out I scrambled up on the wing root and made good my escape. As I went out I shouted to F/O Godfrey, "Be with you in a second Jack." My intercom was still connected but I pulled it loose after I was out of the machine. I then pulled the sliding cockpit hatch back from over the pilot's cockpit, reached in and released the Sutton harness and began trying to pull the pilot free. I cannot say definitely what length of

time elasped during my efforts to free the pilot but as near as the rest of the crew can make out, it was 1-2 minutes. F/O Godfrey was unconscious and his legs seemed caught in some manner. I was beginning to think of leaving the pilot and escaping myself as I feared the port tanks were liable to explode when the flame licked over the edge of the wing catching me across the face and eyes.

I then turned and ran down the port wing, past the exploding ammunition and ran to where F/O Frederick was lying. F/Sgt Clark and I picked up F/O Frederick and began running away from the vicinity of the aircraft with him. We passed a party of men and shouted to them to get us an ambulance. We were taken to hospital and given first-aid for our burns

F/O Frederick sent a letter dated 12 April 1943 to his CO concerning the crash of Hampden AT193 on 1 November 1942 which included:

On the afternoon we took off from Thorney Island in company with an aircraft piloted by S/Ldr W.W. Bean to make a torpedo strike on two merchant vessels which were well beyond our maximum range deep in the Bay of Biscay. After continuing our PLE we returned to St. Eval as instructed; still in formation with our leader. F/O Godfrey was by then very near exhaustion from the strain of flying in formation at nought feet for such a long period in an aircraft which trimmed badly at the slow speed we flew to extend our range. His condition was aggravated by us having been caught without warning by the operation and had nothing substantial to eat since tea the day before.

As we approached the field we found it covered with light haze lying very thick over the downwind area of the runway in use which extends into a valley. F/O Godfrey did not follow his usual practice of flying straight down the flare-path and setting his direction indicator presumably because there was another aircraft in the circuit.

As we circled the field I went to my crash position behind the pilot, put on my goggles and mask and opened the escape hatch above my head and took up a standing position looking over the pilot's shoulder. I did not have my flying gloves. We saw S/Ldr Bean land and shortly after got our green. As we turned into wind we found we could see only two white lights presumably the first two flares and lined up on them. We touched down beautifully right at the end of the runway and at the same time F/O Godfrey shouted "We're off the runway." At the same instant I saw the complete flarepath come into view extending straight away from us on our port bow at an angle of 30-40 degrees from the fore and aft line.

We were rolling very fast across the grass towards a line of Whitleys that showed up in the chance light. Our approach had been perfectly straight along the line on which we touched down but we received no warning from the ground of our danger. We still had our torpedo underneath and I believe that is why Jack did not yank up the undercart—instead he started

applying the left brake to start a swing which would have taken us clear of the Whitleys. I don't believe he saw a lorry and a petrol dump which intervened for I did not until a split second before we hit. Then I saw the lorry flash against our nose and starboard engine which was knocked down and out of the nacelle which burst into flames. The aircraft came to rest in the petrol dump with the starboard wing tip on the ground and instantly burst into roaring flame. I believe that some of the petrol washed in through the nose for the column of fire that rushed under the pilot's seat and out of the escape hatch was absolutely solid.

I found that my left leg was caught. After three unsuccessful attempts to release it I gave up and settled down to wait. Then I felt Sgt Coates grip me at the waist and lift me towards the hatch. This so encouraged me that between us I got my leg free and jumped out onto the wing with Sgt Coates behind me. The aircraft was alight wing tip to wing tip and nose to tail. The wall of flames which surrounded the aircraft was so high on the starboard side that it was impossible to see anything outside.

My clothing was alight from head to foot and the skin was now hanging off my hands like a pair of gloves turned partly inside out, so I ran down the wing and dove through the flames onto the ground where I started rolling in an effort to put out the fire. Sgt Coates went forward to the pilot's cockpit and slid back the cockpit cover which was still closed. He found F/O Godfrey slumped forward unconscious, with the instrument panel driven into his legs. The fire had not yet penetrated the floor of the cockpit. He removed Jack's harness and attempted to drag him out persisting in the impossible task until the fire closed in on him severely burning his face and wrists in spite of the continuous petrol explosions which were going on all around him and entangling him in the holocaust, to say nothing of the torpedo going off.

Meanwhile Sgt Clark had been thrown to the floor by the impact where he was met by a column of fire coming from the petrol cocks. With considerable difficulty he made his way out over his guns onto the port wing and attempted to go forward to assist Sgt Coates, but by the time he got there the fire had reached such intensity that he was unable to do anything. Jumping down off the wing he ran to where I was still rolling about. Throwing himself on top of me he succeeded in smothering the flames which I'd not been able to put out.

Shortly afterwards Sgt Coates appeared out of the flames and between them they got me to my feet and ran with me to a safe place in case the torpedo should go off. Somewhere near the white Whitley's dispersal we met an airman whom we sent after the ambulance which had proceeded to the crash. Looking back at the wreck we saw the fire tender arrive and begin playing a stream of water on the fire but I did not see any attempt to enter the fire although they believed us all to be still there. I did not say this in criticism of their effort, but merely to illustrate the intensity of the fire.

I would like to take this opportunity of expressing officially my appreciation of the courage, coolness and devotion to duty of Sgts Coates and Clark throughout. It was no surprise to me, for both lads always gave of their very best at all times and always acted for the crew before themselves. In spite of the painful burns which he himself had received, Sgt Coates remained with me for over five hours until I was taken to the operating theatre, thereby helping greatly to minimise the shock caused by my experience.

I would also like to record my regret at losing the finest skipper a navigator ever had. Jack was a fine pilot and a good friend. He was never better than on his last flight. It was not through any carelessness on his part that we came to grief—he was just taxed beyond endurance. I would like respectfully to submit that when conditions are such that the automatic pilot cannot be used, some thought should be given to the effect of pilot fatigue, when planning operational sorties for Hampdens. Also that crews should be frequently reminded of the importance of proper escape drill, protective clothing, and special alertness at the end of a sortie.

K.G. Frederick
F/O J8125 RCAF

The tragic but heroic sortie undertaken by F/O Godfrey with S/Ldr Bean perhaps prompted the squadron to consider seriously flights over the Bay of Biscay, as on 7 December 1942 petrol consumption tests were made by three aircraft from Predannack towards the

Spanish coast, taking just over seven hours in total.

W/Cmdr Bean led three Hampdens on a shipping strike to the Dutch coast on 22 December.

They included F/415 X2961, captained by Sgt. G.O Ellergodt, who was airborne from Thorney Island at 2144 hrs. The Dutch coast was reached at 0005 hrs amid both flak and flares from unseen ships. Fifteen minutes later, however, several ships were sighted. They were attacked by releasing torpedoes from 30-40 feet altitude at a range of 800 yards. There was intense light flak and evasive action was taken. Three shells burst in the fuselage of Ellergodt's aircraft and put out of action all of his instruments apart from the gyro, altimeter and compass. The elevator trim was shot away, and the Hampden zoomed up to 800 feet with the cockpit full of blinding smoke. One of Ellergodt's crew—Sgt E.H. Johnson—was wounded in the thumb by a shell splinter. Another of the Hampdens captained by Sgt J.C. McDonald was also badly shot up. They returned to base at 0324 hrs. Sgt Ellergodt was recommended for an award.

References to Chapter Two

1. SWR II p.115
2. GuH para.169
3. JH p.279
4. CCWR p.24
5. CCWR p.20
6. KA p.130
7. RAF I p.372
8. SWR II p.159
9. Naval Intelligence report 1942
10. RAF I pp. 363-75; WSC pp. 98-102
11. RAF II p.94
12. CCWR p.20
13. Ibid
14. Ibid
15. Ibid
16. RAF II p.95
17. RCAF III p.439
18. RCAF p.20
19. RAF II p.95
20. RCAF III p.439
21. WSC IV p.778
22. MM p.281
23. CCWR p.28
24. WSC IV p.613; WSC IV p.404
25. WSC IV p.537
26. SWR II p.312
27. SWR III/2 p.313 and p.320
28. ABC p.482
29 AH S&S p.111; AH FC p.59; AH SS p.56
30. AH S&S p.119
31. SWR II p.340
32. RAF II p.110

Chapter 3

The Flying-Boat Squadrons: April– December 1942

During March and April 1942 the German U-boat Command was aware of increasing RAF air patrols over the Bay of Biscay, but at that time hadn't realised that ASV was being used by patrolling aircraft.[1]

About that time also, submarine tankers, "milch cows," were coming into service which were able to refuel as many as twelve U-boats, enabling them to operate as far as the Caribbean, and were able to cause heavy losses of allied shipping in the first half of 1942.[2]

For Coastal Command aircraft operating from the United Kingdom there was the constant need to protect the vital Atlantic convoys and additionally those sailing to Russia. However, with squadrons such as No. 413 posted to the Far East, Coastal Command was left with only six flying-boat squadrons to operate over home waters, and in April and May two new Canadian units, Nos. 422 and 423, were formed within the Command.[3]

The Formation of the Tomahawk Squadron

The fifth RCAF Squadron to be formed within the RAF's Coastal Command was No. 422. This was at Lough Erne, Northern Ireland, on 2 April 1942, and the unit was initially commanded by an ex-No. 201 Squadron officer, S/Ldr J.S. Kendrick, RAF. He was succeeded by a Canadian, S/Ldr Larry Skey, DFC, RAF who had already served with 210 and 228 Squadrons on Sunderlands.[4] S/Ldr Skey arrived at Lough Erne on 9 July, and another officer from the RAF, F/Lt R.E. Hunter, DFC came from No. 119 Squadron to serve as Flight Commander.

No. 422 Squadron was allocated eight Lerwick flying-boats from Invergordon. Three of these were flown in on 23 July by W/Cmdr Skey, and P/Os Barnett, Bentley, Butler, and Marshall pending the arrival of Catalinas. One of the better known Wop/AGs to join the squadron was the playwright Terence Rattigan. However, the Lerwicks were to prove unsuitable for operational flying and 422 converted initially to Catalinas.

Throughout the war, the RCAF Overseas Branch in London were shown to monitor operational records and F/Lt Thompson from HQ came in July to discuss the unit's welfare and records, etc. as required by Overseas HQ.

The Arrival of Catalina Flying-Boats

On 29 July W/Cmdr Skey left for Beaumaris and Greenock with four skeleton crews to collect 422's first three Catalinas. Lt Honey took over FP103 at Beaumaris and then flew to Greenock; F/O Bellis and W/O Limpert remained at Greenock with crews to take over FP105 and FP106. This was pending the formation of No. 131 OTU. By the end of July 1942 when one Catalina and four Lerwicks were officially on charge, the unit had completed forty hours flying on Lerwicks and five hours on Catalinas. Lt Honey had flown in Catalina FP103 on 31 July; FP105 and FP106 arrived from Greenock on 3 August.

There was an accident with FP103 on 5 August, but with only slight damage and no casualties.

Some intended ferrying by 422 Squadron was deferred due to imminent operations with three Catalinas and with a request to detach three crews with Catalina IIIs to No. 330(Norge) Squadron.

On 16 August W/Cmdr Skey and F/O L.O. Barnett flew Catalinas FP105 and FP106 to the Faeroes to calibrate the RDF station and report on Vaagar as a prospective flying-boat base. They returned to base on the 19th having spent the night of the 18th at Invergordon.

Detachment to Russia

The three Catalinas—FP103, FP105, and FP106—were airborne from Lough Erne at 1400 hrs on 27 August for Invergordon. In the three crews were S/Ldr Hunter, Lt Honey, P/O Beattie, F/O Knox, P/O Omerod, F/O Bellis, P/O Patton, P/O Patience, and P/O Irvine. The purpose of the detachment was to transport key personnel and to assist in covering convoys PQ18 and QP14.

On 30 August A/422 FP103, captained by S/Ldr Hunter, was airborne from Sullom Voe at 1600 hrs for a flight to Grasnya, Murmansk. His second pilot was Lt Honey, navigator P/O Knox, and Wop/AG P/O Beattie. In addition to "key personnel," the Catalina carried spares for Hurricane aircraft. Weather conditions were fair, with heavy winds but good visibility. FP103 touched down at 1740 hrs 31 August.

W/O Limpert captained C/422 FP106 which was airborne at 1520 hrs but scheduled for Lahkta, Archangel. Limpert made landfall at Cape Kanin and completed his trip at 0841 hrs on 31 August.

The third Catalina, B/422 FP105, had F/O J.W. Bellis as captain, and passengers included wireless experts to man a station near Lahkta.

After being airborne from Sullom Voe on 1 September, Bellis encountered violent magnetic disturbances, with a front extending from the White Sea, inland to Russian Lapland, requiring him to fly round the coast to Lake Lahkta, where he arrived at 1320 hrs on 2 September. On 7 September, Lt Honey was airborne from Grasnya in FP103 bound for Sullom Voe, but at 1300 hrs the following day, had to force-land near Whalsey Island. The Catalina was damaged beyond repair, but all the crew and passengers were safe. F/O Bellis, who left shortly afterwards from Grasnya in FP105, was diverted to Invergordon due to bad weather. The third Catalina, captained by W/O Limpert, experienced poor weather conditions with low visibility and cloud base at 1000 feet but made landfall at North Unst at 0711 hrs on 8 September and landed at Sullom

Voe. He had as passenger the British Vice-Consul to Moscow.

W/O Limpert returned to Grasnya with the Vice-Consul on the 15th and two days later undertook a cross-over patrol off Cape North. When 35 miles north of North Cape, a Dornier 18 was sighted, but there was no air-to-air combat. The weather was described as "poor" with low visibility and icing at 300 feet for a trip lasting nineteen hours. W/O Limpert was ferrying personnel from Grasnya to Lake Lahkta in FP106 on the 20th despite a 75-knot wind and icing at low levels. Rear-Admiral Miles was a passenger to be ferried from Lahkta to Grasnya on the 22nd, where he landed during an air raid, with bombs dropping around the Catalina during its approach.

Limpert's final trip in this Russian detachment was to return to Sullom Voe on the 24th with Rear Admiral Miles and L/Cmdr Palmer. FP106 was airborne from Grasnya on 0530 hrs and made landfall at North Unst before being waterborne at 1745 hrs in Sullom Voe. The detachment was such that it gained space in Coastal Command's *Review* for November 1942.

No. 422 Squadron at Lough Erne

In September the Canadians took over the buildings and quarters formerly occupied by No. 119 Squadron RAF. These were being cleaned out on the 5th, and 422 moved in the following day. Lerwick S/422 was on local flying captained by F/Lt Ogle-Skan, on the 10th, but crashed at 1235 hrs when being flown by P/O L.C. Hoare. There were no casualties, but the Lerwick sank. One of the Catalinas, Fp2113, was damaged while taxying on Lough Erne on the 11th.

U-570 had surrendered to a Hudson of No. 269 Squadron on 27 August, and the U-boat was taken over by the Royal Navy as HMS *Graph*. Some of 422 flew to Greenock on 29 September to view the submarine; they included Lt Honey and F/Lt Rawlins who made the flight in Lerwicks "N" and "Y."[5]

Ferrying of Catalinas from Canada to the United Kingdom

As a prelude to the ferrying, a detachment of eleven crews was made to Reykjavik commanded by W/Cmdr Skey, with Lt Honey as his adjutant. Remaining at Lough Erne was F/Lt Murphy taking over administration, with F/Lt S.J. Rawlins acting as Flight Commander.

On 4 October personnel involved with ferrying arrived at Glasgow. From there they were taken by two buses to Preswick, to be informed that their sailing date was delayed forty-eight hours. On 7 October personnel were taken by bus to Greenock and embarked on RMS *Queen Mary*, which sailed that night for Boston, Mass. The following day, while RMS *Queen Mary* was being escorted by a 201 Squadron Sunderland, a message was passed to the aircraft: "422 send T.K." The response from the Sunderland was "201 send G.L." After docking at Boston on 14 October, the detachment was met by embarkation and press representatives from RCAF HQ Ottawa before leaving that evening by train for Montreal.

From Montreal on 15 October the detachment was taken to Dorval airport HQ where W/Cmdr Skey had the distinction of being interviewed by ACM Sir Frederick Bowhill. Sir Frederick had at the time of the battleship *Bismarck* sailing, been AOCinC, Coastal Command.[6] Later

W/Cmdr Skey briefed his crews, saying they would be in two groups, with the first group of five departing on 26 October and the second group of six on 2 November. RAF personnel were given a week leave and assigned to the first flight; RCAF personnel had two weeks leave and were for the second flight. Training was arranged for the RAF Ferry Command's procedure.

At Boucherville, flights were delayed by bad weather until 28 October when four aircraft flew to Gander Lake, followed later by the fifth aircraft. All five had reached Lough Erne by 2 November.

Of the second flight of six aircraft; three arrived at Beaumaris and two at Greenock on 8 November. The ferrying commitment had been completed with two days of the six weeks which had been forecast.

Of the captains detailed for the ferrying, only one had completed a tour of Catalinas, four others had less than five operational sorties as captains, and the other six had not flown as captains prior to the ferrying.

No. 422 (RCAF) Squadron Moves from Lough Erne to Oban

On 5 November the unit had loaded all stores and equipment by 1700 hrs and personnel left Irvinstown by train at 0100 hrs the following morning for Larne. The journey was then by boat to Stranraer and then by train via Stirling to Oban, where they arrived on 6 November. There was a change of Station Commander at Oban coinciding with the arrival of 422 when G/Capt Field succeeded G/Capt Turner, AFC. No. 228 Squadron, RAF, then also at Oban were scheduled to operate from Lough Erne.

Re-equipment of No. 422 (RCAF) Squadron with Sunderlands

From 1 October 1942 the unit was considered non-operational on handing over its three Catalinas to No. 131 OTU at Killadeas. No. 422 was to re-equip from nine Catalinas to Sunderlands. Initially six Lerwicks were to be retained pending allotment of Sunderlands. W/Cmdr Whittaker from HQ No. 15 Group arrived to discuss the new Sunderland establishment. Their first Sunderland "B" arrived on 12 October from No. 246 Squadron and a second one was flown in from Bowmore the following day. There were high winds at Lough Erne on 14 October, and several maintenance personnel from No. 201 Squadron were drowned when dinghy No. 611 sank.

On November 11 Sunderlands W6028 and W6029 were flown to Wig Bay on Loch Ryan for refitting. Two more, W6026 and W6027, were allotted to 422 the following day. The first fully operational Sunderland for 422 was W6026, which Capt Honey collected from Wig Bay and flew to Oban on 17 November.

F/Lt Rawlins collected W6027 from Wig Bay on 20 November and by the end of the month, four Sunderlands were on charge.

On 19 December Sunderland W6029 was returning from a flight to Sullom Voe to change personnel for a detached crew. Weather and sea conditions were considered unsuitable for landing at Oban, and No. 18 Group endeavoured to contact the Sunderland by radio and divert it to Invergordon. It was unsuccessful and W6029 captained by F/Lt J.D. Reed, RCAF, crashed on landing in the Firth of Lorne. Five of the crew and two passengers, Major John Cox and L.C.W.

Allan, were killed or missing. Others were seriously or slightly injured.

The Formation of No. 423 (RCAF) Squadron

No. 423 (RCAF) Squadron was formed at Oban on 18 May 1942 with, as headquarters, a navigation room allocated by the Station. One of the first to arrive was S/Ldr J.D.E. Hughes, DFC, RAF, who was posted from No. 4 C OTU, Stranraer to serve as a Flight Commander.

W/Cmdr F.J. Rump arrived ex-Gibraltar on 26 May to be the unit's first Commanding Officer. The squadron's medical officer, F/Lt "Doc" C. Sheard from No. 518 Squadron, came three days later. LAC Larkman, an RDF mechanic, had the distinction of being the first airman to arrive. Two small rooms on Kerrera Island became available for the servicing party, and one of these served for the signals section. An aircrew of seven, captained by F/O R.Mills, was detached to Greenock for ferrying duties. By the end of June there was still a lack of servicing facilities, although the personnel numbered twelve officers and sixty-two other ranks. No. 423's first aircraft arrived on 17 July, a Mark II Sunderland W6001, flown by S/Ldr Hughes. A second one, W6000, arrived the following day with F/Lt L.D. Lindsay, DFC.

F/Sgt R.S. Long undertook one of the first operational trips. This was an anti-submarine patrol in W6052, which was airborne at 1909 hrs on 4 August and waterborne again at Stornaway at 0731 hrs the following morning.

An officer who was later to become CO of 423's sister squadron, F/Lt J.R. Sumner, made one of the first U-boat sightings on 12 November while flying

W6009 on an A/S sweep. He was at 2500 feet when the U-boat was six miles away. He dived to attack, but the U-boat submerged forty seconds before he reached the scene. Ten seconds too late for a possibly successful attack.

Combat with a Junkers 88

One of 423 Squadron's first air-to-air combats took place on 21 November. F/Sgt Long had been airborne in W6052 on an escort to convoy MKS9 when at 1130 hrs a JU88 was sighted 500 feet above the Sunderland, which was at 1500 feet. It was spotted by his mid-upper gunner, J.R. Matthews. The enemy flew on a parallel track but in the opposite direction before swinging round to the Sunderland's port quarter and attacking from astern at 400 yards, closing to 200 yards range, before breaking away below the Sunderland's starboard bow. The enemy fire was wide, but the Sunderland opened fire at 250 yards and estimated hits on the enemy. The Junkers again attacked, but on the starboard bow of the Sunderland, which banked to give its front gunner a chance to fire a burst from 50 yards range, scoring hits.

The mid-upper and tail gunner followed with more bursts of fire, and suddenly the JU88 dived down to 50 ft from the sea, before turning away and escaping into cloud. The Sunderland suffered just four bullet holes in the mainplane. The calmness of the crew was exemplified by Sgt Clegg in the galley, who carried on cooking lunch during the affray, occasionally viewing the action through the window!

Of 423's early days with Coastal Command, the squadron's first CO,

Air/Cmdre "Freddy" Rump writes in retrospect:

Some time before America entered the war, my flying-boat experience included some adventurous sea voyages to Bermuda via Halifax to collect PB2Ys and PBYs from America, which were then ferried non-stop back to the UK.

These flights were approximately 28 hours non-stop, and apart from an RAD trained navigator, the remaining crew were civilians.

Later I was delighted to be given the opportunity to form, convert and train up No. 423 Squadron. It was quite a unique experience as up until then, the Flying-boat Union was very much a closed shop! On arrival at Oban, I was joined by Johnnie Hughes, an operationally experienced RAF flying-boat captain! Together we had the task of forming and training with RCAF pilots and aircrew (who were mostly inexperienced) in what was a very unusual and completely different change, and indeed, a challenge to us all.

The nucleus of ground crew was eventually built up to squadron strength as RAF were gradually replaced by RCAF tradesmen—meanwhile the aircrew flew with another flying-boat squadron based at Oban to gain operational training and experience.

After approximately six months, 423 was operational and in what was a well-planned and executed move, the whole squadron of approximately 250 personnel flew to Lough Erne in Northern Ireland.

At Lough Erne we settled into somewhat strange accommodation,

including a castle, stables and Nissen huts, and commenced our full operational role. We all worked hard together to bring up to a high operational standard which went on to achieve great success by sinking a number of boats.

A/Cmdre Rump makes particular mention in his letter of 423's first medical officer, Doc Sheard, "who in additon to his valuable medical work,...was always on hand to give us his advice on general medical or psychological problems" and of his RCAF "chiefy," F/Sgt Wright, "the ever willing and cheerful backbone of the ground crew."

During December 1942, 423 Squadron undertook a number of convoy escorts for such as SC111, and MKS3X. For a Wop/AG in F/Lt Mills' crew on the 15th, the sortie was hardly "routine." Their Sunderland W6013 was airborne at 0703 hrs and as the Wop/AG, Jim Wright recalls:

I shall always remember this sortie for its sadness and frustration. We were briefed to fly out into the Atlantic and rendezvous with a secret naval force which comprised HMS *Anson* and four destroyers. Strict W/T silence was to be maintained throughout the flight.

The weather conditions were miserable and on the way we sighted a merchant ship bobbing up and down in the heavy sea and not making any progress. We circled the ship which looked old and battered and the captain flashed a message on the signalling light that it had lost its propeller and had been left behind by the convoy. He asked that we should fly 100 miles away from him and send a wireless signal to Group explaining his predicament with a request for help.

At the briefing our instructions had been peremptory and we were obliged to signal on our Aldis lamp that we were unable to comply. The captain, of course, could have sent a WT message himself but that would have given his position away to U-boats. We felt terrible about this but informed him we would send a report at the earliest opportunity.

On reaching the Naval force we flashed a message giving full details but the Navy was in a similar position; they were not permitted to transmit....The only compromise was for us to cut short our patrol by three hours and one hour from base broke WT silence and transmitted the message. We had not sighted the ship again on the return journey.

After we had debriefed in the operational room we learned that as soon as dusk had fallen the ship had been attacked by a U-boat and sunk. This very sad situation had its parallel in other spheres of the war where men found themselves by reasons of security and for the safety of the largest number of combatants, being forced to withhold assistance against their natural inclinations.

Shortly after F/Lt Mills had taken off on this trip, F/Lt Sumner followed, but in the search for a tanker. Three days later F/Lt Sumner was on escort to HX218 and was requested by the escorting SNO to search for a straggler, which was located. For the remainder of 1942 this was the pattern for 423's sorties: convoy escorts and occasionally looking for stragglers.

References to Chapter 3

1. GüH para.184
2. GüH para.187 and SWR II/p95
3. RCAF IIIp.389
4. AH 'SS' pp.13-19,50
5. AH 'SS' p.107
6. AH FC pp.21-24

Chapter 4

The Flying-Boat Squadrons: January– December 1943

No. 422 Squadron at Oban

The year 1943 began for 422 Squadron with personnel comprising 106 aircrew and 141 ground staff. Aircraft on charge were seven Sunderlands plus one which had been allotted. By the end of February the unit's training was considered virtually completed and it became operational effective 1 March 1943. Six crews were fully qualified and the remaining three were progressing.

Their first Sunderland flying-boat operation was by W6028 C/422 which was airborne from Oban at 0420 hrs, captained by W/Cmdr Skey. He assisted a convoy by "collecting" stragglers, first sighting a trawler steaming at 10 knots and then a merchant vessel of 3000 tons, *Roseform*, despite visibility of 1-2 miles, a cloud ceiling of 800 ft and a 45-knot wind.

W/Cmdr Skey was followed a few hours later by F/O Sargent in W6032, who was to escort convoy ONS169. It comprised thirty-eight merchant vessels, with only two escorts, heading northwards at 5 knots. In position 5652N 1245W he contacted the SNO in the escort K48 by

R/T and received instructions on where to patrol. Due to low visibility, navigation was on occasion by radar. Two days later, another trawler from a convoy was sighted by S/Ldr Hunter; a merchant vessel of 4500 tons, *Mayoress*. S/Ldr Hunter gave the vessel its position and reported to the convoy.

While on an anti-submarine sweep on 11 March, F/O Martin received a message from base: "Proceed to 5830N 2104W and help USA *Bibb* and *Rosewood* to meet; return to Castle Archdale."

Two and a half hours later, in position 5826N 2102W, Martin located a 5000-ton ship with a large hole in the bow which had been abandoned. A few minutes later the bow of a half-submerged vessel was sighted. At 1540 hrs the Sunderland was in position 5819N 2130W to see the stern portion of a blazing tanker which had been abandoned. The tanker, *Rosewood*, of 5889 tons was sunk by U-409 in position 5837N 2232W on 9 March; it had been with convoy SC121.[1]

While still based at Oban there was a successful ASR operation undertaken by F/Lt Limpert. He was airborne at 1825 hrs on 28 April and forty minutes later in position 5628N 0701W sighted a round yellow dinghy ten miles away. There were four occupants. He saw a Beaufort drop a Thornaby bag upwind of the dinghy. F/Lt Limpert circled and directed a small coaster to the scene which picked up all four survivors.

No. 422 Squadron Moves from Oban to Bowmore

Orders were received from No. 15 Group on 1 May for the squadron to move to Bowmore, Isle of Islay, and fourteen airmen with two officers and two NCOs went by air to prepare for the main party's arrival. Arrangements were made with the Royal Navy to transport the main party by LCTs on the 7th. A farewell dinner on the 6th was attended by the Station Commander, G/Capt Field, SHQ officers, and also from No. 330, the Norwegian Squadron which was then also based at Oban.

Six LCTs took the main party and these barges dropped anchor at Bowmore at 2000 hrs on the 7th. Accommodation was for all requirements found to be inadequate, and the following day there was a heavy gale and rain. The weather was to prove a crucial factor for flying-boats, which needed to be moored on open water.

The AOCinC Coastal Command, Air Marshal John Slessor, visited 422 Squadron on 9 May to meet the crews, and the same day, the first of their Sunderlands, F/422, was flown in by F/O A.R. Fair.

The base at Bowmore was found to be quite isolated, and the small village of Bowmore unable to provide facilities for entertainment of personnel. Several cinema shows were given on the station each week and there were also some ENSA concerts. Teams of officers, NCOs, and airmen were formed for games of softball, and during long fine evenings, cycling proved a favourite pastime.

Most Coastal Command aircrew would say that the worst enemy was the weather and such it could prove even in May. On 2 May F/Lt Bellis was airborne at 0548 hrs for a sweep covering convoy ONS6. About seven hours later he was in position 6011N 1159W with heavy snow and icing. There was 10/10ths cloud down at 800 feet ½ mile visibility, a 40 knot wind from the west, a rough sea, and the weather was deteriorating.

F/Lt Butler was on a similar sweep and sighted the convoy steaming westwards at 7 knots in position 5835N 1410W. His navigator was unable to obtain drift sightings due to extreme turbulence, and fixes and courses to steer were obtained by radio. He was able to make landfall six miles south of Barra Head.

The hazards for ships sailing in convoy are reflected in 422's records:

F/Lt Martin was airborne on 21 May in DP831 on a Creeping Line Ahead (CLA) patrol in a search for a lifeboat. He sighted the convoy of forty-eight merchant vessels with apparently only one escort. The convoy was heading due east at 6 knots. For over six hours the wireless operator was picking up various SOS messages but was unable to obtain bearings. Finally in position 5505N 1451W the operator picked up: "SOS rammed trawler KG25 immediate assistance required." Shortly afterwards, a destroyer was sighted steaming at 20 knots and signalled "Have you sighted lifeboat?" "No."

The following day F/Lt Bellis was also airborne from Bowmore in a search for the lifeboat. At 1210 hrs in position 5538N 1245W following a blip on the radar screen, a destroyer was sighted towing the lifeboat eastwards at 15 knots.

On 25 May Sunderland DD846 captained by F/O Paige, DFC, was reported overdue. Paige had been airborne at 0330 hrs on a convoy escort but the following day it was reported that the aircraft had crashed near Clare Island, Clew Bay, Eire, in position 5347N 1000W at 0405 hrs on the 25th. Eight bodies were recovered, including that of F/O Paige, and they were taken to Castle Archdale to be buried at Irvinstown. The chief mourners were the two COs of 422 and 423 Squadrons, W/Cmdr Skey and W/Cmdr Rump. Four others from F/O Paige's crew were still missing.

The AOC No. 15 Group Air Vice-Marshal Sir Leonard Slatter, visited the station on 28 May and gave an informal talk to the officers on the trend in anti-submarine warfare. He gave the opportunity for questions to be asked before visiting other sections. By the end of May, 422 Squadron was still awaiting the completion of a new dental hut located by the medical inspection hut and several personnel were awaiting urgent treatment. Total personnel were then 367, including fourteen WAAFs.

An Encounter With Three U-Boats

During June 1943, 422 Squadron sent a number of aircraft and crews to operate from Castle Archdale, since there was a maintenance detachment of twenty airmen also at Wig Bay on Loch Ryan to assist with inspections for squadron aircraft. On 16 June F/Lt Butler was airborne from Castle Archdale in Sunderland W6031 at 0840 hrs. Just under

eight hours later he was in position 4404N 1342W flying at 300 feet altitude. There was a westerly wind of 30 knots, cloud base down to 100 feet, visibility 1000 yards and the weather generally bad. Through the haze, however, three vessels were sighted and then identified as U-boats. They all opened fire with 20 mm cannon and their main armament but the Sunderland suffered no hits. Butler closed the range and circled the vessels, which were still firing their rear guns. A sighting report was transmitted before contact was lost completely due to haze. This, perhaps, would have prepared F/Lt Butler when at a later date he was able to attack a U-boat successfully under more suitable conditions.[2]

Escort to Force H

F/Lt Limpert had the distinction of acting as escort to the Royal Navy's Force H on 19 June. About the time of operation Torch, Force H was based at Gibraltar but in June 1943 was using Scapa Flow in preparation for the invasion of Sicily. It comprised the battleships HMS *Nelson*, *Rodney*, *Warspite*, and *Valiant* with the aircraft carrier *Indomitable*.[3] There was thick fog and Limpert located the force by radar when it was in position 5245N 1454W before undertaking a sweep ahead of the vessels.

Dominion Day was celebrated at Bowmore on 1 July by 422 Squadron with, in the afternoon, a Field Day with games including softball, badminton, and tennis. Dances were held in the evening for the officers in their Mess, and at Bowmore Hall for other ranks. For the personnel who were lost on 25 May, a memorial service was held at Bowmore church on 13 July. The service was conducted by S/Ldr

H. Porter, and W/Cmdr Skey read the lesson.

Some of the squadron made a pilgrimage to Bowmore in 1975, and asked why Bowmore had built a round church? The minister replied that it was to avoid any corners which might harbour the Devil.

Sightings of U-Boats

In July 1943, No. 422 Squadron had detachments to Pembroke Dock including the CO, W/Cmdr Skey, who flew there with his crew in W6028 on the 13th. On 28 July P/O J.F. Wharton captained W6028 C/422 which was airborne from Castle Archdale at 0753 hrs. Four hours later, in position 4821N 1257W he sighted wreckage extending over ten yards. At 1614 hrs two U-boats were seen at eight miles on the starboard bow. They were fully-surfaced and heading due west at 12 knots. As Wharton flew in to attack, an American Catalina was sighted apparently releasing four depth charges which failed to explode. A second drop was made from the Catalina followed by smoke floats. A Sunderland from No. 201 Squadron appeared on the scene and circled with the other aircraft for half an hour. P/O Wharton made no attack, as the U-boats submerged minutes before his approach. After resuming his patrol, a 19 Group message instructed him to home on an aircraft in position 4425N 1210W, but no further sighting was made.

The Senior Air Officer (SAO) from HQ Coastal Command, Air Vice-Marshal Maynard, visited 422 Squadron on 8 August to discuss with the Commanding Officers at Port Ellen and Bowmore on the Isle of Islay the requirements necessary to make Bowmore an operational base for flying-boats. They realised later, however, that prevailing strong winds precluded any success in that respect.

The RCAF appeared ever conscious of the need to keep good records and on 15 August, G/Capt K.B. Konn from the Historical Records Section, RCAF HQ Ottawa, visited 422 Squadron to gain some background on squadron life. He flew three days later to No. 409 Squadron at Acklington.

Some secrecy prevailed on 26 August when two Sunderlands arrived from the RAF Marine Aircraft Experimental Establishment, Helenburgh. They undertook experimental flights "with new devices at Bowmore."

On 4 August, a signal from the AOC of No. 15 Group RAF referred to the anti-submarine patrols of both British and American Squadrons undertaken during July and included the statement..."the enemy can't get away with it by passing through the Bay in packs and fighting on the surface.... The Chief of Air Staff in particular sends his congratulations on the notable victory on 30 July when a whole pack of U-boats was destroyed."

The term "British" in this context certainly included the RCAF Squadrons in Coastal Command.

About this time, No. 422 Squadron was using bases at Bowmore, Castle Archdale, and Reykjavik. Thus on 4 August F/Lt Butler was airborne in W6033 at 1215 hrs from Castle Archdale for a "Moorings 2" patrol in the North-Western Approaches but became waterborne again the following morning at 0109 hrs on the 5th at Reykjavik.

The Ditching of Sunderland DD861

Sunderland DD861, captained by F/O Jacques de le Paulle, was airborne at Castle Archdale at 0100 hrs on 3 September for an A/S patrol of thirteen hours duration over the Atlantic, with an ETA at base of 1425 hrs. At 0630 hrs de le Paulle had reached position 4700N 1350W and commenced his patrol.

Two and three-quarters hours later the Sunderland was in position 4430N 1320W when as Don Wells, the third pilot at that time recalls:

Without any warning the starboard outer engine caught fire and soon after a violent explosion occurred. The engine fell forward in its mountings, hung for a moment, and then fell free from the aircraft taking the outboard part of the wing and the float with it. Power was lost in the inner engine and the port engines had to be cut to maintain stability. Barely a minute passed from the time the engine caught fire until we were in the drink.

The hull was badly crushed and the plane started to sink; there was a lot of shouting of orders but no panic. I went to see if the rear gunner was all right and to release the dinghy which was stowed by the back door. The aircraft was sinking by the nose, and by the time the dinghy was pushed out of the rear door, we were high in the air, almost 40 feet I believe.

I dived feet first, came up spluttering and heard someone shouting about the DCs not having been defused. As it turned out this was a false rumour because the tail disappeared without event. We counted heads and found that everyone was on the surface; the whole crew had survived. The only injury was to the navigator Bolton who had a nasty cut on his head. One dinghy had been torn and had to be repaired before we were all out of the water.

The skipper was cool and confident as though this sort of thing had happened to him lots of times...a more efficient skipper no one could want. He set about taking stock of things. We knew we were about 250 miles from the northern coast of Portugal and although an SOS had been sent it was probably very short. Skipper calculated that our rations could be apportioned on the basis of a fourteen-day voyage; this worked out to ½ pint water, one Horlicks tablet, ½ oz chocolate, and one stick of chewing gum per man per day. We were also equipped with a couple of spray sheets, canvas pails for bailing, flares, paddles and some small lines which were used to lash the two dinghies together. The portable radio transmitter had been left in the aircraft; someone said it had been jammed in under the navigator's table.

The rubber dinghy is not a comfortable place to spend time, especially in rough water. With six men in each rubber ring there was little room to move; the only worthwhile occupation was talking. Considering that we had crew members from England, Scotland, France, Canada and USA, I feel we were reasonably civil.

By mid-afternoon we were adjusted to our situation and I managed to doze off in the night despite the discomfort of having a wave break over our heads every little while. Time tended to drag, baling was a constant chore, the cigarettes had all disappeared, we took turns watching the horizon for ship or plane.

The second day was quite warm but a stiff gale came up in the night and we had to hold on to avoid capsize.

Two separate aircraft flew over that day; we fired off our flares but were not seen. We were somehow cheered by this and there was a general discussion about what we would do when we next got leave in London.

Just after noon on the third day a Liberator with USA markings flew right over us, turned and circled. Great excitement and useless shouting. After a few more laps he came over with flaps down and dropped a parachute bag with fair accuracy. The bag hit the water about 200 yards off and our skipper dived in and struck out through the waves. After a longish swim he managed to bring the bag back and was pulled aboard. A note therein told us to hold on as help was on the way. Also a dozen oranges and several packs of American cigarettes. A couple of long hours later a beautiful Sunderland appeared from the north and again we cheered. But a wind came up and we were afraid that it was too rough to attempt a landing. We tried to wave him off but the pilot found the right trough and dropped in like a real pro. We were all rather weak after three days soaking in salt water and had to be helped into the aircraft. I was given a cup of tea and a place in the bomb bay with my back to the wall. The take-off was awesome; we were sure the aircraft would come apart but

the pilot finally got it into the air and set course for home.

The journey was not entirely uneventful as we came a bit too close to Brest (it was dark at the time), and the AA gunners had a go at us. Not too long after we were landing at Pembroke Dock. The aircraft was out of fuel and the tide was out as well.

After an interminable wait we were towed to the pier and managed to climb to the top of a lot of steps and walk a very long way along the pier to dry land.

The day after, we met the 228 Squadron crew briefly, and the day after that our CO flew to Pembroke Dock and took us back to our base which was Bowmore on Islay.

The Liberator (B24) which dropped the parachute bag for de le Paulle's crew was commanded by Lt Dudock and was from No. 6 Squadron of the AAF which had been deployed from the United Kingdom to operate with Coastal Command from July and was from the 479th A/S Group.[4] It was thought that the Liberator had been attracted by the flash from a mirror held by one of the survivors. The Liberator then homed in a 228 Squadron Sunderland captained by F/Lt Armstrong. Armstrong was allowed by No. 19 Group to use his own judgement and opted to touch down. During the take-off, the Sunderland bounced 50 feet into the air at 45 knots but after sinking, just managed to get airborne at 60 knots. In January 1944, S/Ldr H.C. Armstrong was diverted to Castle Archdale but crashed into a hillside in Eire. There were two survivors.

No. 422 Squadron suffered a further crash-landing on 28 September. F/O G.E. Holley was airborne from Castle Archdale at 1830 hrs on 27th for an A/S patrol in W6033. At 0910 hrs, the following morning, however, he crashed near Kaldadarnes at the entrance to Hvalfjord. The crew were unhurt and the Sunderland was beached.

The mooring area for flying-boats lacked shelter against strong winds and gales, and there was a lack of proper maintenance facilities such as a slipway. The squadron made a plea for "a more suitable base" in its operational records, "without undue and costly delay."

With the posting of the CO W/Cmdr Skey, to other duties, a dinner was held in his honour on 4 October and three days later a squadron party was held during which a presentation was made to W/Cmdr Skey. News of the hoped-for move from Bowmore came on 25 October. It was to be Castle Archdale but with some accommodation at St. Angelo, albeit all at Lough Erne.

W/Cmdr J.R. Frizzle, who succeeded W/Cmdr Skey as CO, arrived at Castle Archdale on the 28th to supervise final arrangements for the move.

The Loss of Sunderland JM712 S/422

Acting F/Lt Paul Sargent was airborne on 17 October at 0145 hrs from Castle Archdale as captain of JM712. He had been detailed as one of five on an anti-submarine sweep flying in parallel and to cover convoy ON206. There was 2/10ths cloud at 1000 feet with visibility 25 miles. The wind was 35 knots and the sea swells were 10-20 feet high. At 1245 hrs Sargent was passing 20 miles south of convoy ONS20 when two blips on the radar appeared at 5 miles range, while the Sunderland was in rain cloud. On

emerging, two wakes were seen and, using binoculars, two fully surfaced U-boats were sighted heading due west at 16 knots. U-boats had been instructed in August to work in groups of two or three, and their AA armament was being increased with the intention of remaining on the surface and to fight it out with lone aircraft.[5]

Both vessels opened fire on the Sunderland at 2000 yards range with cannon and machine guns. Sargent's gunners responded with their machine guns and initially were able to clear the U-boats' decks. Three 250 pound torpex DCs were released from 50 feet at 240 knots, but they undershot by 30 feet.

Sargent circled tightly to port for a second run from ½ mile range at 100 feet but took no evasive action. The Sunderland was heavily shelled by both U-boats: a radio was shot away, the front turret recuperator destroyed, the auto-pilot blown out of the aircraft, the radar and the radio transmitter destroyed. The control quadrant was hit, propeller and throttle exactors destroyed, a dinghy was blown out from a wing, the mid-upper turret hit, and the hull generally riddled. The navigator, F/O Steves, had his left leg and part of his body blown away but was able to give a course for the aircraft to the convoy before he died. The gunnery officer who had joined this crew was killed at his post, as was also Needham, the front gunner.

Two depth charges had however straddled one U-boat's conning tower. It lifted before disappearing, while the second U-boat remained on the surface firing continuously. It was last seen heading south-west at 10 knots. Sargent flew towards the convoy 20 miles away and reported by Aldis lamp to HMS *Drury* and signalled that he would need to ditch ahead of the vessel.

The Sunderland touched down at 75 knots on top of the swell, rose, and in one second buried its nose in the swell and disintegrated, with the whole tail assembly breaking off. Paul Sargent was entangled in the wreckage and, despite attempts to free him, he went down with the aircraft along with the three killed by AA fire: F/O Steves, F/Sgt Needham, and Gunnery Officer F/Lt Woodward.

The Sunderland had been losing height en route to the convoy and ditched at 1330 hrs.

F/O Bellis, one of two brothers on the squadron from Victoria, BC, had been wounded in the shoulder and lost consciousness. He became entangled in the aerials after being thrown through the pilot's window. A rating from HMS *Drury*, Robert Leitch of Glasgow, swam to the Sunderland wreckage and released Bellis before fighting his way back to the ship.

Two others in the Sunderland crew, Rutherford and Mesney, found themselves on the underside of the plane; Mesney with four fractures in a leg and with an arm temporarily paralysed, Rutherford with concussion and lacerations. They escaped through the gap left by the tail breaking off. HMS *Drury* broke off from the convoy and steamed for port. From the 422 Squadron record, a second escort vessel went to the scene and was thought to have sunk the second U-boat. The nearest sinking to the Sunderland's position was of U-841 by HMS *Byard* on 17 October.[6]

The estimated position of F/Lt Sargent's attack was 5950N 3000W. If the two depth charges straddled one of the U-boats, severe damage, if not a "kill" could be expected and the Coastal

Command record credits Sargent's aircraft with damaging a U-boat requiring it to return to port. The U-boat however, is not identified.[7]

LCTs (Landing Craft Tank) were used to ferry both heavy equipment and personnel from Bowmore to Londonderry on 1 November 1943. Personnel were accommodated by the United States Navy at their Springtown camp just outside Londonderry. Two days later a special train transported the squadron from Londonderry to Inniskillen and from there, heavy equipment was taken by train to Irvinstown. The maintenance party then went to Castle Archdale, other personnel to St. Angelo.

Convoys SL139 and MKS30

On 14 November two homeward bound convoys from Sierra Leone and North Africa, SL139 and MKS30, had combined south of Cape St.Vincent but on the 15th were sighted by German aircraft. A great battle was to follow involving escort vessels, U-boats, Coastal Command aircraft, and long-range Heinkel 177 Luftwaffe aircraft with glider bombs. A total of twenty-six U-boats in three groups were ordered to attack.[8] L/Cmdr Peter Cremer in U-333 was the first to intercept on the 16th at 1130 hrs but U-333 was located by Asdic, suffered a pattern of ten DCs and was rammed by the frigate HMS *Exe*.[9]

A Wellington from 179 Squadron sank U-211 on the 19th, and the following morning the frigate HMS *Nene*, together with the Canadian corvettes HMCS *Calgary* and *Snowberry*, sank U-536.

F/O J.D.B. Ulrichsen of 422 Squadron undertook a fateful part in this battle. He was captain of W6031 on the centre patrol of three aircraft flying parallel tracks which were to cover the convoys SL139 and MKS30. Ulrichsen was then to land at Gibraltar.

He was airborne from Castle Archdale at 1145 hrs and six hours later a sighting report was received. There was no further signal until an SOS included the position 4500N 1920W of the first sighting. The SOS had been received by Gibraltar, Malta, and the Azores when the Sunderland's DR position was 4240N 1920W and it was assumed that Ulrichsen had set course for Gibraltar. The following day an extensive ASR search was undertaken from the Azores, but W6031 was lost with a crew of eleven; it was shot down by U-618. Also lost about that time was a 53 Squadron Liberator which was shot down by U-648.[10]

In this battle against the combined convoys, the enemy claimed one vessel of 4,405 tons sunk and one other damaged by glider bombs; HMS *Chanticleer* was damaged by an acoustic torpedo. A third U-boat, U-538, was sunk by HMS *Crane* and HMS *Foley;* U-333 despite serious damage, docked at La Pallice on 1 December. Peter Cremer, its commander, records that he was the only one to reach the merchant ships.[11]

The German U-boat war diary's account of this action is headed: "Complete failure against MKS30 and SL139."[12]

A Liberator Interlude

One of the outcomes of an Atlantic Convoy Conference held in Washington during March 1943 was that Britain and Canada should become entirely responsible for convoys on the North Atlantic route. Canadian and British controls were to be at Halifax, Nova Scotia, and Liverpool respectively. There had been a gap in air defences for convoys south of Greenland and that gap was now closed by operating VLR Liberators.[13] By April there was a shuttle service between Newfoundland and Iceland. As a result, No. 10 Squadron RCAF came within Coastal Command's area of control.

ONS18 sailed from Milford Haven on 12 September 1943, a convoy of twenty-seven ships with twelve escort vessels. It was followed by a faster convoy, ON202 from Liverpool: forty-two merchantmen with six escorts.[14]

The German U-boat command anticipated that a convoy would follow a great circle route and estimated it would reach about 25° West on the afternoon of 21 September. The *Leuthen* group of U-boats, nineteen in number, was ordered to form a line across the convoy's course and the U-boats were expected to sail submerged.[15]

Winston Churchill had attended a conference at Quebec and returned to the United Kingdom in the battlecruiser HMS *Renown*, which had been provided with an escort from Gander by Liberators operated by No. 10 Squadron RCAF.[16]

These aircraft landed at Reykjavik prior to a return flight to Gander. Fog had been limiting coverage by air, but when that lifted, No. 10's Liberators were used during their return flight to act as escorts to the convoys.

Liberator B/10 captained by F/O C.M.M Harper was airborne from Reykjavik at 0600 hrs on 19 September and likewise, A/10, captained by F/Lt R.F. Fisher. At 0900 hrs Fisher was flying at 3000feetjust below cloud when his co-pilot, F/O J. Dale, sighted a U-boat two miles away. Fisher dived to attack but overestimated. In a second attempt, one of the squadron, John Jamieson recalls: "they were so low they had to pull up to miss the conning tower." Six DCs were released, followed by another four. The Liberator remained in the area for twenty-five minutes before returning to Gander to touch down at 1845 hrs, making it a flight of almost thirteen hours.

Of this episode, F/Lt Harper writes:

I was flying as captain of a Liberator at that time. On September 16th 1943 on a sweep out of Goose Bay, Labrador on an anti-submarine patrol; we landed at Reykjavik after an 11 hr 50 mins flight. We departed again on September 19th on another patrol and landed at Gander, Newfoundland after 13 hrs 10 mins."

According to F/Lt Harper's log, this was Liberator 587. Harper later flew as a pilot with Air Canada but F/Lt Fisher was killed in a flying accident.[17]

The German U-boat attacks on the convoys were exceptional in that this was the first time their acoustic torpedoes (*Zaunkonigs*) were used. Furthermore they were directed against the escort vessels rather than the merchantmen. The intention was to first break through the "cordon" provided by the escorts, and then to attack the merchant vessels at comparative leisure. They had not anticipated such a strong defence which had been increased with the addition of the 9th Escort Group.

F/Lt Fisher's victim was U-341, which had sailed from France on 31 August commanded by OL Dietrich Epp; it sank in position 5840N 2530W. The final toll in the five-day battle between convoys ON202 and ONS18 and Group *Leuthen* was three U-boats sunk and three damaged; three escort vessels sunk, one severely damaged, and six merchantmen

sunk. Although F/Lt Fisher's attack is the only one by No. 10 Squadron RCAF to feature in the Coastal Command War Record, further sorties were undertaken by the unit.

No. 423 Squadron in Northern Ireland

For January 1943, No. 423's base is given as Lough Erne. W/Cmdr Rump was the Commanding Officer but for 26 January he is recorded as proceeding from Bowmore, Isle of Islay, to London for a Coastal Command conference, leaving S/Ldr J.R. Sumner to act as OC 423 Squadron.

The unit received a number of eight-inch discs with a $\frac{1}{2}$ inch outer blue roundel and an RAF blue centre with the red Canadian maple leaf superimposed. These were placed on the port side of 423's Sunderlands forward of the leading edge of the wing.

Quite exceptionally, on the 19 January one of the Sunderlands had some difficulty in overtaking and circling a convoy! This was DD828 A/423 captained by F/Sgt S.H.E. Cook who was detailed to escort convoy TA34. At 1426 hrs he set course down the convoy's track, but his ground speed was 75 knots and the convoy was steaming at $26\frac{1}{2}$ knots. There was thick sea haze and the conditions were bumpy. F/Sgt Cook seemingly cut short his sortie and returned with 1600 gallons fuel in addition to a full bomb load.

Convoys SC122 and HX229

Sixty ships in convoy SC122 with escort vessels sailed from New York on 5 March, and forty ships in HX229, also with escorts, sailed three days later.

German intelligence had decrypted signals from either the Western Approaches HQ or the Admiralty and had HX229's position for 13 March and its intended course.[18] By the 15th, a group of twelve U-boats was deployed in a line across the track of convoy SC122, but a total of forty U-boats came to be used against the two convoys. The U-boats were initially from *Raubgraph* but were deployed in two groups, *Sturmer* and *Dranger*.[19]

The first air support came from Liberators from Iceland and Northern Ireland on the 17th and 18th, but by the 20th the Sunderlands of shorter range were able to take part. F/Lt Clare Bradley was on a parallel track sweep in W6053 when at 1115 hrs a message was intercepted from another aircraft of an attack on a U-boat. Bradley set course for the reported position and at 1145 hrs sighted a periscope ten miles away which was heading due east at five knots. He was too late to attack but was able to warn a tanker by Aldis lamp of the enemy. Less than two hours later a surfaced U-boat was sighted also heading 90°. At five knots and at eight miles ahead of the Sunderland Bradley was able to attack but only two DCs released out of six, with one exploding 40 feet ahead of the swirl. Before leaving the scene at 1445 hrs, further DCs were released to "scare" the U-boat. F/Lt Bradley considered that the U-boat was shadowing the tanker *Roman*, which was a straggler from a convoy.

F/O A.B. Howell was airborne in W6011 F/423 at 0535 hrs on a parallel track sweep, and F/O T.F.P. Frizell captained W6008 E/423 which was airborne ten minutes later. Both aircraft formed part of the cover to two convoys.

Frizell set course down the track of the convoys and at 0910 hrs saw an oil slick and air bubbles 100 yards long on the surface but resumed his patrol after fifteen minutes. His rear gunner then saw a conning tower four miles away. Frizell turned to attack but it disappeared before he could reach the area, only to see another oil slick. After resuming patrol his wireless operator intercepted an attack report from Howell's aircraft.

F/O Howell, after patrolling down the convoy's track, at 0955 hrs sighted a fully-surfaced U-boat eight miles to starboard. Four men were seen on the U-boat's deck as Howell went in to attack. The vessel was straddled with five DCs when it was partly submerged. Howell resumed patrol and forty minutes later saw debris and an oil slick a mile long by ¼ mile wide.

At 1427 hrs F/O Howell sighted another U-boat fully-surfaced but eight miles away and heading south-west at 10 knots. He attacked with two DCs but one failed to release. AA fire from the U-boat had been returned by the Sunderland and 2-3 feet of the U-boat's stern was seen as the DCs exploded.

According to Martin Middlebrook this was U-631, and it was only "badly shaken."[20] U-631 had sunk the merchant vessel *Terkoelei* in position 5145N 3115W on 17 March, just one out of twenty-one ships totalling 141,000 tons sunk for the loss of one U-boat.[21]

It was the increased air support beginning on 20th which decided the enemy to call off further attacks.[22] While 423 could not claim any "kills," they may well have prevented the loss of further valuable ships with the lives of their crews plus vital cargoes. For the Germans, it was the "Biggest convoy operation of the war."[23]

Atlantic Sweeps, Searches, and Escorts by No. 423 Squadron

F/Lt C.W. Bradley captained Sunderland W6008 H/423 on 5 April as escort to convoy TA39. He was airborne at 0817 hrs but while flying at 5500 feet on a parallel track to the convoy at 1541 hrs, a fully-surfaced U-boat was sighted. It was ten miles away and heading eastwards at 15 knots. Bradley turned to attack down sun at 175mph, releasing four 250 pound DCs from 50 feet and set at 25 feet with 30 feet spacing. The entire underwater shadow with propellers turning was visible as the depth charges were released to fall directly on the shadow. They all exploded.

Aircrew in the upper and lower turrets saw at least a dozen pieces of solid debris 5x3 feet thrown into the air with spray from the second and third depth charges. While circling after the attack, most of the Sunderland crew clearly saw objects in the water, some appearing as bodies. The captain, second pilot, and front gunner were positive that at least one body clad in a sweater was floating amongst the debris. Forty-five seconds after the attack, there was a violent explosion, followed a minute later by a violent eruption. Oil rose 1½ hrs later, forming a patch 500 feet by 300 feet. The convoy was informed of the attack before F/Lt Bradley left to land at base after a flight of seventeen hours twenty minutes and with only 100 gallons of fuel remaining. Despite all this evidence of a "kill," post-war records give no U-boat being sunk at that time.

Sunderland W6053 E/423 was airborne at 0424 hrs on 8 April captained by F/O Al. A. Bishop for a parallel track sweep. While flying at 200 feet at 1321 hrs, a fully-surfaced U-boat was sighted heading due south at 10 knots, one mile away.

Bishop lost height and, due to the close proximity, made a circuit while all his three gunners opened fire. After 1½ minutes as the U-boat began to dive, Bishop attacked down track at 140 knots releasing three Mark XI and three Mark VIII torpex depth charges from 50 feet and spaced at 100 feet with a 25 foot setting. This attack was within 20 seconds of the U-boat diving, but no damage was claimed by the Sunderland crew.

A mercy mission was undertaken by F/Lt Russel from Castle Archdale on 15 May. He undertook a CLA search in W6068 for a lifeboat. The lifeboat was located and a Thornaby bag was dropped to its occupants. The Thornaby bag contents included a transmitter which ultimately was instrumental in the rescue of the survivors. A corvette was sighted heading north-east at 15 knots and a lifeboat with twelve survivors 75 miles south of the corvette. The lifeboat had hoisted a white sail and was on the same course as the corvette. Russell climbed to obtain a W/T fix and requested permission to land, but visibility was bad and sight was lost of the lifeboat.

The Sinking of U-456

Convoy HX237 sailed from New York on 1 May but in mid-Atlantic, together with convoy SC129, was attacked by three groups of U-boats, *Elbe*, *Rhein*, and *Drossel*.[24]

Sunderland W6008 captained by F/Lt J. Musgrave from 423 Squadron was one of many aircraft employed as escorts to HX237. F/Lt Musgrave was airborne from Castle Archdale at 2343 hrs on 12 May to meet the convoy reported as being composed of 43 merchant ships with eight escort vessels. At 0815 hrs while flying at 3000 feet he sighted a fully-surfaced U-boat heading north at 15 knots. Musgrave used cloud cover before diving to attack the U-boat, which opened fire at one mile range after its initial surprise.

In accordance with Coastal Command's orders, finding that the U-boat remained on the surface, Musgrave abandoned the attack and signalled the convoy. While the Sunderland exchanged fire with the U-boat, a corvette arrived on the scene at 0837 hrs. The Sunderland suffered a shell hit, but scored hits on the conning tower, and within two minutes the U-boat submerged, choosing the moment when the aircraft was out of range. Musgrave turned to attack and released two DCs thirty seconds after the vessel had submerged. From L/Cmdr Schull's account, the corvette was HMCS *Drumheller*, one of three Canadian corvettes in the escort group. She released depth charges before leading the Royal Navy's frigate HMS *Lagan* which followed with a "hedgehog", attack and gave the coup-de-grace.[25]

U-456 had sailed from France on 24 April, captained by KL Max-Martin Teichert; it was sunk in position 4837N 2239W on 13 May.[26]

Featured in the defence of these convoys was the presence of the carrier *Biter* and the use of "hedgehog" a battery of 65 pound bombs which were fired ahead of the escort vessel deploying them and which, unlike depth charges, would only detonate when the target was struck. Thus was detection by asdic unaffected in a search.

On 23 May W/O R.S. Long was one of those detailed for a parallel track sweep to cover convoy HX239, which was estimated to consist of forty-two merchant vessels escorted by eight warships. He was airborne at 1347 hrs in Sunderland DD828 and while flying at 1500 feet at 2102 hrs sighted the conning tower and foredeck of a U-boat five miles to port. W/O Long dived to attack and within 1½ minutes had released four DCs which straddled the track of the U-boat fifteen seconds after its periscope had submerged and twenty feet ahead of the swirl. There was no sign of damage to the vessel, however. After circling the area, W/O Long subsequently met the convoy when it was on course 065° at 10 knots.

The German account of the battle against convoy HX239 refers to it as a "failure" and of "numerous short signals from boats, reporting attacks from the air." A number reported "serious damage" and on the same day as Long's attack, the action against convoy HX239 was discontinued. [27]

On 8 June Air-Vice-Marshal W.A. Curtis arrived at Castle Archdale to present No. 423 Squadron with the unit's badge, which had earlier been approved by the King. The end of June marked the change of command, with W/Cmdr Archambault succeeding W/Cmdr Rump. Of this Air Commodore Rump remarks: "Sadly for me personally as part of the RCAF Canadianisation policy, I handed over my command to a new RCAF commander. On my departure I was formally presented with a large silver tankard suitably engraved 'From RCAF Squadron *Fog Hogs*' as a reminder of the weather in which we normally operated!"

Combat With FW200 Kondors

F/Lt J. Musgrave was airborne in Sunderland DD860 at 0921 hrs on 22 July for a "Seaslug patrol." At 1405 hrs the cloud lifted from 500 feet to 1500 feet and the rear gunner reported an enemy aircraft astern. It was an FW200, which opened fire with cannon from 1500 yards range, the first burst putting the Sunderland's hydraulic system out of action and thus its gun turrets. The rear gunner had been able to fire only fifty rounds; he received slight splinter wounds to his face, the second pilot was wounded in an arm, and the front gunner suffered a wound to a knee. There were many holes below the waterline in the Sunderland, the trimming controls, the port carburetor cock, and the port jettison cock were shot away. Two depth charges were hit by rockets but did not detonate. Musgrave entered cloud and set course for base.

On September 14th the Australian captain, F/O H.C. Jackson, had a similar experience. While on patrol in DP181, a Kondor was sighted three miles away. It later emerged from cloud 3000 yards astern and prepared to attack from below the Sunderland opening fire with cannon from 1500 yards range and closing to 300 yards. The Sunderland responded with 800 rounds of machine gun fire, and the enemy broke off the engagement.

Sunderland DD859 and U-Boat U-489

F/O Al Bishop and his crew had picked up Sunderland DD859 G/423 on 21 June from Wig Bay, a maintenance base on Loch Ryan, and flown it to Castle Archdale. They had a few hours training before starting operations two days later and up to 4 August had logged 200 ops hours.

On 4 August F/O Bishop captained DD859 on a "Moorings 2" patrol between Iceland and the Faeroes and was airborne from Castle Archdale at 0455 hrs. Al Bishop continues:

At about 0900 hrs while flying at 5000 feet my crew sighted a fully-surfaced U-boat which made no sign of diving. During that period of the ASW some of the U-boats were staying on the surface to fight it out with attacking aircraft so we did not find this unusual.

As we circled the U-boat we soon saw the advantage we might have was to attack down sun. We proceeded with such an attack descending to sea level. As we approached, the U-boat started shooting at us with what appeared to be cannons with exploding shells and machine guns. I took evasive action by undulating the aircraft. As I levelled out at 50 feet for the final bombing, the shells began to hit the aircraft.

Two of my crew forward in the Sunderland returned fire with a .5 on a swivel and a .3 gun in the front turret. I was successful in tracking over the submarine and dropped six DCs straddling the sub.

After the attack the crew advised me that there was a fierce fire in the galley and bomb bay areas with flames coming upstairs.

The starboard engines were running at full power and there was very little aileron control. This was apparently caused by a shell which had burst under my seat severing the exactor controls to the starboard engines. I had slight flak in the back of my left knee which I did not know at the time. I had to stop the starboard engines and attempt to maintain control with the rudder. I decided to make an emergency landing and advised the crew over the intercom.

All this happened in a few seconds.

In trying to land we bounced and I had trouble controlling the aircraft; as we hit the water again the port wing dropped a little, the port float caught in the water, and we cartwheeled in the sea.

I recall putting my right arm in front of my face and the next thing I recall was being underwater and rising to the surface. I came up slightly behind the port wing. What was left of the aircraft was on fire and there was fire on the water around it. I swam through an open space.

As I was swimming, I heard Sgt Finn call, "Skipper can you give me a hand?" I turned and swam to him and discovered he had no Mae West and was obviously badly hurt.

He did not struggle probably because of his injuries (he had been on the front gun), and his extensive swimming experience. I grabbed hold of him with my right arm.

I saw one of the aircraft floats and was able to reach it but as soon as I grabbed it, it started to fill with water and sank.

I could not see any of the other crew members but a short while later I saw the submarine, stern down, not too far away. The crew were getting onto Carley floats or rafts. As the sub sank there was a big explosion. Its crew made no attempt to come over to us.

For the next while (I was in the water about fifty minutes), I don't recall anything. I attempted to change Finn to my left arm but every little move caused him to scream with pain.

Next I recall looking round and

seeing the RN destroyer. Apparently they were patrolling in the same area and an alert lookout had seen the Sunderland dive down. Then after the crash they could see black smoke from the fire. They launched lifeboats and picked us up. I was able to scramble up the scramble net at the side of the destroyer. While in the water I recall seeing a Sunderland overhead. It was from a Norwegian Squadron and I later met the captain.

Once aboard we were taken to the wardroom. There we started shivering violently. Before I could bed down, I was called to the deck to identify one of my seargeant's bodies and witness his burial at sea. After that I saw a doctor briefly and climbed into a bunk.

I was awakened at about 0230 hrs 5th August as we were entering Reykjavik. We survivors were taken to the hospital. Two of us were able to walk. The other four were badly injured and were in hospital in England for some time. I returned to Ireland on 13 August via a Liberator and went on a month's sick leave. I returned to flying on 19 September and to ops on 2 October. I was repatriated to Canada in March 1944.

U-489 had sailed from a home port on 22 July as one of "two remaining tankers" which had been sent to the North Atlantic to refuel U-boats operating in distant areas. Due to attacks such as that by F/O Bishop, many U-boats were recalled.[28]

From the RCAF's official history[29] the destroyer was HMS *Castleton* which picked up fifty-eight of the U-boat's crew and six of the Sunderland crew.

From Capt Roskill's account, U-489 was one of ten type XIV ocean-going 'milch-cows' of which seven had been lost. Captained by OL Schmandt, it sank in position 6114N 1438W.[30] F/O Bishop was awarded the DFC.

Italy Surrenders to the Allies

At Castle Archdale on 8 September 1943, 423 Squadron received news that Italy had surrendered unconditionally to General Eisenhower's forces. Armistice terms had been signed on 3 September, and it was General Alexander who informed Churchill.[31]

One outcome of the armistice was that the Italian fleet, including three battleships, sailed on the 9th for Malta to be met at sea by the Royal Navy.[32]

While the Allies had Italy as an enemy, her numerous submarines and powerful surface fleet had gained the attention of other Sunderland Squadrons such as 228 and 230.

Convoys SC143 and HX259

The *Rossbach* group of U-boats had expected to encounter convoys SC143 and HX259 at 30° West on 8 October and had a BV222 reconnaissance aircraft in support.[33]

On that same day Sunderland J/423 captained by F/Lt A.H. Russell was airborne from Castle Archdale at 1027 hrs to escort SC143. Exceptionally on this trip was W/Cmdr J.R. Frizzle who writes:

When I was selected to be OC of 422 Squadron I was given a quick and abbreviated conversion course on Sunderland aircraft at Alness and it was planned that I should be given three ops trips with 228 Squadron at

Pembroke Dock and three trips with 423 Squadron at Castle Archdale before taking over as OC 422 Squadron. This was because I had considerable water time in Canada on Stranraer aircraft. I completed the three trips with 228 Squadron and went to Castle Archdale for three trips with 423 Squadron. This one on 8 October was the first of those three!

F/Lt Russell met the convoy at 1734 hrs and set course to patrol the area astern of the convoy. Just two hours later the wake of a fully-surfaced U-boat was sighted at 100 yards on the port bow. G/Capt Frizzle continues:

I was flying the aircraft when we flew directly over a sub at about 300 feet in pouring rain and very poor visibility and extremely rough seas. The aircraft captain, Russell was down below having breakfast when the sub was sighted and a call went to him to come to the flight deck.

In the interval I set up the aircraft for an attack on the sub and was well into the final run in by the time Russell took over the controls. Russell continued my approach and selected four DCs keeping the extras in reserve if we needed a second attack. I stood directly behind Russell for the attack and according to the rear gunner we blew the sub out of the water and it broke in two. The U-boat made no attempt to submerge and I could see tracer bullets going just under our starboard wing.

Russell did a quick 180° turn at about 200 feet and as we passed over the sub's position it was gone and about fifteen German crew were in the water with considerable debris around.

From the Squadron record, the 4th DC hung up but it was the explosion from the 2nd DC which lifted the conning tower of the U-boat 15 to 20 feet. F/Lt Russell had been recalled to base over ½ hours earlier with the weather still bad and cloud base at 500 feet. He advised the escort group with the convoy and returned to base, completing a trip of over sixteen hours.

The U-boat, U-610, had sailed from a French port on 12 September, captained by KL Walter Freiherr von Freyberg-Eisenberg-Allmendingen; it was sunk in position 5545N 2433W on 8 October. It was one of three U-boats lost during their intended encounter with the two convoys from which was lost just one escort, a Polish destroyer, *Orkan*.[34]

The official publication Coastal Command Review gave the following report: "This excellent attack is another example of quick decision in bad visibility showing a high degree of training and gunnery." After this initiation, W/Cmdr Frizzle took command of 422 Squadron then at Bowmore, Isle of Islay succeeding W/Cmdr Larry Skey. In 1993 G/Capt Frizzle led a contingent from Canada to the Battle of the Atlantic commemoration at Liverpool, England.

Arrivals and Departures at Castle Archdale

The AOCinC Coastal Command, Air Marshal Sir John Slessor, arrived on 9 October with the AOC No. 15 Group, AVM Sir Leonard Slatter, and made an inspection of the station. After dinner, Sir John Slessor discussed matters pertaining to the Command. Congratulations from both Coastal Command and the CinC Western Approaches were received following F/Lt Russell's success.

For the 15 October, No. 423 Squadron gives an entry in its records: "It was with genuine regret that officers, NCOs and airmen in turn held farewell parties for the Station Commander, G/Capt F.A. Pearce, OBE, and Mrs. Pearce. They were tops with British and Canadians alike and the esteem with which they were held indicated itself in countless ways." Air Commodore Pearce, as he became, had earlier in his service been senior officer in West Africa and had organised, exceptionally, a Hurricane flight within a Sunderland Squadron.[35]

In October 423's adjutant F/Lt Langdale and medical officer "Doc" Sheard, were posted to "drier if not greener pastures."

On 23rd October Sunderland DD858 from No. 201 Squadron, but flown by a 423 Squadron crew, overturned in the Lough at Belfast with two of the crew, F/Sgt Eastaway and Sgt. G.A. Saunders, dangerously injured.

Coastal Command summed up the situation in the North Atlantic battle against U-boats for October 1943 with:

The lack of sightings in Moorings area indicates that the enemy is using extreme caution tactics in that region, at the expense of his batteries and regardless of the length of time taken. Recent prisoners of war confirm that they were finally forced to surface when through the Rosengarten and when sighted by Iceland aircraft were unable to submerge again, both crews and batteries being exhausted. The value of these continuous patrols is considerable and crews should know that their apparently unprofitable patrols have contributed greatly to recent successes further west.

Sunderland Losses and Casualties

DP181, captained by F/Lt M.D. Lee, crashed at 2040 hrs on 11 November while landing. The aircraft sank, and missing were F/O R.W. Hill, P/O W.G. Arnold, and P/O G.T. Raymond. Seriously injured was F/O L.R. Hobbs and killed, Sgt. W.D. Scott. W/O C.M. Hardcastle died of injuries. Others in the aircraft were slightly injured. The wreckage of the aircraft was raised on the 22nd, and the body of Sgt. Scott was recovered.

On the 13th Sunderland DP863, captained by F/Lt A.F. Brazenor, was airborne for an A/S escort at 0946 hrs. Brazenor reported engine trouble at 1130 hrs and 1½ hrs later an SOS was received and then nothing more. Wreckage from this Sunderland was washed ashore from where DP863 was believed to have crashed due to very rough seas. F/Lt Brazenor and his crew of ten were all reported missing.

Attack on a Blockade Runner

On 25 December Sunderlands from No. 423 Squadron in addition to those from 422 were detailed to search for a blockade runner, and on the 27th the *Alsterufer* was sighted by F/Lt H.C. Jackson, an Australian pilot serving with the Canadians. He was airborne at 0219 hrs in EK581 to begin a CLA search. At 1026 hrs the blockade runner was sighted steaming at 15 knots on a course 120°. The ship opened fire, but Jackson continued to shadow after sending a sighting report. As a prelude to an attack,

Jackson broke cloud hold a mile from *Alsterufer*, but there was intense AA fire precluding any success and he set course for the Scillies where the Sunderland was waterborne at 1930 hrs.

F/Lt W.Y. Martin captained EK576 Q/422 for a similar mission. He was airborne at 0112 hrs and at 0255 hrs sighted a hospital ship before reaching his patrol area at 0840 hrs. He later intercepted a message from Sunderland T/201 and set course for the position given. At 1049 hrs the wake of a merchant vessel was seen heading 120° at 15 knots and then shortly after, two Sunderlands circling.

F/Lt Martin attempted an attack on *Alsterufer* by flying out of cloud but overshot and didn't release his bombs. He made a second run, also out of cloud, from 1500 feet and flying at 160 knots, and released two 500 pound bombs with instant fusing spaced at 30 feet. The decks of the vessel were raked with machine-gun fire. One bomb was seen to explode, but 40 yards from amidships. The Sunderland suffered a hit in the port wing by a 4 pound shell. Martin had now reached PLE and set course for base.

Ultimately it was left to a Liberator "H" from the Czech Squadron No. 311 to achieve the *coup-de-grace* by attacking *Alsterufer* with both rockets and bombs. The vessel was set on fire and about 70 survivors were picked up by ships of the 6th Escort Group.[36]

References to Chapter 4

1. JR p.155
2. Ibid
3. SWR III/1 p.57
4. C&C II p.394
5. GüH para.373
6. USSL p.165
7. CCWR p.16; RCAF III p.404

8. SWR III/1 p.50
9. PC p.155
10. SWR III/1 p.51
11. PC p.159
12. GüH para.393
13. WSC V pp6-7
14. SWR III/1 pp.38-40
15. GüH para. 374
16. WSC V pp.126-128
17. RCAF II p.562
18. GüH para.311; SWR II p.364
19. SWR II map 38
20. MM p.277
21. JR p.158
22. GüH para.311; SWR II p.365
23. GüH para.311
24. GüH para. 329
25. JS pp.172-175
26. USSL p.163
27. GüH para.331
28. GüH para.365
29. RCAF II p.584
30. SWR III/1 p.31; USSL p.164
31. WSC V p.99
32. SWR III/1 p.167
33. GüH para.382
34. GüH App.III/p.113; SWR III/1 p.41; USSL
    p.165
35. AH SS p.66
36. SWR III/1 p.74.

Chapter 5

Shipping Strikes and Anti-submarine Operations:January– December 1943

No. 404 (RCAF) Squadron Moves to Chivenor

The Squadron had been deploying aircraft from Dyce, Skitten, and Sumburgh, but on 18 January 1943 W/Cmdr Truscott went to Chivenor regarding the intended move of 404 to that base. The main party arrived at Chivenor on the 22nd, followed by the Beaufighters and one Blenheim the next day. The Air Officer in Chief of Coastal Command, Air Marshal, Sir John Slessor, visited Chivenor on 9 February and discussed the re-equipping of 404 Squadron.

On 23 March 1943 six of 404's Beaufighters were airborne for a line patrol led by F/Lt A. de le Haye. While flying in company, seven JU88s were sighted 2 miles dead ahead at 200 feet. Three of the enemy remained at that altitude, while the other four JU88s climbed for cloud cover. R/404 attacked one JU88 from astern by firing four cannon bursts. Hits were seen on the enemy's port wing and engine, which emitted heavy black smoke, and pieces fell from the wing. The JU88 turned

violently to port, and R/404, in trying to turn within the enemy's manoeuvre, stalled before firing two more bursts of cannon at close range.

Only one other aircraft of the Canadian Squadron—H/404—was able to make an attack before all the JU88s escaped into cloud at 6000 feet. This brief encounter demonstrated the German opinion of Beaufighters. At the beginning of 1943, flights of JU88s were being used to protect U-boats crossing the Bay of Biscay. The enemy was prepared to attack lone Coastal Command aircraft (albeit with some respect for such as the Sunderland), but when Beaufighters were encountered, the JU88s "had to clear off" and in fact expected to operate in flights of at least six![1]

No. 404 (RCAF) Squadron to Scotland

On 1 April, 404 Squadron commenced another move from Chivenor, Devon to Tain in Scotland where the main party arrived the following evening. Twelve days later, they were warned of another move impending—to Wick, Caithness.

While at Tain, three of 404's Beaufighters undertook an exercise with Torbeaus of 144 Squadron. On 19 April F/Sgt K.S. Miller was pilot of JM105, one of three Beaufighters on a Norge recce. At 1228 hrs while flying at 50 feet, he sighted a merchant ship of 1500–2000 tons steaming at 8 knots with its escort vessel. He attacked the ship at 600 yards, closing to 75 yards on its starboard beam and scoring strikes on its superstructure aft of the bridge.

The Squadron completed its move, to Wick on 21 April when twelve of 404's aircraft arrived there with the CO, W/Cmdr Truscott.

Shipping strikes remained a feature of Coastal Command's duties right up to the end of the war in Europe, largely along the Norwegian and Dutch coasts. No. 404 (Buffalo) Squadron was ever in the forefront of this dangerous activity, frequently sharing the honours—and the losses— with other units.

Six of 404's Beaufighters were on a Rover patrol on 27 April from Wick, but their duty changed to escorting four torpedo aircraft from 144 Squadron on a shipping strike. This was from 6320N and then following the shipping lanes southwards along the Norwegian coast. After refuelling at Sumburgh, the formation was led by F/O R.A. Schoales in Q/404 JM160. After 1.40 hrs flying, landfall was made at Lister before heading easterly at 50 feet. Five minutes later an enemy convoy of one 4000-5000-ton merchant vessel with two escorts was sighted. F/O J.D.W. Campbell in A/404 JM112 attacked one escort with machine gun fire and then the second escort with both machine guns and cannon, despite

AA from both vessels. F/Sgt K.S. Miller in B/404 JM105 made quarter attacks on the escorts with machine gun and cannon fire, and F/O Schoales raked the escort to port of the merchant ship with 400 cannon rounds. Such attacks on the escorts by 404 enabled 144 Squadron's Torbeaus to release torpedoes.

Schoales' aircraft was damaged by flak, and his arm was struck by a bullet which then pierced the armour plating behind him. A fire extinguisher was knocked from its bracket and burst in the cockpit. His port engine was also damaged by flak. An HE shell had jammed and exploded within the barrel of his port inner cannon, and all the doors to the cannons apart from that on the rear starboard were blown off. G/404 attacked the same escort and suffered flak in the fuselage and elevators. S/404 scored hits on the bridge and superstructure of an escort. With his port engine smoking, Schoales was escorted back to base by F/Sgt Miller. The merchant ship had been left with a 25-degree list to port and largely shrouded by smoke and steam.

Coastal Command's record credits the Hampdens of 144 Squadron with sinking *Trondjemfjord* of 6753 tons but 144 Squadron crews considered their success was largely due to 404 drawing the fire of the escorts.[2]

There was a major operation involving 404 Squadron then based at Wick, on 1 May. They provided eight aircraft headed by the CO, W/Cmdr Truscott, in JM114. The first wing were airborne with twelve from 235 and eight from 144 Squadron, closely followed by a second wing comprising thirty Beaufighters. Landfall was made north of Lister at 2018 hrs, and the formation followed the shore line within 100-400 yards northwards. They experienced much heavy flak from shore batteries throughout the patrol, and one of 404's aircraft was attacked by two enemy fighters on its tail suffering 100 bullets on the port engine, fuselage, mainplane, tail assembly, and both propellers. Only one of 404's Beaufighters failed to return, however, JL124 crewed by F/O S.J. Flannery and F/O B.J. Wright. When FW190 fighters were sighted coming from the south, the formation took evasive action.

No. 404 (RCAF) Squadron Receives Its Emblem

The original copy of the squadron's emblem signed by King George VI was received by the unit on 5 May 1943, and three days later, a new Canada ensign arrived.

Eight of 404's Beaufighters were detailed to escort eight 489 Squadron Hampdens on 13 May. Of 404's aircraft, two were in action against the enemy. P/O J.D. Hart and F/Sgt J.H. James were airborne in JL947 at 1232 hrs preceded by JM173 with F/O G. Bell, DFM, and F/O W.R.White at 1218 hrs.

Hart lost sight of the other Beaufighters due to bad weather but saw an enemy convoy of a merchant ship with two escort vessels. He attacked one of the escorts, firing 360 rounds of cannon and 420 rounds of machine gun fire despite much light and heavy flak from both ships and shore batteries. He noted the Hampdens attacking with torpedoes at short range. F/O Bell had been flying for almost three hours when he sighted a JU88. He left the formation to attack. At one stage the JU88 passed directly overhead of the Beaufighter, and Bell made a tight turn to attack from dead

astern. He opened fire at 500 yards, closing to 300 yards firing 360 cannon rounds and 420 rounds from machine guns. He broke off when black smoke was pouring from both engines of the enemy. Bell's Beaufighter suffered hits to windscreen, engine, hydraulic tank, and port aileron. He landed at base with a punctured tire.

The Squadron was again in action the following day with four Beaufighters headed by W/Cmdr Truscott in JM132. They were on a Rover patrol from 1155-1552 hrs to escort six Hampdens armed with torpedoes from 489 Squadron. A 4000-ton ship was sighted with two escort vessels and a single-engined aircraft. F/Lt J. McCutcheon sighted a B&V138 above the convoy and at 1000 yards range. He turned to attack with cannon and machine guns closing the range to 100 yards. Hits were seen on both engines of the B&V, so that they were in flames with the enemy losing height rapidly. McCutcheon flew over the convoy, but the merchant vessel was flying a balloon, and he broke off his attack. Heavy AA from an escort vessel damaged his port engine nacelle, which caught fire; his hydraulics were damaged and the port wheel dropped. As McCutcheon turned to port he saw two FW190 fighters crossing his bow to port at 100 feet, flying in close line-astern formation. He banked to port and fired a short burst at the rear FW190, which made a steep climb and, doing a stall turn, made a head-on attack on A404, which dived beneath the FW190s. They were not seen again. Flames from McCutcheon's engine reached his observer's hatch and then ceased. He set course for base, overtaking four Hampdens and, after escorting them for twenty minutes, made a successful crash-landing at base with an unserviceable undercarriage.

Crewing Up—The Luck of the Draw

One of 404's two-man Beaufighter crews first met at Catfoss OTU. They were a Canadian pilot, John Symons, and an English navigator, Len Barcham. Both at one stage were without their respective pilot or navigator. Symons describes their first encounter one evening while he was just finishing dinner:

> Len came along, sat down on a chair just vacated and introduced himself, explaining that he had just been fired and would I like to crew up with him? I quickly agreed. We got on well in the air and on the ground. At the end of our course a raffle was held to decide which crews would be posted to 404 Squadron at Wick and which would go to a Squadron posted to the Far East. Finally there were three ballots left and only one vacancy for 404, when out came our names.

Later, due to the arrival of six pilots without navigators (initially, some pilots, including Symons, had had to give up their navigators), this was followed by a further raffle when it was found that one pilot could have back his English navigator. Symons won, and Len Barcham returned to him! He was convinced that they were destined to stay together for the rest of the war.

Len Barcham gives a navigator's viewpoint:

> We always flew at 50 feet on the outward journey to avoid radar; this gives a tremendous impression of speed, by contrast when you sighted the target ship you at once went up to 1800 feet to prepare for attack and this gave such a strong feeling that you had "stopped" and would stall and fall out of the sky and no matter how many times this happened I could never suppress this fear.
>
> The other thing that frightened me most was the angry menace of the North Sea itself—even on its super calm days, it was still a danger, then the sea and sky merged with no horizon, not a good thing at 50 feet!
>
> Of the nav's work—-if you tried to do it conscientiously, there was just too much of it, and in cramped conditions. A small chart table on which nothing would stay except the chart which was pinned down, everything else finished on the floor and getting down to retrieve it or take a drift was difficult.
>
> Apart from the normal navigating job, there was a large, pivoted wireless set to look after and to listen out, also the great help to navigation the GEE set which often took longer to come up with the answer than there was time for. We had a. 303 Browning in the cupola and it was a confounded nuisance, it was pivoted and in flight would centralise and swing round and hit one in the ear. I tied it with a bootlace and on the one occasion I thought to use it, it couldn't be untied quickly enough. We were followed by two ME110s, one on either side thus we couldn't turn towards one without putting the other in a good position... eventually they gave up. On reflection we decided they were beginners. It was not a good idea to keep one's head in the office all the time!

While at Wick, Len Barcham was mainly on shipping strikes along the Norge coast, but also, as he adds:

Escorts to Naval units we seldom saw but particularly MTBs coming from Sweden. They would leave Gothenburg as soon as dark, go west up the Kattagat, then SW through the Skagerrak and across the North Sea making, I believe, for Newcastle. It needed a great deal of nav work to search up their track. We had a number of detachments to Sumburgh which enabled us to go further up the Norge coast. We had four squadrons at Wick, one RAF, one RCAF, one Australian and one New Zealand and worked together as a wing.

No. 404 Squadron at Wick

In June 1943 No. 404 (RCAF) Squadron was equipped with nineteen Beaufighter XICs and one Blenheim IV. They were based at Wick but with a detachment in the Shetlands at Sumburgh.

On 4 June F/O W.D. Thomsett was airborne from Sumburgh in Beaufighter JM117 at 0424 hrs for escort duties. There was 10/10ths cloud at 600 feet with visibility 3 miles. He was flying at 50 feet altitude when a JU88 was sighted. Thomsett climbed for cloud cover before diving to attack from 700 yards range with cannon and machine guns closing to 500 yards. Although the JU88 escaped into cloud, it was seen with smoke coming from both engines. The only damage to the Beaufighter was due to a bullet through the windscreen.

There were two missions for 404 on 4 July; four of their aircraft were on a Rover patrol escorting Hampdens, and three others took part in a shipping strike with No. 235 Squadron Beaufighters. S/Ldr Gatward in JM174 led the three which included Sgt. G.A. Pothecary in JM173 and P/O J.H. Rumbel flying JM166 "K." The three were airborne at 1705 hrs with initially heavy rain and poor visibility. The weather cleared near the Norwegian coast and landfall was made at Erkna Island. They turned north at position 6224N 0556E and sighted a ship with an escort vessel, and then, off Kristiansund, two more ships with an escort vessel. While flying along the coast there was heavy and light flak from shore batteries, as well as from the enemy ships. When some unescorted vessels were located, 404 Squadron aircraft circled a fjord to draw the fire, while 235 Squadron attacked the ships. The Beaufighters were over Norway for 45 minutes and they were attacked by ME109 fighters. K/404 was believed by 235 Squadron to have been hit and was last seen off Kristiansund. P/O Rumbel, with his navigator Lalonde, failed to return.

RAF station Wick was visited by Air Marshal Sir Philip Joubert, then acting as Inspector General, on 7 July. He was one of Coastal Command's Air Officers who obviously took a personal interest in individual personnel such as, it happened, a pilot who was with 404 Squadron, S/Ldr Gatward. As a Flight Lieutenant with 236 Squadron, Gatward had been specially briefed at Northwood by Sir Philip Joubert in May 1942 to fly over a German parade in Paris and release the French tricolor.[3]

Many Squadron records indicate that successful attacks not listed in the post-war records were made on ships. One of these occurred on 10 July when six of 404's Beaufighters escorted four aircraft from 235 Squadron on a Rover patrol. Led by S/Ldr Gatward they made landfall at 6030N 0450E and on turning north sighted a *sperrbrecher*-type armed vessel. Four of 404's aircraft climbed to give cover while the other two, with 235 Squadron Beaufighters, attacked the ship. It was left listing and smoking. One aircraft from 235 Squadron failed to return and one of 404's aircraft suffered slight damage to its tailplane. The AOC of 18 Group thanked 404 for "putting up a good show."

On 17 July five of 404's Beaufighters were with four from 235 Squadron while S/Ldr Gatward led those from 404 in JM119. They were airborne from Sumburgh at 0309 hrs and made landfall at Feje, position 6045N 0404E where a merchant vessel of 2000–3000 tons was sighted with one escort vessel. The ships were attacked with rocket projectiles and reported to have been heavily damaged and left ablaze. P/O McDonald in M/404 machine-gunned small flak ships but was himself wounded in a leg and his right arm. His instruments were shot away and on return he made a belly landing, as the Beaufighter's wheels had also been damaged. Due to a seriously wounded arm, he was flown from Sumburgh to Wick by F/O Hodson. The post-war record credits 235 and 404 with sinking the auxiliary UJ1705 of 548 tons.[4]

Escort to HMS Belfast

No. 404 Squadron provided escorts for the 10,000-ton cruiser HMS *Belfast* and its screen of destroyers on 28 July. S/Ldr de la Haye in "P" JM113 and F/O Shulemson in "D" JL947 were airborne at 0825 hrs and sighted the naval force at 0902 hrs when they were directed by the SNO to a JU88 which, however, escaped into cloud. When a B&V138 appeared it was first attacked by de la Haye, who scored hits on an engine and wing. Shulemson followed with a stern attack, and the B&V138 burst into flames and force-landed in the sea. There was one survivor who fired 5-star cartridges. Both Beaufighters vectored on another B&V138. De la Haye made a stern attack setting fire to its starboard engine, wing and hull. The enemy aircraft dived into the sea and there were no survivors. Both enemy aircraft were confirmed as destroyed.

Two more Beaufighters from 404 Squadron—JM123 with F/O Kefe and JM119 flown by F/Sgt Miller—followed in this escort duty at 1643 hrs. They lost contact with each other, and at 1807 hrs one was instructed by the SNO to return to base. About half an hour later, the remaining Beaufighter "H" sighted two single-engined enemy fighters which dived from cloud and dead astern. "H" took evasive action and then sighted two B&V138s. The Beaufighter turned to make a stern attack and pieces were seen falling from the hull of the first enemy. Two more attacks were made on the same aircraft with hits scored on its port engine and hull. The port engine burst into flames and the hull caught fire. H/404 broke away with its port engine unserviceable. A belly landing was made at base as the undercarriage was damaged.

Beaufighter J/404 JM130 was one of four from the squadron detailed to escort three aircraft from 235 Squadron for a Rover patrol and shipping recce airborne between 1309 and 1319 hrs on 4 August. At 1430 hrs when in position 6100N 0450E, four enemy escort vessels were sighted heading south in line astern. Five minutes later the enemy convoy was dead ahead. Two merchant vessels were immediately attacked with cannon and machine gun fire. There was intense and accurate flak, and J/404 flown by Sgt Dale was hit in the port engine, which burst into flames. The Beaufighter, now in flames, was ditched.

A Change of Command for No. 404 Squadron

It was while No. 404 Squadron was at Wick that the CO, G/Capt Truscott, relinquished command and W/Cmdr C. Willis succeeded him on 9 September 1943. No. 404 Squadron was able to claim a definite success on 30 September. Six of their Beaufighter Xs were led by W/Cmdr Willis in "Z" LZ295 on a Rover patrol. They were all airborne from Wick and in formation by 1605 hrs. There was low cloud over the Norwegian coast and they decided not to enter the leads but headed north from Stadlandet. Fifteen minutes later they sighted a merchant vessel in position 6211N 0404E. It was attacked by all the Beaufighters, scoring hits from amidships to astern. The whole of the vessel's superstructure burst into flames, and was left heading for shore and burning fiercely. There was only light flak from shore and the ship. It was recorded as *Sanet Svithin* of 1,376 tons, sunk by 404 Squadron Beaufighters. This ship was almost certainly the one sighted by F/Sgt Hobson who, while on a recce the following day sighted a ship beached on its side in position 6206N 0510E.[5]

The Four Brothers

The Stratford Beacon published in Stratford, Ontario, on 14 February 1945 gave an account of four brothers who had enlisted in the three fighting services. One of these was a navigator of a 404 Squadron

Beaufighter, and a letter written to the father of the brothers by W/Cmdr Willis includes the following:

At 1125 am on October 14 [1943] your son took off in a twin-engined aircraft on a reconnaissance of the Norwegian coast. Your son acted as navigator to the pilot Flt/Sgt J.W. Adamson...of Hinchliffe, Saskatchewan.

A message should have been received from the aircraft about three hours after it took off. When this message did not come through, and before the aircraft was actually overdue, six aircraft took off at 4 pm to carry out a search along the return route which the aircraft was to have taken. Although these aircraft flew low and covered as completely as possible the entire area in which the aircraft should have been found, the searchers were unable to find any trace. I myself joined in this search which continued for approximately four and a half hours.... The following day a further search was carried out by three aircraft which took off between seven and eight a.m. Just as light conditions allowed. Visibility was considerably improved on this day and the search lasted approximately five and a half hours. The same complete area was covered and the aircraft proceeded within twenty miles of the Norwegian coast...These two searches were carried out by comrades of your son who are members of the squadron... At present there is no indication available as to what occurred to your son's aircraft.

This extract from W/Cmdr Willis' letter is quoted to show the effort made to recover personnel who might be in distress. A copy of the letter was sent to the author by one of the four brothers, Tom Prest, who served with No. 410 Squadron, and who mentions that his navigator brother's daughter was born "after he went missing" and now resides in Ontario.

There was an exceptional peaceful mission for the squadron on 24 October when F/O J.S. Cummins in "Q" LZ189 was on a sortie from 0939 to 1405 hrs. This was to escort the ships *Empress of Russia, Atlantis,* and *Drottningholm,* which were bringing home to the United Kingdom ex-British POWs from Germany, via Sweden.

No. 404 Squadron at Wick received specific instructions from the Overseas Branch on 18 November regarding the compilation of records "especially the F.540" (operational records). They stated that it was generally the responsibility of the Squadron Adjutant. The Overseas Branch considered that the F.541 giving results should be the responsibility of the Intelligence Officer. Such formal directions did not preclude the Canadian Squadrons from voicing their own feelings with the phrasing tending to be not unlike the "line books" of RAF Squadrons on many occasions for both losses and successes.

Shipping Strike to Stadlandet

From Wick on 22 November eight of 404's Beaufighters acted as anti-flak escort to No. 144 Squadron's aircraft on a Rover patrol to the Stadlandet area. Chuck Page captained N/404 LZ296 and recalls:

I was one of eight 404 fighter escorts with cannons only to 144 Squadron

Torbeaus...We flew most of the outbound trip at nought feet to avoid enemy radar. Zipping along just above the waves was quite an exciting experience in itself. We climbed to 1500 feet as we reached the patrol area and almost immediately sighted a small convoy rounding Stadt corner, and I finally got to fire on the enemy, diving on one of the small escort vessels.

A convoy including three merchant vessels was attacked by both squadrons but no hits from 144's torpedoes were seen. Chuck Page explains that this failure was due to the torpedoes being set to run at 10 feet depth and passing under their targets, adding: "Much to the disgust of the Torbeau leader!"

While on a second run over an enemy vessel, the main hatch came off F/O W.Wilkie's aircraft, and his cap and Irvin jacket floated down onto the deck of the ship. One of 144's aircraft had to ditch on the way home, but S/Ldr de la Haye circled the dinghy until relieved by an Anson, an ASR Walrus, and an ASR launch. There was one survivor from 144's aircraft. De la Haye returned with only enough fuel to make base.

Coastal Command Squadrons lucky or unlucky enough to operate over the North Sea area were able to appreciate one of Bomber Command's aids to navigation—GEE. This was a radar system used in conjunction with a special chart and, in the writer's brief experience, could certainly pinpoint one's position. On 26 November, four of 404 squadron's navigators were put on to GEE training.

L/404 flown by S/Ldr de la Haye and navigated by F/Sgt C.A. Smith was one of four aircraft from the squadron on a Rover patrol on 28 November with four aircraft from 144 Squadron. When 200 miles from base, de la Haye had to turn back due to fumes from the windscreen de-icer fluid. He was almost overcome and asked Smith to go forward and be instructed on how to fly the Beaufighter, just in case. They returned safely, and as the squadron record states, the aircraft was "undoubtedly saved."

A Beaufighter Strike with Rockets

No. 404's operations for November 1943 concluded with a Rover patrol to Sogne fjord, of which F/Lt Chuck Page recalls:

I think this was my most effective of the eleven strikes I was on as I was able to fire on three ships in "one fell swoop" so to speak. We were five Beaus armed with rockets this time, a small enough formation to enter a fjord, and that's what we did.

We entered the northside channel around Bermanger, turned right and started out the southside channel, here we ran smack into five ships steaming in line ahead into the fjord; two merchant vessels escorted by what appeared to be two armed trawlers with a destroyer bringing up the rear. I attacked the lead merchant vessel, opening up with cannon and then firing my SAP rockets at roughtly 600 yards range, and I'm quite sure I scored with some of them. Since I had done a beam attack I now had to turn to port sharply to avoid the steep sides of the fjord, and lo and behold, there was the second MV dead ahead.

I managed to spray it with cannon fire and then headed towards the open sea, only to realise I had to pass over the destroyer in order to exit from the

fjord. I was quite low by now but was able to get off a quick squirt before passing over him.

I could see all his guns blazing away and wondered how he missed me. A few minutes later, homeward bound, I realised I was sweating and my feet were juddering on the rudder pedals. I had experienced my personal "baptism of fire." On landing back at base we looked over our kite and found a number of small holes in the tail assembly caused by shrapnel—a near miss.

In addition to Page, who flew N/404 LZ296, there were P/O Miller, F/Sgt French, F/O Shulemson, and F/O Decloux. They were all airborne by 0938 hrs and two hours later were in positon 6133N 0440E when they turned south. Five minutes later, the convoy was sighted. F/O Shulemson in LZ291 claimed eight hits with RPs on a merchant vessel causing serious damage, but was hit by flak in the starboard engine, with a shell punching a hole in the bottom cylinder. The elevator was also damaged, with a trimming tab shot away. A shell entered just below navigator Peter Bassett's seat, ripping a hole in the nav. bag. The engine functioned on 13 cylinders and Shulemson kept with the formation. P/O Miller in LZ466 had the main electrical line in his Beaufighter cut by flak.

P/O Miller with his navigator P/O Young in LZ294 led seven Beaufighters from 404 Squadron for a Rover patrol on 7 December. Landfall was made at position 6127N 0440E where the formation turned north into the leads favoured by the enemy-controlled shipping. Four of the aircraft were armed with 25 pound armour-piercing projectiles, and three with 60 pound HE RPs. At position 6210N

0509E a convoy was attacked from 600-800 yards range. Despite heavy and accurate flak from both ships and shore batteries, the convoy was considered seriously damaged. Only three of the Beaufighters were slightly damaged.

Losses for No. 404 Squadron

F/O D.N. Turner, RCAF, with his navigator P/O H.W. Duckitt, RAF, flew to Stadtlandet the following day to photograph the results but failed to return to base.

There was a serious accident on 16 December when the squadron was still based at Wick. F/O J.S. Cummins and navigator W/O W.K. McGrath were in one of four aircraft intended to escort 144 Squadron, but their starboard engine failed. The propeller was feathered, and an attempt was made to circuit on one engine when that also failed. They crashed in a field south of the base, making a heavy landing. The aircraft broke up with the tail almost severed, and the undercarriage 50 yards away. The aircraft caught fire. F/O Cummins was trapped by the control column and was unconscious. McGrath, who was unhurt, forced the control column back but had to remove one of Cummin's boots and safety harness to free him, suffering burns on his hands, hair, and eyebrows. Despite the danger of 60 pound HE RPs exploding due to the intense heat, McGrath lifted the unconscious Cummins from the cockpit and dragged him 100 yards to safety.

The squadron MO, F/Lt G.E. Beacock, arrived when the aircraft was burning furiously, with no sign of the crew. He warned spectators away and, despite exploding ammunition and petrol tanks, dashed to the aircraft to remove the crew.

They, unknown to him, had been taken to a farmhouse by locals. F/O Cummins, the pilot, suffered only first and second-degree burns to face and hands, thanks to his navigator McGrath.

On 22 December five of 404's Beaufighters undertook a Rover patrol together with four Torbeaus from 144 Squadron. They took off at 0932 hrs and landfall was made near Listeer. When in position 5759N 0652E a destroyer and U-boat were seen sailing in line astern. Visibility was poor, but the Beaufighters attacked with cannon at 700 yards range, and strikes were observed on the U-boat's conning tower. P/O K.S. Miller followed with a port beam attack, scoring hits. F/Lt Munro with his navigator F/O Conn dived from 700 feet, meeting intense flak. They were unable to pull out from the dive and went straight into the sea. Beaufighter NE323, flown by F/O I. Gillespie with P/O J.E Glendinning, turned to attack from landward with two other aircraft, but Gillespie's Beaufighter was seen to be on fire before nosing down and crashing into the sea. There were no survivors from 404's lost aircraft.

The U-boat is recorded as U-1062, which was damaged in these attacks.[6]

Christmas 1943

Christmas 1943 was marked by 404 Squadron standing down aircrew while the Headquarters staff closed their office at 1100 hrs, as they record "to build up strength to tackle the Christmas dinner." Season's greetings were received from the High Commissioner for Canada, the Rt. Hon. Mr. Vincent Massey.

No. 404's record for 27 December gives emphasis to No. 144 Squadron. The weather was good, and six aircraft from

404 escorted four from 144 to the Stavanger and Egera area. A convoy of two merchant vessels with three escorts was located. One of the escort vessels was left on fire due to 404's attacks, while one torpedo hit was claimed by 144. F/O R.S. Harrison, flying M/144, released his torpedo and then sighted a B&V138 at 800 feet, 1½ miles away. The Torbeau was then at 200 feet in position 5840N 0500E and doing 230 knots. Harrison made a tight climbing turn to starboard up 1000 feet when the enemy was diving to port. M404 closed firing first at 300 yards range and then at 150 yards on the centre nacelle and port engine of the enemy. The centre engine caught fire, and pieces were seen to break off. There was a green flash followed by red flames in the cabin. The B&V138 made a gentle turning dive to sea, appeared to level off very high from the water, then struck the surface and cartwheeled onto its back. No survivors were seen. M/144 then sighted two FW190 fighters and flew for cloud cover.

The last major operation for 404 Squadron in 1943 was led by the CO, W/Cmdr Willis, in "C" LZ449 on 28 December. Nine aircraft were detailed for a shipping strike with seven of those armed with RPs and the two flown by F/Sgt Hunt and Lt F.E. Huntley used cannon only. The weather, although windy, was good and all were airborne by 1202 hrs. Landfall was made at Krakanes before turning north around Stadtlandet. Writing in general terms about such operations, Chuck Page, one of the pilots on this strike remarks:

The very irregular Norwegian coastline with its many islands and deep, steep sided fjords provided good protection for enemy convoys because they could do most of their sailing in the inside passage [the leads], behind the islands. This made it practically impossible to manoeuvre a formation effectively, and going "in line astern" would have provided great target shooting for the flak gunners.

So, we had to catch them at places like Stadtlandet and the Mandel to Lister coastline where they were forced to sail in open waters. Often, even if shipping had been reported in the open seas they had disappeared by the time we reached the Norge coast. However, we sometimes managed to get small flights of five or six aircraft in behind Bermanger and into Vanelos fjord. We then had two things to worry about—flak and rock walls! some hundreds of feet high and almost vertical. Our favourite spot though, was Stadt corner where we could catch them in the open and hammer them. It became evident that we could use our RPs as main weapons and this facilitated the use of small formations. A semi-armour piercing rocket could rip as many as three plates out of a ship's hull and the 60 pound HE heads were equivalent to a six inch shell.

On this occasion the enemy was sighted in the entrance to Vanelos fjord: a convoy of two merchant ships with two escort vessels ahead and a destroyer behind an island further up the fjord. Six of the Beaufighters attacked a 2000-ton merchant ship with RPs, with F/O Decloux straddling the target and W/O Hallatt claiming two probable hits. The vessel was obviously damaged, given the emission of smoke and debris. There was intense flak from both shore and the escorts, but both merchant ships and two escorts were damaged. There was no time for the destroyer to move up, although it fired a constant barrage.

Three enemy aircraft were sighted but they all made for cloud cover. Three of the Beaufighters were slightly damaged by flak, including that flown by W/Cmdr Willis, who made a good landing although sustaining damage to undercarriage, tire, wing root, and elevators.

No. 407 Squadron in Transition

While at Docking in January 1943, 407 was still operating Hudsons on strikes off the Dutch coast. On the 18th their CO, W/Cmdr Archer, led three of 407's Hudsons with three from 320 Squadron. All were airborne at about 1745 hrs. The Dutch crews reported sighting a convoy in positon 5338N 0455E. It was attacked and 320 Squadron claimed direct hits on ships of about 2000 tons. Two of 407's crews claimed near misses. However, the sinking of a merchant vessel, *Algeria* of 1,619 tons, was credited to both squadrons.[7]

Two days later P/O Anderson took off at 1945 hrs in Hudson AM551 on a reconnaissance to the Dutch coast. He was last seen by an aircraft from No. 320 Squadron dropping flares and was plotted at about forty miles off Orfordness but failed to return.

Conversion of No. 407 Squadron to Wellingtons

There was a signal for W/Cmdr Archer and his crew together with the Engineering officer to report to the OTU at Cranwell. He returned on 30 January after a three-day conversion course on Wellingtons. On the same day, two Wellington aircraft were received by the squadron.

No. 407 became non-operational on 8 February and four days later the unit prepared for another move, this time to Wick's satellite—Skitten—but personnel were not sorry to leave Docking. The main party left by train for Wick at 1020 hrs on 15 February and arrived at Wick at 1330 hrs the following day. Trucks and buses took them to Skitten, where accommodation was limited and conditions cramped.

By 21 February more Mark XI Wellington aircraft were being received, and on 7 March 1943 F/O Jordan and Sgt Munch were airborne in Wellingtons MP534 and MP523 on anti-submarine patrols. S/Ldr Weightman and F/Lt Pickard left for Chivenor, to undertake training on Leigh-light Wellingtons. Ground crews left by train from Wick on 31 March for Chivenor which was to be the squadron's new base. Eighteen aircrews arrived at Chivenor the following afternoon.

No. 172 Squadron RAF had been operating Leigh-light Wellingtons for a year on anti-submarine patrols and two of their officers—S/Ldr Thomson and F/O Triggs—gave talks to 407 on A/S operations and ditching a Wellington respectively.

One of 407's first attacks on a U-boat occurred on 21 April. F/Lt D.G. Pickard was airborne at 2057 hrs on a Derange A/S patrol at 2057 hrs. The Derange area began approximately west of Brest and extended southwards, thus largely covering U-boat routes to and from the French ports. While flying his Mark XII Wellington at 1000 feet a radar contact was obtained at four miles distance. The sea was calm and visibility was good. He was homed down by his radar operator to 100 feet altitude and in position 4547N

0856W sighted a fully-surfaced U-boat which was heading eastwards at 10 knots. The U-boat opened fire with cannon and machine guns. As Pickard turned to port for an attack, his rear gunner opened fire and silenced the U-boat's gunners. The U-boat had submerged for only fifteen seconds when Pickard released all his ten DCs from about seventy-five feet altitude. They fell along the U-boat's track spaced at 100 feet and with the centre of the stick 200 feet ahead of the swirl.

The wisdom or otherwise, of releasing all ten DCs was apparent when another sighting was obtained thirteen minutes later with a U-boat silhouetted by moonlight one mile ahead and heading south-east at 8 knots. The rear gunner was able to obtain hits on the conning tower before the enemy crash-dived.

A week later F/O Cross was airborne from Chivenor at 2243 hrs on a similar patrol. He was flying at 1200 feet altitude $4\frac{1}{4}$ hrs later when a radar contact was made at 8 miles. He lost height as he was homed onto the contact and the U-boat's wake was sighted at $\frac{1}{4}$ mile. The Leigh-light was switched on to illuminate a fully-surfaced U-boat heading due east at 12-15 knots. Cross released six DCs from 200 feet at 90 degrees to the vessel's track, which was straddled forty feet astern of the U-boat. The rear gunner was able to silence cannon and machine gun fire from the U-boat. F/O Cross circled the area but no further contact was made.

The Demons lost one of their Wellingtons on 29 April. F/Sgt Fergusson had been airborne at 0020 hrs in MP652 for a Derange A/S patrol. Flying Control was in contact at 0330 hrs but at 0405 hrs the police at Woolacombe reported an aircraft crashing into the sea 330° 8-10 miles off Morte Point at 0335 hrs. The

squadron record gives also a report of F/Sgt Fergusson crashing three miles off the coast while returning from his patrol. The body of his navigator, F/O Flemington, was recovered and his funeral was held at Brookwood. The body of one of the wireless operators, Sgt Summers, was recovered off Ilfracombe on 4 June and buried at Heanton Church three days later.

By 4 May, F/Lt Pickard had obviously improved his technique for attacks on U-boats. At 2132 hrs again airborne on a Derange patrol in Wellington MP593, the sea was rough and visibility hazy when, while flying at 1500 feet a radar contact was obtained at nine miles range. While being homed, he lost height to 400 feet and at $1\frac{1}{2}$ miles range sighted a U-boat's wake. The vessel was heading north-east at fifteen knots; Pickard turned to port and at $\frac{1}{2}$ mile switched on the Leigh-light, which just showed a conning tower.

Six DCs were released from 40 feet ten seconds after the U-boat had submerged. This was from 200 feet ahead of the swirl and at 30-40° to the track. One large explosion was seen by the rear gunner. Pickard remained on the scene, position 4928N 0908W, for twelve minutes but no further contact was made.

The Canadian press were with No. 407 Squadron during 6-7 May and various members were interviewed. No. 407 Squadron's badge was presented to the unit on 11 June by the OAC of No.19 Group, RAF, Air Marshal Bromet, an officer who in World War I had commanded No. 8 (Naval Squadron).[8]

On 25 June, Wings for Victory week at Chivenor opened with a dance in the Officers' Mess. There was a station parade on the 27th and an address was given by G/Capt Chilton, and in the afternoon there were station sports with all personnel permitted to attend.

Blockade of the Bay

The German U-boat Command was aware of increased air activity over the Bay of Biscay following the withdrawal of their U-boats from the North Atlantic, and the Wellingtons of 407 Squadron continued to take an active part in what the German Command described as a "Blockade of the Bay".[9]

F/O G.C. Walsh was airborne at 0955 hrs in MP541 for an A/S patrol and was flying south-west at 1200 feet with 10/10ths cloud at 500 feet above him when his second pilot sighted a wake two miles to starboard. The wake was from a U-boat heading north-east at 8 knots and was about to dive. Walsh altered course to attack and lost height. At one mile distance the U-boat submerged, but Walsh was able to release six DCs from 70 feet within 18 seconds with them falling eighty yards ahead of the swirl. They straddled the track and all were seen by the rear gunner to explode. Walsh flew over the area and sighted air bubbles followed later by an oil patch which spread to 400 feet diameter.

No. 407's Domestic Affairs

At the beginning of July, Dominion Day was marked by the release of all personnel who could be spared. Some cycled, others were content to sunbathe. A few days later, S/Ldr Howe from the RCAF District HQ at Exeter, visited 407 Squadron to interview personnel. The biggest complaint from ground crews was the Pool Maintenance system. This would have been in sharp contrast to having both aircrew and ground crew allocated a specific aircraft. The pool system nullified personal involvement; the latter enabled ground and aircrew to make personal contact and to be aware of each other's work. The writer was able to appreciate this aspect during only six months of his service.

During the visit of S/Ldr Howe, NCO aircrew complained about the lack of promotion. The operational record includes a report by the Medical Officer on skin complaints suffered by airmen. At that time the Service did not provide bed sheets for airmen, and there were cases of boils and impetigo thought to have resulted from dirty blankets which had not been changed for months. Further skin infections were pediculosis, scabies, virulent impetigo, and dermatitis.

For recreation and amusements, games were laid on, such as softball, and 407's teams played teams from 172 Squadron RAF and an American Naval Unit from Instow. Films were screened twice a week in each of the three messes, and there were occasional ENSA shows.

On 28 July the George Medal was awarded to F/Sgt Coates for an act of bravery when he was serving with 415 Squadron. Two days later a farewell party was arranged for S/Ldr R.Y."Happy" Tyrrell, RAF, who had been on operations for 2½ years and had been in charge of B Flight since January.

In August 1943, the twelve Wellington Mark XIIs and three Mark XIVs used by 407 Squadron were on the Station's charge. On 2 August W/Cmdr Archer was airborne in HF127, a Mark XIV at 0534 hrs. While flying southwards four hours later at 2000 feet just below cloud, the wake of a U-boat was sighted 10-12 miles ahead.

Gp Capt V.H.A. McBratney, No. 413's first
Commanding Officer.

Hudson crews were typically four: pilot, two WAGs, and 2nd pilot or navigator. Here, rather more
with transport and RR-H possibly AM811 in the background.

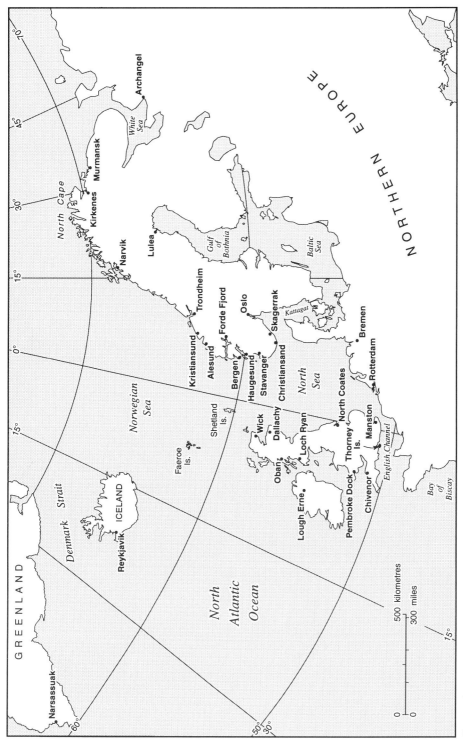

Chart of Northern Europe including areas over which RCAF squadrons in Coastal Command operated.

No. 407 (Demon) Squadron on parade with three of their Hudsons in the background.

Beaufighters of No. 404 Squadron en route to Norway; identifiable is EE-B NE687.

Christmas 1942 in the Sergeants' Mess, Oban. No. 422 Squadron was based there until May 1943.

Sunderland 3-H coded for No. 423 Squadron on Lough Erne.

No. 422's emblem depicting the arm of a brave
holding a tomahawk. The motto is taken from
Shakespeare's *Richard II*.

A No. 422 Squadron Sunderland crew of eleven awaiting the arrival of a pinnace.

The rescue of all the crew of DD861 by F/Lt Armstrong in a Sunderland of No. 228 Squadron on 4 September, 1943.

Pembroke Dock, a Coastal Command flying-boat base in South Wales as seen from the air.

The electronically operated Boulton & Paul turret on a No. 407 Squadron Hudson.

Jack Bellis and crew of No. 422 Squadron. F/O Bellis was in Sunderland JM712 on 17 October 1943, when it was shot down by a U-boat.

F/Lt Sid Butler, DFC, of No. 422 Squadron who sank U-625 while with Frank Morton's crew, but shown here with his own Sunderland crew (front row 2nd from left).

A Hudson coded RR-B for No. 407 Squadron, and possibly a Mark V AM679.

F/Lt David Hornell with four of his Canso crew at Wick in 1944.

The radio position in No. 162 Squadron's Canso 11081 with Doug Johnson.

The navigator's position in a No. 162 Squadron Canso with F/O Ron Wales.

John McRae, DFC, who flew with No. 162
Squadron from January 1943 until March 1945.
He was co-captain of Canso 9816 which sank
U-715.

Cameron Taylor, here with two of his Hudson crew. While flying a Wellington of No. 407
Squadron on 30 December 1944, he sank U-772.

U-625 being attacked by Sunderland EK591 U/422 in position 5235N 2019W on 10 March 1944, when flown by F/Lt Butler with W/O Frank Morton.

Pembroke Dock with Sunderlands at moorings.

F/O Ken Ashfield, DFC, with his Wellington crew of No. 415 Squadron. They successfully attacked two ships off the Dutch coast on 20 April 1944.

No. 404 Squadron aircrew at Davidstow Moor on D-Day, 6 June 1944.

W/Cmdr Ken Gatward, DSO, DFC, after his last trip with No. 404 Squadron on 8 August 1944.

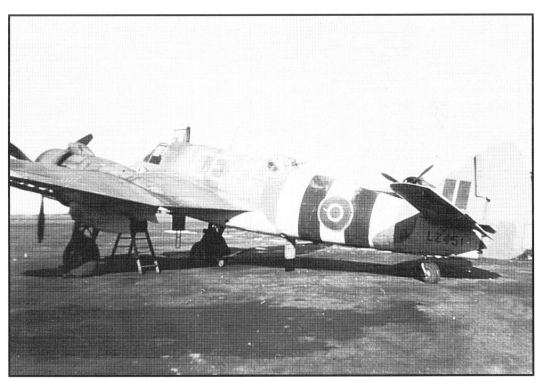

Beaufighter EE-M LZ451, one of No. 404 Squadron's aircraft which flew on the raid against *Monte Rosa* on 3 March 1944.

Sydney Shulemson, DSO, DFC, who as a Flying Officer took the lead in some notable shipping strikes of No. 404 Squadron.

Beaufighter NE355 coded EE-H for No. 404 Squadron at Davidstow Moor in July 1944, armed with cannon and rocket projectiles.

A shipping strike by No. 404 Squadron over Egersund harbour on 24 March 1945 when two ships, *Thetis* and *Sarp* were sunk.

Nonte fjord on 9 February 1945; "Black Friday," when No. 404 lost six out of eleven Beaufighters in a strike by the Dallachy wing led by No. 455's CO.

A memorial at Dallachy on the Moray Firth to the strike wing, with emblems of five squadrons including that of No. 404 (RCAF).

F/Lt Pengelley's Wellington crew on No. 407 Squadron at Chivenor, Devon, in 1945.

He followed appropriate tactics by climbing into cloud to get ahead of the vessel and then, using binoculars, sighted a surfaced U-boat at 7-8 miles when it was heading due west at 12 knots.

Height was lost two miles ahead of the vessel and six DCs were released from 50 feet. The U-boat had altered course to port and the DCs fell almost at right angles to its track. W/Cmdr Archer's rear gunner saw all the DCs explode in a straddle, although the nearest was apparently twenty feet from the conning tower. The U-boat remained on the surface, circling and firing at the Wellington, which remained in the area for fifty minutes but out of range of the AA fire. When PLE was reached at 1020 hrs, W/Cmdr Archer set course for base.

The 13th August was ill-fated. F/Lt B.W. Pritchard, while taking off from Beaulieu, Hampshire, collided in mid-air with a Halifax from Homsley-South. The funeral of the 407 Squadron crew took place six days later with 75% of the squadron on parade. On 20 August, the squadron suffered further losses, due to foggy weather.

The crews that had been in night operations were diverted to Beaulieu and the aircraft flown by P/O Dalgleish crashed. He was killed, together with most of his crew: P/O Hirtle, F/Sgt Clancy, F/Sgt Peters, and F/Sgt Clark. A W/AG F/Sgt G.O. Buckman, was seriously injured and was taken to Bristol Infirmary. The funeral of P/O R. Carl Dalgleish and four of his crew took place at Heanton churchyard overlooking the aerodrome. F/Sgt Peter's commission had just come through and he was to have married Miss Betty Moss from Newcastle-on-Tyne on 1 September. She attended the funeral with some of her family.

No. 407's OC B Flight, F/Lt C.W. Taylor, was promoted to squadron leader on 30 August and must have been one of the Squadron's longest serving members.

No. 407 Squadron's First U-Boat Kill

The weather on 6 September at Chivenor was gusty with intermittent rain, but flying operations continued, with six of 407's crews airborne. One of those, P/O E.M. O'Donnell, took off in Wellington HF115 at 2157 hrs on an A/S patrol. While heading east at 1500 feet visibility was 2-3 miles, with 5/10ths cumulus cloud at 2-3000 feet and no moon. A radar contact was made at 8 miles range and while homing, O'Donnell lost height to 600 feet and at ¾ mile range the Leigh-light was switched on, illuminating a U-boat. It was low in the water at position 44536N 1013W heading south-west at 10 knots. P/O O'Donnell was in an unfavourable position to attack and flew over the vessel, turning sharply to port. The U-boat opened fire with guns and cannon; the Leigh-light was switched off and the rear gunner fired up to 2000 rounds, but his ring sight would have been diffcult to use under such conditions. O'Donnell circled the area and saw the U-boat's wake at two miles range when it was steering a zig-zag course. At one mile the Leigh-light was switched on to see the U-boat at the same level in the water as before and maintaining the same heading and speed. Just before the U-boat submerged and with the conning tower and stern still visible, O'Donnell released five DCs on hanging up. The rear gunner saw at least four explosions straddling the U-boat's track 20-30 yards ahead of the swirl. The Wellington circled and marked the attack position with flame floats. The Leigh-light was switched on, but there was no sign of the U-boat. Nineteen minutes after the attack a marine marker was dropped and P/O O'Donnell returned to base.

U-669 had sailed from a French port on 29 August captained by OL Kohl and was sunk in this attack.[10]

Losses for No. 407 Squadron

The squadron lost three more aircraft before the end of the month; Sgt George Munch crashed on the 12th. With him were Sgt Russell, W/O Haughey, and P/O Pincock; all four were killed instantly. Two others, W/O Cote and W/O West, were severely injured and taken to Devon Infirmary where W/O J.A. Cote died the following day. W/O James Haughey was from Lurgen and his body was taken to Northern Ireland; the other casualties were buried at Heanton. Wellington MP693 was airborne at 2043 hrs on the 26th for an A/S patrol. An SOS was received, and a fix on its position obtained, but it failed to return. Lost with MP693 were F/O J.C. Austin, P/O C.R. Booth, W/Os R.W. Revell, K. Rolfstad, A.R. Merritt and L.G. Smith.

At 0546 hrs the following morning, the English CO, W/Cmdr J.C. Archer, with his crew of five, was airborne in HF124 on a search for F/O Austin's crew. A distress signal was received but that Wellington also failed to return.

Many attacks by Coastal Command aircraft on U-boats must have caused considerable damage, but not enough to require them to return to port. Such attacks would thus not appear in the Command's lists of successes but must

have left the U-boats prone to subsequent affrays with the Navy.

Such an attack was made by F/O Thomson on 15 October. He was airborne from Chivenor in Wellington MP688 and just before midnight was flying at 1000 feet above broken cloud when a radar contact was obtained. Thomson kept on course to avoid attacking down moon. A turn to port was made and height lost. At 200 feet altitude he was 3/4 mile from the contact; the Leigh-light was switched on and a fully-surfaced U-boat was seen heading north-west at 10 knots. There were shells bursting about the Wellington, which responded with front guns, and the AA became erratic. Six DCs were released from 50-75 feet and straddled the vessel. The U-boat turned with its stern higher out of the water, and later was still on the surface sailing at reduced speed. Some minutes later it disappeared.

Chivenor-St. Eval-Chivenor

There was a further move by the squadron, beginning with the air party arriving at St. Eval on 3 November. Following the loss of W/Cmdr Archer, S/Ldr Pickard had taken command, but on 4 November, W/Cmdr R.A. Ashman arrived to succeed as CO. A Wop/AG who was to join W/Cmdr Ashman's crew as Gunnery Leader was Bill Parrott from Newfoundland. An inventory of 407's Leigh-light Wellington armament states that they would have had six 250 pound depth charges, four .303 machine guns in the tail turret, and one .303 in the nose. The latter is surprising; many Coastal Squadrons on anti-submarine warfare did their best to increase the forward firing armament to counter AA from U-boats before releasing depth charges.

While at St. Eval, the squadron recorded how good the catering was, being "marvellous in all messes" and added that the station went "out of its way to co-operate with squadrons which helps to make life worth while." Chivenor received less favourable comments.

Rats were obviously attracted to the parcels sent to Canadians as they were likely to contain food items. However, the only health problem recorded at St. Eval was influenza, and most cases responded within a few days to treatment.

On 2 December the main party arrived at Chivenor from St. Eval, and four crews which had been airborne from St. Eval on operations returned to Chivenor, with the balance of the air party arriving with S/Ldr Taylor the following day.

One of those who had been on operations was F/Lt D.W. Farrell, who was airborne at 1734 hrs on 2 December in HF228 for an A/S patrol. While heading southwards at 600 feet altitude, a radar contact was obtained at 14 miles range. There was no moon, the sea was rough, and there was 10/10ths cloud at 1600 feet. A flame float was dropped and a further contact was made at 12 miles. Farrell homed to within 1½ miles when a phosphorescent line was seen. At ¾ mile, while flying at 400 feet the Leigh-light was switched on to see a fully-surfaced U-boat sailing south-west at 10 knots. At 2142 hrs five DCs set for 25 feet were released from 100 feet and at 100° to the U-boat's track. There was tracer from the vessel, but some DCs were seen by the rear gunner to explode between the conning tower and the stern.

AA from the U-boat ceased. Flame floats which were dropped indicated a straddle with the DCs. The U-boat remained on the surface and was shadowed for six minutes before contact was lost. F/Lt Farrell remained in the area until PLE was reached and marine markers were dropped.

As early as September 1943 the Admiralty was aware of potential blockade runners in the Far East and in December, 407 Squadron was one of the many Coastal Command Squadrons to be involved when the blockade runners were attempting to reach the French ports.[11]

On 24 December 407's Wellingtons were armed with bombs instead of DCs for a shipping strike. F/O D.E. Rollins was airborne in HF184 at 2251 hrs but for an A/S patrol when he sighted eight enemy vessels which he shadowed and attacked. During this sortie he collided with a Liberator and although both aircraft were considerably damaged, both returned to their bases, with Rollins touching down at 0824 hrs on Christmas Day.

Operations had been laid on for Christmas but were scrubbed just before briefing. An excellent dinner was served in all messes and crews which had been diverted on Christmas Eve arrived back in time for the meal. That evening there was a fancy dress ball for all ranks, and on Boxing Day a party for 75-100 children of members of the station was held. They received gifts of toys and candies. There had been performances of "Blackouts 1943" in the hall hired at Braunton for £2 for the 27th and 28th and the cast were entertained at a dance held in the Sergeants' Mess on the 29th.

When 1943 was being rounded off for the Demons, a New Year's dance was held in the Officers' Mess at which photographs were collected and a squadron album prepared outlining personalities and 407's historical data. The record refers to an influenza epidemic throughout Britain in

December 1943 and noted that for 407 "there were more than the usual number of cases." Most required treatment and a stay of 3-4 days in Station Sick Quarters, and aircrew with colds were grounded for 48 hrs or more. Squadron morale was lowered by the standard of messing, pariculary for the airmen, in whose mess the crockery was reported as "consistently dirty."

No. 415 Squadron: Detachments at Predannack and Docking

Seven of 415's aircraft with their crews and thirty-three ground staff had been on detachment at Predannack for servicing since 4 December 1942. Six of those Hampdens were airborne at 1244 hrs on 3 January 1943 led by F/Lt J.G. Stronach for a shipping strike to the French coast, following the report of a merchant vessel of 2000 tons west of Lorient and heading due east. The ship was sighted by the Hampdens ten miles off the coast, and they divided into two flights so as to attack from both sides of the vessel which, however, proved to be only a 500-ton coaster. One aircraft was instructed to release a torpedo while the other Hampdens used gunfire. The torpedo ran twenty yards behind the ship and exploded 400 yards beyond. The Hampdens were close to the enemy coast and were without fighter cover, but a strong force of Fortresses was bombing Lorient and diverted the enemy's fighters.

On the 18 February, Sgt J.C. McDonald was airborne at 2040 hrs in D/415 armed with a torpedo for a shipping strike off the Dutch coast. After flying for $1\frac{1}{4}$ hrs he sighted three merchant vessels heading south at 7 knots. He attacked the ship nearest the coast from 80 feet altitude but with unknown results. There was intense, accurate flak, and he had to take evasive action in poor visibility.

F/O A.B. Brenner, who was airborne in Hampden P1157, had seen flares and flak which had probably been directed against McDonald and followed in an attack just one minute later. This was against two ships in echelon. He made his attack such that if his torpedo missed the first vessel, there was a chance of it striking the second. He had to take violent evasive action towards the enemy coast and on turning passed over what was probably a heavily armed *sperrbrecher*, and the Hampden was severely damaged by AA fire. His two gunners had looked back to see a merchant vesel estimated at 4000 tons on fire in the bows. Due to severe flak damage, with rudders, fins, and elevators shot away, perspex smashed in many places, and the port engine unserviceable and starboard engine erratic, Brenner had to ditch his aircraft at 2257 hrs. The Hampden sank in eight seconds, but its crew had been able to board their dinghy. Brenner and his crew were picked up on 20 February at 1750 hrs by a Walrus piloted by F/O Brown and taken to Martlesham Heath. They were back with the squadron at Thorney Island two days later.

Nine aircraft with their crews were detached to Docking on 24 February. An ex 489 Squadron officer S/Ldr G.H.D. Evans, assumed command of No. 415 Squadron on 16 March, succeeding W/Cmdr W.W. Bean who was returning to Canada.

There were more losses suffered by the squadron in March. On the 19th four of their aircraft, armed with four 500 pound bombs each, were on patrols from Thorney Island along the French coast. Two

Hampdens covered from Boulogne to Dieppe, while the other two aircraft patrolled from Dieppe to Le Havre. Hampden AE418 captained by Sgt W.L. Hurl crashed just prior to landing at 2315 hrs, and all four on board were killed. On the 23rd F/O J.D.P. McLeod was captain of AE395 airborne on a shipping strike from Thorney Island at 2125 hrs but failed to return.

Enemy-Controlled Ships Sunk or Damaged

A shipping strike was laid on to the Dutch coast on 14 April which proved to be very successful. F/O P.N. Harris in B/415 armed with a torpedo was airborne from Bircham Newton at 2116 hrs. At 0018 hrs on the 15th he sighted a convoy of six ships, four large merchantmen in line astern and two smaller vessels following abreast. Harris attacked the third merchantman estimated at 6000 tons, by releasing his torpedo from 600 yards range and 80 feet altitude. It was seen to run true, and both his air gunners saw thick black smoke gushing from the ship. F/O Harris claimed only damage to his target, but it appears likely that he sank the 4,821 ton *Borga* off Ameland. He returned to base after a trip of over five hours.[12]

P/O K.C. Wathen was airborne in Hampden K/415 shortly after Harris, similarly armed with a torpedo. At 0046 hrs on the 15th he sighted the same convoy and made four runs before releasing his torpedo from 50 feet altitude at 600 yards range. Dense smoke was seen gushing from a ship, and it was claimed as damaged. From 415's operational record, this was the same ship as was attacked by F/O Harris, but from Coastal Command's

war record, another ship, the 2,092 ton *Tom*, was damaged.[13]

A month later P/O K.C. Wathen and his crew were lost together with F/Sgt L.E. McGee and his crew. Both were airborne from Thorney Island at 2149 hrs on 17 May for a shipping strike, but failed to return. F/O P.N. Harris who was on the same strike released a torpedo against a ship but didn't see it strike as there was much smoke over his target. His crew, however, saw an aircraft sinking in the water which could have been either Wathen's or McGee's. Shipping strikes at low altitudes were one of the most dangerous occupations in World War II whatever armament was used and for torpedo aircraft particularly so.[14]

S/Ldr C.G. Ruttan in R/415 saw two ships awash smoking and sinking and several lifeboats. Another Hampden captain, Sgt W.N. MacEachern, had his aircraft damaged in several places, and he himself was wounded in the hip but managed to return to base. From the Coastal Command war record, No. 415 was successful on the night of 17-18 May in sinking two ships, the Auxiliary VP1106 *Ernst von Briesen* of 408 tons off Ameland and also an M-class minesweeper, M.345 of 750 tons, off Calais. It is not clear who claimed the latter.[15]

Nationalities in Coastal Command

Many nationalities were represented in Coastal Command Squadrons, which Canadian aircrew appeared quite happy to accept, but which the Canadian authorities deplored, wishing their units to be "Canadianised." An English pilot, Ken Ashfield, crewed up with a Scottish navigator and two Canadian Wop/AGs at No. 32 OTU Patricia Bay in October 1942 after he had completed a GR (General Recconnaissance) course at Charlottetown, Prince Edward Island. Although all four reached Britain separately, they met up at a torpedo training unit at Turnberry, Scotland. Given the choice of Wick, Leuchars, or Thorney Island, they opted for the latter and joined 415 Squadron in May 1943. As Ken Ashfield adds:

> When we joined the squadron all the pilots and observers were RAF as was the CO, but over the months this changed as more and more RCAF personnel arrived, also a Canadian CO, W/Cmdr Ruttan. After joining 415 we were immediately detached to Tain for further training in dummy attacks against shipping. HMS *Reading* being the target. We returned to Thorney Island and started operations, at that time our Hampdens had no radar so torpedo operations were confined to the moon periods.
> The Battle of the Atlantic was at its height and my crew carried out their first sortie at the beginning of June 1943 positioning to St. Eval with six DCs to operate on anti-sub patrol down the Bay of Biscay next day. This completed we slept and returned to Thorney Island. This pattern of operations continued with three anti-sub patrols each taking three days every two weeks. The trips down the Bay lasted eight hours plus. Towards the end of June 1943 during the moon periods we carried out Rover patrols along the Dutch coast with a torpedo.

On 26 June they were airborne from St. Eval on a Musketry patrol in the Bay of Biscay when, after flying for about seven

hours, both engines cut, due, Ashfield suggests, to airlocks developing when the fuel was low. They were ten miles from base and jettisoned much equipment and prepared to ditch when the port engine picked up at 300 feet. They landed at St. Merryn with the undercarriage up, and although the aircraft was damaged, none was hurt.

A/Cmdre F.L. Hopps, CBE, AFC, a former Station Commander at Wick, but now deputy senior Air-staff Officer Coastal Command, visited No. 415 Squadron on 27 July. At about this time the unit was notified that F/Sgt D.M. Coates had been awarded the George Medal for his gallantry on 1 November 1942.[16]

The Sinking of U-706

The United States Army Squadron No. 4 was credited with sinking U-706 in position 4615N 1025W on 2 August 1943, but 415 Squadron must surely share the credit.[17]

On 2 August S/Ldr Ruttan was airborne at 0553 hrs from St. Eval for a Musketry patrol. After flying for just over three hours he sighted a U-boat about to surface. In his initial run there was AA and he broke away to attack from the starboard quarter. His front gunner fired only ten rounds before the gun jammed. S/Ldr Rutan released six 250 pound DCs from 100 feet altitude across the course of the U-boat but was unable to see the result. The U-boat, however, appeared low in the water with its speed only 3 knots and apparently disabled. At 0917 hrs the AAF Liberator was seen attacking the U-boat with DCs and the vessel was not seen again. Three minutes later the Hampden crew sighted about fifteen bodies and much wreckage and diesel oil. S/Ldr Ruttan's part in this sinking is now recognised at least in the official RCAF history.[18]

F/O W. Savage was airborne four hours after S/Ldr Ruttan for a similar Musketry patrol over the Bay of Biscay but with a very different experience. He first sighted a Sunderland flying-boat circling two flame floats where there was a large oil patch. He resumed his patrol but at 1446 hrs was attacked by five JU88s. Visibility was 6-7 miles and there was cloud cover. Savage jettisoned his depth charges and took evasive action, but the enemy fighters attacked from all angles. His gunners saw their tracer hitting and entering nearly all the enemy aircraft, but F/O Savage continued evasive action by cork-screwing and making for any available cloud cover.

When his rear gunner had almost exhausted his ammunition and had some trouble with his guns, the JU88s concentrated on the tail of the Hampden. After a combat of about twenty minutes, F/O Savage managed to escape and returned to St. Eval.

The Hampden's hydraulics had been shot away, there were holes throughout the fuselage and mainplane, the elevators were damaged, and perspex from the cockpit was blown away but none of the crew was wounded. The squadron records: "Mighty good show."

An official World War II publication, *Coastal Command Review* was ever ready to report on squadrons which had distinguished themselves in any way, and No. 415 was given an appropriate mention in the issue dated October 1943. The unit was then credited with sinking three ships totalling 9,821 tons and damaging one of 2,092 tons during the period April-September 1943.

On 6 September P/O R.E. Ritscher, P/O O.K. Main and Sgt H.J. Hanson were detailed for practice night flying. Their Hampden was airborne from Thorney Island at 2205 hrs, but about four minutes later when halfway round their first circuit, the Hampden crashed in shallow water. It caught fire and burned for some time. A party reached the area within a few minutes and the search continued throughout the night and the following day when another aircraft was sent to cover the area.

Six days later wreckage was located in water and salvage operations were commenced. On 14 September wreckage was hauled ashore in Chichester harbour and the body of P/O Ritscher removed. Those of P/O Main and Sgt Hanson were recovered the following day. The three were buried at St. Nicholas cemetery, West Thorney, on 17 September.

No. 415 Squadron Re-Equipped

In September the unit was informed that it was to receive ten Albacore biplanes and ten Mark XIII Wellingtons. While in Coastal Command Albacores could be considered as torpedo aircraft, the Wellingtons served not only as anti-submarine aircraft but also as markers or pathfinders, carrying flares for the latter purpose.

The first of 415's experiences with Wellingtons was on 2 October when W/Cmdr Ruttan checked out S/Ldr Brenner and P/O Watt. Six days later the squadron's Wellington HZ725 was ditched in shallow water a short distance from base. P/O W.R.R. Savage during take-off found the propellers had stuck in full fine pitch, and he was unable to reduce engine revs below 3300 rpm. The only minor injury in the crew was to P/O Savage who was taken to St. Richard's hospital in Chichester with lacerations over his eye.

By the end of October 1943, 415 Squadron had on charge twelve Mark XIII Wellingtons and four Mark I Hampdens. Seven crews were considered fully trained for operations on Wellingtons.

One of 415's first Albacore pilots must have been Norman Chadwick, who was attached to the squadron on 14 October. He had been trained for Hampden torpedo operations but when 415 was split into two flights, one with Wellingtons at Bircham Newton, the other with Albacores at Manston, he opted for the latter. As F/Lt Chadwick recalls:

> We took over from a Fleet Air Arm squadron and our assignment was night-bombing in the English Channel, primarily against German E-boats although we attacked any target of opportunity. Most of the time we were controlled by radar direction from Dover, sometimes on routine patrols, at other times from a standby situation, awaiting orders to scramble. Our armament was six 250 pound bombs initially with time delay penetration fuses, but latterly using a special air burst detonator.[19]

No. 415 Squadron Moves to Bircham Newton

On November 6th, W/Cmdr Ruttan went by road from Thorney Island to Manston for the inspection by the AOC Coastal Command, Air Marshal Sir John Slessor, of 415's torpedo detachment. The main body of the squadron moved from Thorney Island to Bircham Newton via Emsworth and Docking on the 15th.

On 25 November five of the Albacores flew from Manston for an anti-shipping strike off the French coast with aircraft armed with six 250 pound bombs, but with some intended to serve as Air-Sea-Rescue (ASR). The following evening two of the Wellingtons were airborne captained by W/Cmdr Ruttan and P/O Ashfield in "Operation Deadly." This was in co-operation with the Royal Navy against German E-boats. The Wellingtons were airborne from Bircham Newton at 1809 hrs but after completing the patrol over three times, were recalled and landed at Sculthorpe, Norfolk.

F/O D.C. Thomson with his navigator F/O A.H. Bartlett was airborne in Albacore E/415 at 0002 hrs on 21 December from Manston for an anti-shipping patrol. Six vessels were sighted north-east of Calais. Thomson attacked from ahead and at the centre of the first three vessels, releasing six 250 pound bombs from 900-1000 feet. The bombs straddled the vessels and there was a red flash and explosion due to a direct hit. There was some intense flak from the other ships, which were not hit.

F/O Thomson was airborne again from Manston on 30 December for a patrol of the Calais to Dunkirk area. A mile off shore and half a mile north-east of Calais, two stationary barges tied together were sighted. Thomson released six 250 pound bombs from 750 feet altitude and although they burst twenty feet from the vessels, Thomson believed that the barges had been severely damaged.

References to Chapter 5

1. GüH para.357
2. CCWR p.25
3. PJ p.178
4. CCWR p.25

5. Ibid
6. CCWR p.16
7. Ibid
8. HAJ III App. xii
9. JuH para.359
10. JuH App.III p.114; CCWR p.12; USSL p.165
11. SWR II/1 p.73
12. CCWR p.21
13. CCWR p.13
14. RAF II pp.94-99; JT p.456
15. CCWR p.21
16. Ibid
17. SWR III/1 p.366; USSL p.164
18. RCAF III p.398
19. OT p.156 [841 Sqdrn FAA]

Chapter 6

Iceland and No.162 Squadron RCAF: January– December 1944

No. 162 Squadron RCAF Moves to Reykjavik

No. 162 squadron was formed on 19 May 1942 at Yarmouth, Nova Scotia, from a Catalina detachment of No. 10 Squadron. It was commanded by F/Lt N.E. Small, and some of the unit's first pilots were F/O Aldwinkle and P/O R.E. McBride. By 18 March the squadron had built up to full strength and on 31 August, S/Ldr C.G. Chapman assumed command.

On 7 December news was received of an impending move to overseas for the squadron and in January 1944 the unit transferred to Reykjavik, Iceland. This resulted in the squadron during January 1944 being dispersed between Dartmouth, Goose Bay, Bluie West 1 in Greenland, and Reykjavik, Iceland.

Fifteen Cansos transported 180 personnel via Goose Bay and Bluie West 1 to Reykjavik; others were flown by Dakotas or Liberators. Equipment went by sea on *Eskimo* and *Beaver,* RCAF marine craft.

Of the landing stage in Greenland, their scribe remarks:

The stop-over midway between Labrador and Iceland is certainly mis-named. On approaching the island, the view from the air of glaziers and fjords is wonderful. A pilot's first thought is "Where do they hide the aerodrome?"; but after twisting and turning up the fjords, it suddenly appears before, nestled at the base of mountains. The hospitality of the Americans stationed at BW1 is really wonderful. The American and RAF Ferry Command personnel were most helpful and gave considerable assistance to our F/Engineer and maintenance crews when they were held up by engine changes and other repairs.

The first to arrive at BW1 was F/O A. Hildebrand in Canso 9841 on 5 January. He was followed the next day by eight others including W/Cmdr Chapman and F/O McCrae.

Navigating to Reykjavik

No. 162's first Canso arrived on 6 January and all were safely there by the end of the month. They lacked transport and maintenance facilities but expected to be operational within a week. Flying control was considered "highly organised" and D/F bearings could be "relied upon with the utmost confidence" but weather forecasts were treated with caution. Runways were of average length but "rather rough."

Of relations with others, according to the 162 record:

> Generally all personnel of other services (RAF, RN, USAF, USN), as encountered by this squadron in Iceland, are co-operative and congenial. Civil relations—very little can be said. The peoples of Iceland definitely regard us as foreigners, but at the time show no malice and are in many cases openly friendly.

The navigation officer, F/Lt J.M. Thomson, reported on the ferry trip to Iceland. Batteries in some sextants froze at 12,000-15,000 feet; some experienced a compass deviation of 30° and found the sun in January at those latitudes with a maximum altitude of 8°. Reverting therefore to "old reliable DR with three-course winds holding first place in daylight if contact flying is possible."

On flying from BW1 to Reykjavik he considered that a flight plan was required for every 5° zone of the route, rating the track via BW3 to Cape Farewell, thence to Iceland the easiest route given a minimum ceiling of 12,000 feet and with minimum height after taking off of 8000 feet over the airfield before setting course over the icecap. Throughout, his navigation was a "combination of DR, D/F, astro and radio range flying with some QTEs and QDMs."

Technical Problems

Of the engineering and other problems; on running up engines there was a mag. drop which was cured by changing the plugs. Some suffered leaks to fuel tanks and some oil coolers became unserviceable. Fuel consumptions varied from 60 to 89 gallons per hour with an average of 75 gals/hr.

One of the pilots, F/Lt James M. McCrae, DFC, recalls:

> Our crew were to fly Canso 9808; each aircraft carried its normal crew of eight plus four tradesmen. We also carried as many spares as weight restrictions would allow. On 3 January we did a compass swing and on 4th flew the first leg from Dartmouth to Goose Bay.
>
> At Goose Bay we were plagued by extremely cold weather and when we attempted the second leg to Bluie West 1 in Greenland on 5 January, Hildebrand in 9841 was the only one to get away. I finally got away from Goose Bay on 14 January and the next day we made it from BW1 in Greenland to Reykjavik.
>
> Our first couple of weeks in Reykjavik were not remembered for their comfort. We were housed in Camp Corbett which had been used by the RAF. Our Nissen huts had only small coal stoves and they were the only means to heat water for washing up. Fuel was scarce and we had to make night forays in search of coal. Fortunately we were soon moved to Camp Kwitcherbelliaken, one of which had been occupied by the Americans. Here we had heat and running water and it seemed like heaven after enduring Camp Corbett.

Later it was called Camp Maple Leaf. The squadron lost no time in preparing for operations; on 24 January we took 9808 up for a test flight and some local flying and the next day were assigned to do an anti-sub sweep, the first operation by the squadron from Iceland.

On 1 February we provided escort for the *Queen Mary* in Canso 9766 flight time 11¼ hrs. On 7 February we escorted the *Pasteur*. On that day gale force winds were in effect. The ship, which was westbound had to slow to 3½ knots in the highest seas I had ever seen. Without a homing procedure, we would never have located the ship, she was so far from her estimated position. When we did make contact, we exchanged the usual recognition signals, and by Aldis lamp asked for instructions and her position, course and speed (to confirm our navigation). The ship looked almost like a small fishing vessel in those huge waves and I didn't envy the signaller on board who must have had to direct his lamp almost straight up at times and almost horizontally at others as the ship climbed one wave and buried its bow in the next. Because of our ground speed, would be low on return, we bid adieu but then came a message from Coastal Command to remain until PLE and then land at Stornaway.

No. 162 Squadron's First Attacks on U-Boats

F/O C.C. Cunningham was credited with the squadron's first attack on a U-boat. This was in position 61N 21W on 22 February, but the submarine was apparently undamaged. He was requested to remain on the scene pending the arrival of a No. 120 Squadron Liberator, making a trip of fifteen hours for the Canso.

It was rather different for F/O Cooke on 17 April. He was airborne at 0705 hrs for a CLA patrol and a Met. flight in Canso 9767. Just over three hours later while flying at 800 feet, his co-pilot sighted a wake at six miles on the starboard bow. At four miles and with binoculars a U-boat was identified.

Cooke prepared to attack out of sun and at 3000 yards there was flak; he took evasive action closing to 1200 yards when his front gunner opened fire scoring hits on the conning tower. There were bursts of flak all around the Canso, which was not hit, and at 300 yards the flak ceased. Three depth charges were released from 50 feet altitude, the first one entering close to starboard and forward of the conning tower. The other two DCs fell to port. Three men were seen in the conning tower by the gunners. As Cooke circled to port the U-boat emerged from the plumes made by the exploding DCs as it made a tight turn to starboard at 12 knots. As Cooke circled, his port blister gunner opened fire.

Nine minutes after the attack, the U-boat was sailing at 6 knots at conning tower depth and appeared to submerge. There was a violent explosion 15 feet forward of the conning tower and the vessel sank immediately. Wreckage appeared covering 100 sq.yards. There was a continuous stream of air bubbles for over an hour after the U-boat had sunk, and there was a large oil patch 3000 x 600 yds. This marked the demise of U-342 which had sailed from Norway on 4 April commanded by OL Albert Hossenfelder to report on weather conditions west of the

British Isles only to be lost in position 6023N 2320W. Both F/O Cooke and his navigator F/Lt E.W. Wiskin were awarded DFCs, others in the Canso crew were mentioned in dispatches (MiDs).[1]

F/Lt R.E.McBride and U-477

During spring and early summer of 1944, No. 162's operational flights ranged from both Reykjavik in Iceland and Wick in Scotland. It was the period when the U-boats were being forced to vacate French ports following the invasion of Europe in June and when U-boats were increasingly relying on Norwegian ports.

No. 162 Squadron was asked on 25 May how many aircraft could be sent to Wick on temporary detachment due to the U-boat activity north-east of Scotland. Three were sent in addition to one already there.

On 3 June Reykjavik was bright and clear with scattered clouds and good visibility. No. 162 Squadron had three aircraft on operations including F/Lt McBride's which was airborne from Wick. At 0211 hrs he was flying south at 1700 feet when a U-boat was sighted four miles away. The U-boat was on a northerly course at 15 knots, and McBride turned to port losing height and closing to 1000 yards range when his gunner opened fire, scoring hits on the conning tower. The U-boat endeavoured to keep stern on to the Canso, but McBride attacked from 60 ft, tracking over the vessel and releasing four DCs. Explosions straddled the U-boat; McBride made a steep turn to port, and saw the U-boat lift bodily and swing to port losing all forward movement before submerging. At least five survivors were seen in the water apparently waving to the aircraft. When the Canso left the

scene 3 3/4 hrs later, there was an oil patch a mile long and 400 yards wide. Although the Canso had experienced some intense and accurate flak, the aircraft suffered no damage. Captained by OL Karl-Joachim Jensen, U-477 had sailed from Norway on 28 May to be lost on 3 June in this attack.[2]

The Sinking of U-980

F/Lt L. Sherman was airborne from Wick on 11 June and at 1515 hrs a U-boat was sighted on the starboard bow. He was then flying at 1000 feet and turned to starboard, losing height. At 800 yards range his gunners in the nose and starboard blister opened fire on the U-boat, which was turning to port to keep its stern to the Canso. AA fire was light but fairly accurate and Sherman adopted evasive tactics. Four DCs were released from 50 feet as the aircraft tracked over the U-boat from port quarter to starboard bow. Two dropped to port with one close, midway between bow and conning tower. The vessel emerged from the plumes and circled slowly, leaving a trail of oil. There were further exchanges of fire but the U-boat was getting lower in the water. It sank within ten minutes of the attack, leaving wreckage and about thirty-five survivors in the water. They were from U-980 which had sailed from Norway on 3 June and sank on the 11th in position 6307N 0026E.[3]

Two days later, Sherman's crew reported attacking another U-boat in position 6410N 0011W but nothing more was heard from Sherman, and two Warwicks with ASR equipment were airborne on a search for the Canso. It was learned later that F/O Sherman had been shot down outside Alesund with three of the crew killed immediately. Four others were lost after they had drunk sea water and jumped overboard. The sole survivor, F/Sgt J.E. Roberts, was picked up by a fishing vessel owned by the Remoy family of Volda. At the time of the rescue his dinghy was "very far out in the ocean" and although a wind was blowing towards the land, it was unlikely that Roberts, who was very ill, could have survived until the dinghy reached land. To save his life it was necessary to take him to Alesund hospital but with the realisation that the Canadian would become a POW. F/Sgt Roberts was repatriated after the war and Knut Remoy, who was present at the time of the rescue, kept up correspondence with the airman's wife, Mrs. Stella Roberts of Toronto.

The Disposition of U-Boats on 6 June 1944

From the German U-boat diary, there were twenty-two non-schnorkel types of the *Mitte* group at the Norwegian ports of Bergen, Stavanger, and Christiansand and, en route from Norway to the Atlantic, a further ten non-schnorkel and seven schnorkel U-boats. From the latter, however, five had been sunk and one damaged. In French ports were thirty-seven of the *Landwirt* group, including nine fitted with schnorkels, thus making a total of seventy-three potentially hostile U-boats.[4]

From Capt Roskill's account, twenty-five were ordered to the English Channel, but five gave up, seven were sunk, and three were damaged.[5] The Germans anticipated a possible second landing in Norway and the *Mitte* group of U-boats was kept at short notice.[6]

The Sinking of U-715

W/Cmdr Chapman with co-captain Jim McCrae were airborne on 13 June for a search north of the Shetlands. Their Canso was armed with "six .303" Brownings, twins in the front turret and each of the two blisters; a contrast from the eighteen guns including .5s which some Sunderlands carried.[7]

They were flying at 1000 feet when McCrae sighted what proved to be the schnorkel and periscope of a U-boat. McCrae continues:

At the action station signal, Staples was manning the nose guns, Bergevin was at the radio, Cromarty was in the Flight Engineer's position and Leatherdale and Read were in the blisters. I turned to check the bombing circuits and to make sure the depth charges were armed and the master switch on. Waterbury, the navigator handed our position to the WAG and he transmitted a sighting report. Chapman turned in the direction I'd indicated but could still not see the wake....I had the feeling we had been spotted but using binoculars saw it a little to right of our heading. Chapman began the attack run down to 50 feet releasing four depth charges which straddled the vessel. Just we passed over the enemy I caught a glimpse of the conning tower railings just breaking surface. We continued straight ahead getting pictures with the rear facing camera, then turned back and climbed to 1000 feet. Our intercom became unserviceable. The sub came to the surface and slowed, turning 45 degrees to starboard with the rudder and screws visible, proceeding

200-300 yards before coming to a stop as we circled out of range.

Chapman opted to use the rear camera instead of the hand-held one...we made several runs diving down to 50 feet; the stern had disappeared but in levelling out, enough of the conning tower resurfaced to get their guns into play...we were hit...we were a sitting duck...just a little intimidated flying with the Wingco and were hesitant to suggest what to do.

Our port engine was hit but we were unable to feather the propeller although our speed had enabled us to reach 1000 feet, we could not maintain height.

We set course for the Shetlands, 150 miles away but were soon down to wavetop height. The sea was relatively calm, the wind was light and there was a long swell with waves 5-6 feet high. Cromarty lowered the wing tip floats; we struck the top of a wave; the impact was not too hard but it bounced us a few feet and we kept going. The second time we hit much harder and flying speed was gone. I held the throttle back and with Chapman and I both holding the control yoke back in our chests, we settled into the crest of a wave with hardly any shock at all.

Once in the water, we discovered that one of the shells had holed the hull and the aircraft was sinking. There was plenty of time though to launch the two five-man dinghies. Bergevin remained at his radio and got a distress signal out. We donned our immersion suits and loaded the dinghies with emergency equipment. Everything was well in hand when

suddenly one of the dinghies exploded. Everything in it went down. Almost immediately the other dinghy got a three-corner tear and from then on we had trouble keeping it inflated enough to be any use.

The aircraft settled slowly until the wing went under and as the nose sank lower, the tail disappeared as well. We were left with one, half serviceable dinghy.

During the next few hours we discovered that the immersion suits did not keep out the water; I could feel the cold creeping up my legs as the water came in. We changed positions several times but with the damaged dinghy, no more than three could occupy it. Eventually a Sunderland came into view and he spotted us. We knew that help was coming but it was just a matter of time. An ASR Warwick came on the scene and shortly after dropped an airborne lifeboat. It landed downwind just as it was supposed to do.

If all else had been normal, our dinghy would have drifted down upon it or on one of the lines which were deployed by rockets when it landed. Even with sea anchors though, it was drifting faster than our dinghy which had five of us in the water holding it back. It was then that Dave Waterbury stripped off his heavy clothing, put on his Mae West and swam for the boat. After at least an hour of superhuman effort, he got it back to us. It had been damaged on landing, and although it had oars, the deck and oarlocks were under water.

The lifeboat was also equipped with a gasoline motor, but it, like the rowlocks, was under water. The boat itself was only kept afloat by inflated sponsons at each end, and Dave had to sit on one of those and paddle it back in the manner of paddling a canoe.

Some time during this, Leatherdale succumbed and released his hold. One minute he was there; the next minute he was gone. Staples and Reed were also in bad shape. The Warwick realised we were still in trouble and dropped Lindholme gear to us. It included a ten-man dinghy which we eventually retrieved.

Altogether, more than seven hours had gone by when one of the aircraft which had remained over our position began making low approaches from the south and it was not long before the rescue launch he was leading in appeared.

It was a welcome sight and we were soon high and dry aboard. However, all efforts to revive Reed and Staples failed. We were brought back to Lerwick and spent a day or two in the military hospital there before being flown back to Wick in a Ventura.

Some comment is required regarding our experience with the dinghies. In every ditching drill we had done, the final instruction after launch was "top up the dinghy." This seemed appropriate enough, as on our dry drills on a hangar floor, the dinghies seemed to be only half inflated. Someone decided to increase the size of the CO_2 bottles. Naturally we did not think to check for overinflation. It was stated later that the CO_2 charges were increased for operation in the extremely cold climate of Goose Bay and had not been changed.

It was about this time that our forward armament was modified. A small dome was placed in the forward gunner's position and the two moveable guns were raised enough to mount four fixed .303 Brownings below them. These were fired by the pilot by means of a button on his control wheel. To my knowledge these guns were never fired in anger as the flurry of submarine activity we had encountered in June seemed to be over.

Flight Lieutenant David Hornell, VC

No. 162's entry for 24 June 1944 gives six aircraft on operations and two in transit from Wick to Reykjavik. Canso A 9754 captained by F/Lt Hornell was one of those on operations and detailed for an anti-submarine sweep. At 1900 hrs a fully-surfaced U-boat was sighted and Hornell closed to attack. At ¾ mile range the U-boat opened fire with severe and accurate flak; at 1200 yards F/O G. Campbell in the front turret responded but one of his two .303 guns jammed. At 800 yards the Canso was hit and one engine dropped into the sea. Hornell continued with his attack and straddled the U-boat with his depth charges. The Canso was unable to maintain height and Hornell ditched about a mile from the U-boat survivors. No signal was received from the Canso but by chance a Catalina from No. 333 (Norge) Squadron captained by Lt. Carl Krafft sighted the U-boat survivors and then the Canadians in their dinghy. Despite severe weather conditions with cloud base at one stage down to 50 feet, the Norwegian circled the dinghy for twelve hours transmitting homing signals. The Norwegian Catalina was relieved by a

Norwegian Sunderland captained by S/Lt Ole Evensen who witnessed the pickup of the survivors by an ASR launch.

From F/O Denomy's account, the Canso suffered two 2 feet diameter holes in the starboard wing and a $1\frac{1}{2}$ feet diameter hole in the fuselage. The aerials were shot away and when oil from the starboard engine caught fire, fabric on the aileron and trailing edge burned off.

They bounced three times before the Canso remained down; the two pilots escaped through the hatches, the remainder of the crew through the blisters. St. Laurent launched the starboard dinghy and it drifted away. The others used the port dinghy which had been inflated by Scott. F/Sgt Cole passed the emergency rations and a can of water. Cole, although wounded and weak, jumped into the water and attempted to swim back for the dinghy radio but was restrained by the others, who feared the petrol tanks might explode.

Hornell, Matheson, and Denomy slipped into the water to propel the dinghy to St. Laurent's, but one of the dinghies exploded. Those three remained in the water for an hour when it was decided all should enter the remaining dinghy although it was found necessary for one to be in the water to allow room for baling. This was done by using Hornell's trousers which had the legs knotted, plus a flying helmet. It was to be so for twelve hours.

Four hours after the ditching Lt Krafft's Catalina was sighted and Campbell released flares; the last one was seen by the Norwegians who reported also forty men spread over a mile and whom they took to be German.[8] Waves were then 18 feet high with a wind of 20 knots. Krafft released markers periodically to keep the dinghy in sight. After about eight hours, the Canadians saw one of the bodies from the U-boat pass 50 feet away followed by one of the deck boards. They would have been from U-1225 which, captained by OL Ernst Sauerberg, had sailed from a home port on 17 June only to be sunk in position 6300N 0050W.[9]

The waves reached 25 feet high with the wind at 30 knots and both Hornell and Campbell were seasick and Hornell suffered from cold. When the waves increased further, the survivors shifted their weight from side to side as the dinghy went trough to crest and down again. Hornell and St. Laurent began to weaken, with the latter becoming delirious before he passed away. "We slipped his body out of the dinghy and made way for Scott who had remained partly in the water."

After sixteen hours a Warwick dropped an airborne lifeboat which drifted away; Hornell would have swum for it but was stopped by Denomy. Scott had been in the water for a long time and had grown weak and died. "We also slipped his body out of the dinghy."

After twenty hours and thirty-five minutes under such conditions, the ASR launch arrived and, from F/Sgt Bodnoff's report, Hornell was then unconscious; Campbell and Matheson very weak, and only Denomy and Cole were able to board the launch without help; the others were winched up. According to Bodoff, Hornell did not regain consciousness despite prolonged effort. F/O Denomy paid this tribute to his co-captain: "Outstanding about F/Lt Hornell was his marvellous ability in flying such a badly damaged aircraft especially in the face of strong enemy fire. His courage and bravery throughout marked him as a great man. Words cannot do justice to the fine job he has done."

129

David Hornell had enlisted in 7 January 1940; he died on 25 June 1944 at the age of thirty-four. On 28 July the BBC announced that a posthumous VC had been awarded to F/Lt David Hornell.

A Flight Engineer, Chuck Walker, recalls an incident when F/Lt Hornell was acting as Transport Officer and supervising the unloading of a supply ship where there was some indifferent behaviour. "Very quickly it was obvious some order was needed, Hornell appeared and, without fuss or raised voice or show of arms, looked us over, gave some advice, weeded out the bad ones, and established order. He gained immediate respect and became known as 'grandaddy', after all, he was a decade older than most of us."

Attacks on U-478

On 30 June F/Lt McBride sighted a U-boat which submerged before he could attack. When he saw it again and attempted to attack, his depth charges hung up. A Liberator from 86 Squadron was homed to the scene and sank the U-boat. U-478 which had sailed from home on 20 June commanded by OL Rudolf Rademacher was lost with all hands in position 6327N 0341W.[10]

At the end of June, W/Cmdr Chapman's report for 162 Squadron refers to fourteen men and three aircraft being lost in action but adds: "Our own losses in this period might be said to be due to the fortunes of war, but in our opinion are directly the result of poor, inadequate and insufficient armament." He referred specifically to the nose gun, stating that a power operated, quadruple gun, .5 or .303, in a nose turret was required. He continued: "With good aircraft armament,

the U-boat hasn't a chance; with poor aircraft armament, we haven't a chance."

By 20 August, No. 162 Squadron was testing a two-gun nose turret and four fixed nose guns.

Lighter Moments for 162 Squadron

On 10 July a dance was held for airmen in the Laugavegur Hall, Reykjavik. This was followed two days later with a formal one in the Officers' Mess. Members were able to invite guests who included Col. Klinkerman, USAAF, Miss Imba Gisladottir and Miss Gerda Johansen, a secretary to the British Minister, and twenty couples from other services. The event was highly organised with an orchestra and waiters and was reported as "the most gentlemanly party ever attended."

The US Army band gave a concert in the camp theatre on 23 July of "very fine music" by No. 228 Army Band under its conductor, W/O Korlie.

The Intelligence Officer, Adjutant, and Navigation Officer went on a fishing expedition guided by an Icelander at one of the national resorts. They caught sixty-four "very nice trout."

At the end of the month thirty of 162's personnel were guests of the Royal Navy at Akraness. The same evening there was a show, "Bits and Pieces," put on by the Americans.

Mercy Missions in Iceland

Just before midnight on 25 July the AOC Iceland, A/Cmdre Wigglesworth, requested an aircraft to fly north on a mercy flight. No. 162's CO investigated possible landing facilities and decided it should be tried. At 0030 hrs on 26 July F/Lt McBride with W/Cmdr Chapman flew 150 miles north of Reykjavik to Adalvik, where he found a stretch of clear water to land. He taxied round a bay for an hour while the patients were brought out in a rowboat. The patients were a baby of 3 months suffering with severe mastoids, the mother, father, and the grandmother, who also was ill. They were all flown back to base.

F/Lt Orr flew to Eisa fjord on 19 November with a surgeon from the Royal Navy. At Eisa fjord, a fishing village on the north-west coast of Iceland, a Navy seaman who had broken a leg was picked up.

F/O A. Hildebrand was detailed for an A/S sweep in Canso 11062 and had taken off at 1255 hrs on 29 July but at 1930 hrs, crashed on Foula Island due to bad weather. Seven of the crew were killed and there was one survivor, F/S J.H. Knight, who was taken to Lerwick hospital with multiple injuries.

On 4 August F/O Marshall was airborne at 1050 hrs on an A/S patrol when he attacked a U-boat as it was about to crash-dive in position 6225N 1430W.

After two attacks by Marshall, the U-boat surfaced and attempted to shoot it out before vanishing in a patch of fog. It was U-300 which had sailed from a home port on 13 July and due to the damage caused by the Canso returned to port on 17 August.[11]

Subsequently all 162's Cansos were withdrawn from Wick to search in the area off Iceland.

Viewpoints of 162 Squadron Personnel

Chuck Walker served with 162 Squadron from November 1943 to October 1944 as a flight engineer. After arriving at Dartmouth, Nova Scotia, to join the unit he states:

At briefing the word was given that we were headed for Iceland via Labrador and Greenland. At least we would be closer to the real action and operate in a new area. In Iceland we became accountable for assigned operational tasks and weather could never be an excuse. Gone were the days of half-hearted fair weather flying. My reaction to this duty was first of excitement and interest. As the duty became routine in March and April, I adopted a ho-hum attitude. However in May and June when the squadron scored kills on the U-boats and suffered casualties, a feeling of pride prevailed, but along with this a degree of fear became a part of our lives. There was no time to dwell on these factors because of our busy schedule. Another factor to be felt by mid-June was fatigue. Six months without leave, long flight times, heavy buffeting from winds and, on some flights, low temperatures down to 50° combined to take its toll on a person.

Chuck's best friend was lost with Hildebrand's crew and he adds: "After that event I failed to regain the spark that had carried me for six months. The attitude was 'Let's get the job done as soon as possible and get out of here.' Out of a total of 1358 hrs flying, Chuck Walker had completed 901 ops hours.

A navigator, Ron Wales, flew with an American pilot, F/O Jeff Davies, on 162 Squadron. He comments on the Canso crew comprising two pilots, two engineers, three wireless operator/air gunners, but only one navigator. Two navigators were later used but with the second one straight from a navigation school. Wales used largely dead reckoning (DR) navigation until LORAN became available. Of the LORAN system he comments that in conjunction with special charts, a pin-point fix could be obtained in about five minutes compared with fifteen minutes for astro shots.

One of the wireless operators to fly with Ron Wales was Doug Johnson, who wrote about the equipment he used in Cansos:

The main transmitters were three AT12's, which I believe were made by General Electric. Each transmitter was tuned to one frequency—two operational and one emergency. The main receiver was an AR6. The R/T command liaison set was AR6, AT7 also used for intercom. At OTU in Canada we used Bendix crystal controlled transmitters. Initially their Cansos were equipped with Mark II (ASV) radar but later as for other squadrons in Coastal Command, Mark III radar became available with its rotating scanner and with the CRT screen giving outlines of such as coastlines instead of just "blips" as prevailed with the Mark II equipment. It was in the latter stages of 162's service within Coastal Command that sonobuoys to track U-boats also came into use.

Emergency Equipment with 162 Squadron

In July 1944, following a number of ditchings by the squadron, further drills were undertaken. Experience gained with emergencies had shown that the two "S" dinghies carried in the Cansos were not suitable to take all the crew and if one failed, the second one could not hold eight men. They became equipped with one "H", and two "S" and eight "K" type dinghies. The latter were essentially individual ones, able to take just one person. Hooks were placed in the Canso to accept the "K" types.

A new type of Mae West from the RAF was issued to all aircrew. These lifejackets contained one "ever hot" bag, two "two star" distress signals, and a first aid kit. Floating lights for all aircrew were ordered. Only thirty-four exposure suits were on the squadron and 110 were ordered. A number of modifications were made to the equipment for the "H" type dinghies.

Changes in Command

Wing Commander C.G.W. Chapman, DSO, had commanded No. 162 Squadron from September 1943 until September 1944 and thus had contended with all the problems of administration due to the move from Canada to Iceland and with a detachment to Scotland. His service covered a notable period in June 1944 with the sinking of U-boats and the award of the RCAF's first VC of World War II.[11]

He was succeeded by W/Cmdr W.F. Poag who in turn relinquished command to W/Cmdr J.F. Sully at the end of November 1944.

In the latter months of 1944, the squadron's operations comprised anti-submarine sweeps with an occasional convoy escort. There were many night sorties, some as long as fourteen hours. There was still intensive training in the use of such as LORAN and the deployment of sonobuoys.

On 19 December, Canso 11061 was airborne for an A/S sweep at 0740 hrs, captained by F/Lt E.P. Oakford. At 1950 hrs the Canso crashed in the mountains of Iceland with all eight on board killed.

References to Chapter 6
1. JuH para 417 & USSL p.167
2. JuH App.III p.112 & USSL p.168
3. JuH App. III p.116 & USSL p.168
4. JuH para.433
5. SWR III/2 p.68
6. JuH para.433
7. AH SS p.1
8. Lt.Krafft's report to No.333 Sqdrn.
9. USSL p.168 & JuH App.III p.117
10. JuH App.III p.112 & USSL p.169
11. CCWR p.18 & JuH App.III p.111

Chapter 7

Anti-Submarine Operations: January–December 1944

No. 407 Squadron at Limavady

In January 1944 while still at Chivenor, No. 407 had the use of a dual-control Wellington from No. 172 Squadron and it was hoped that second pilots could be trained as captains and thus avoid the need to attend OTU.

On 25 January, however, 407 was ordered to Limavady, Northern Ireland and the first five of their aircraft left at 1500 hrs. The following day the main party left with No. 612 Squadron and arrived at Stranraer at noon on the 27th, where they were billeted in an Army transit camp before reaching Limavady on the 28th.

When the writer was based at Limavady in 1942, the standard of messing was the highest he was ever to experience at a Coastal Command base. It compensated for the very wide dispersal of billets. Peat was provided as fuel for heating billets and, although effective, burned rapidly.

No. 407's experience in 1944 was similar; limited transport made the dispersal very obvious, but of messing: "All ranks are commenting on the good food on this station. The few extra eggs available here are most appreciated."

In early 1944, U-boats were operating individually west of the British Isles between approximately 10° to 30° west and from 45° to 63° north, although by 14 February the U-boats were directed against convoy ONS29.[1]

Attacks on U-Boats by No. 407 Squadron

F/O P.W. Heron was airborne from Limavady at 1520 hrs on 7 February in Wellington HF207. Just 5½ hrs later he was flying south-east at 1000 feet when a radar contact was obtained at 9 miles range. He was then in position 5130N 1840W. With moon on the starboard beam he homed until contact was lost in the ¼ mile ring of the scanner. At ½ mile range the Leigh light was switched on and illuminated a fully-surfaced U-boat heading southwards at 10 knots in position 5145N 1850W. F/O Heron attacked from 50 feet altitude at 150° to the U-boat's heading, by releasing six DCs set at 25 feet depth and spaced at 60 feet. Three explosions were seen from the astro hatch. The Wellington circled the area for 1½ hrs until PLE but radar contact was not regained.

F/O Owen Campbell was also active that night; he had been airborne at 1617 hrs in HF115 and at 2353 hrs was heading due west at 800 feet when a radar contact was made at 12 miles range. It was on the port bow, but Campbell turned to starboard so that the contact would be silhouetted by the moonlight. He closed the range to a mile and although cloud was shrouding the moon, sighted a U-boat and its wake. At 1000 yards the Leigh light showed a fully surfaced U-boat. An attack was made from 100 feet at 165° to the U-boat's heading, releasing six DCs set at 25 feet and spaced at 60 feet. Course was held for 15 seconds before circling and taking evasive action from the U-boat's AA. Campbell closed the range to 500 yards and his gunners opened fire. A bunch of weak blue lights were seen on the surface of the sea. The Wellington remained in the area until PLE, and returned to base after a trip of almost eleven hours.

On the night of 10 February, F/O Peter Heron was again airborne but this time in Wellington MP578. He had been flying for six hours when a radar contact was made six miles ahead. He was then flying at 1000 feet but height was lost to 100 feet and closing the range to 1½ miles when the navigator saw a conning tower. At one mile the Leigh light was switched on for a U-boat to be seen with decks awash. It was in position 6045N 1250W and heading due west.

Six DCs set at 25 feet depth were released and an explosion was seen on the U-boat's starboard beam abaft the conning tower before the whole of the vessel was obscured by other explosions on the port beam. When they had subsided, a large red glow was seen on the surface and there was light AA from just forward of the

glow. The light AA was accurate and estimated as 20 mm. This was the demise of U-283, captained by OL Gunter Ney who had sailed from a German port on 13 January.[2]

An American serving with the Canadian squadron, Lt. Daniel B. Bleser, USAAF, from Wisconsin was captain of Wellington HF142 on the morning of 15 February. He crashed while taking off and all the crew were killed instantly.

There was another loss on 11 March; F/O Edmund O'Connell, DFC, from Toronto captained HF311 which was one of three aircraft on an anti-submarine patrol. The Wellington had been airborne with a total crew of six but failed to return to base.

No. 407 Squadron Moves Back to Chivenor

At the beginning of March 1944, 407 was advised that it would be undergoing intensive training and the following month it moved back to Chivenor in Devon. The squadron recorded the high standard of health and fitness while at Limavady which was attributed to good food, ample billet space, agreeable working conditions, and favourable weather. There was mild dissatisfaction, with aircrew lacking operational sorties but partly compensated by intensive training. The training paid dividends.

Wellington HF134, captained by F/O Lorne J. Bateman, was airborne from Chivenor at 2147 hrs on 3 May. While flying at 800 feet six hours later, a radar contact was made at seven miles range. The sea was calm and visibility 2-3 miles in moonlight. Bateman lost height and at two miles a fully-surfaced U-boat was sighted in position 4604N 0920W. At 500 yards range there was concentrated AA fire from the U-boat and the Wellington's front gun jammed. Six 250 pound DCs were however released from 150 feet altitude. After they exploded, the AA ceased. Bateman climbed to 1500 feet and circled; only an oil patch extending for half a mile was seen. U-846 captained by OL Erich Hashagen had sailed from a French port on 29 April; it was sunk in Bateman's attack.[3]

This success was followed on 22 May by F/O C.M. Balger, who flew on an A/S Channel patrol. He was airborne in HF306 at 2233 hrs and at 0247 hrs the following morning obtained a radar contact at seventeen miles range. It was still dark at that hour with haze, but the sea was calm; Bolger began losing height from 600feet and at eight miles range, ten minutes later, he was in position 4918N 0338W. When ½ mile from the contact, the Leigh light was switched on to sight a fully-surfaced U-boat heading south at 17 knots. There was intense flak to which the front-gunner responded as the Wellington tracked over at 300 feet. Bolger turned to port and climbed to 400 feet for a second approach but rapid evasive action by the U-boat and AA frustrated this attack, as well as a third attempt. In a fourth attempt, six 250 pound Torpex DCs were released from 75 feet altitude and set for 25 feet depth. The AA ceased and the contact disappeared. F/O Bolger was awarded the DFC—he deserved it for his persistence. The U-boat however, was apparently able to continue on operations.

The lack of success by the Wellington crew may be attributed to the minimum forward firing armament of just one .303 machine gun against intense AA from the enemy.

U-989 sailed from a French port on 6 June but was so badly damaged by a 224 Squadron Liberator and a 407 Squadron Wellington that it returned to port on the 7th and was there for a month before sailing again.[4] The Wellington was HF149 captained by S/Ldr Desmond W. Farrell from Montreal, which was airborne at 2235 hrs from Chivenor for a Channel and Bay of Biscay patrol. It failed to return to base with its crew of six.

Of two more attacks by 407 on U-boats in June, one was apparently unsuccessful; the other required the U-boat to return to port. S/Ldr A.H. Laidlaw in HF286 made a Leigh-light attack in position 4531N 0133W on a fully-surfaced U-boat at 0418 hrs on 14 June. His six DCs appeared to straddle the vessel abaft its conning tower but apparently without causing any damage.

On 20 June F/O F.H. Foster was airborne at 2142 hrs in HF134 and about two hours later was heading south at 800 feet. There was a moderate sea, no cloud, and visibility ½ mile. At 2½ miles range a radar contact was obtained but moving to port when the Wellington was at 200 feet altitude. At ½ mile range a wake, and then a U-boat was seen heading due east at 15 knots. The training 407 had shows through in the records; Foster turned to port to get ahead of the vessel and three minutes later he approached on the port bow at 36° to the U-boat's course. Six DCs set (exceptionally at 14-18 feet) and spaced at 60 feet were released from 100 feet but at 135° to the U-boat. The rear gunner saw some explode just aft of the conning tower, two having fallen to port and four to starboard. The U-boat apparently submerged with only the conning tower visible but later was stationary on the surface and began inaccurate AA fire. Radar contact was lost but Foster remained until PLE before setting course for base. U-971 which had been damaged in this attack, had sailed from a Norwegian port on 8 June captained by OL Walter Zeplin; it was sunk in the English Channel by HMCS *Haida*, HMS *Eskimo*, and a 311 Squadron Liberator.[5]

From Captain Roskill's account, five schnorkel-fitted U-boats reached Biscay ports as part of Germany's anti-invasion forces.[6] While still based at Chivenor, 407 lost another aircraft. F/O J. Allen crashed at 0915 hrs on 7 July. He was returning from operations when the Wellington's port engine cut after he had entered the circuit and he went down at Woolacombe. W/O Albert Telford from Montreal had taken the place of one of Allen's usual crew and was in the rear turret. He subsequently died of his injuries. One other in the crew was injured—W/O H.E. Meston. A further loss occurred on 13 August. F/O F.J. Kemper from Toronto had taken off with his crew of five in E/407 HF825 for a patrol in the Bay of Biscay but failed to return.

The officer sometimes known as "The Father of the RAF," Marshal of the RAF Lord Trenchard, visited the station on 18 February and gave a talk to the officers. By then another move for the squadron must have been imminent, as three days later 407 was ordered to Wick in Scotland. The main party left by train on 23 August. This move from the English Channel and Biscay area reflected the land situation in France and the deployment of U-boats.

The Americans had broken through at Avranches on 4 August and three of the U-boats' bases were threatened; some attempted to move south but about 50% arrived out of a total of sixteen.[7] U-boats were being recalled from the English Channel and on the 24th and 26th seven were ordered to Norway but with five only arriving there.[8]

No. 407 Squadron at Wick

There was an exceptional sortie for one of 407's crews. F/O Gordon Biddle was airborne from Wick at 0050 hrs on 26 September 1944 to patrol the south-western Norwegian coast in Wellington NB811. At 0538 hrs he reported being unable to reach base and altered course to land in enemy-occupied Norway. A fix had placed the aircraft between Bergen and Herdle, and it was presumed to have force-landed after 0622 hrs. There being no further information, his crew was reported missing. On 13 October M.I.9 reported the safe arrival in the United Kingdom of all six of the crew, and six days later they returned to the squadron to collect their kits.

In 1949 further details came to light; F/O Biddle had crash-landed his Wellington south-east of Bergen in the middle of an airfield but the Germans didn't notice that it was an Allied plane as they were changing the guard. The crew escaped and were hidden by the Norwegian underground movement before being brought back to the United Kingdom by "Shetland" Larsen following the escape arrangements being made by another Norwegian, Kjell Harmans.

The German U-boat diary summed up the situation in October 1944 that Allied A/S operations would be concentrated against the Atlantic route, the North Sea, the approach to the Baltic, and off Norway. By 19 September they had lost the use of the French ports and were using ones in Norway and some in Germany.[9]

U-1060 captained by OL Herbert Brammer sailed from Norway on 25 October while U-1061 followed from Germany on the 26th. F/O John Neelin was airborne from Wick at 2346 hrs on the 29th in Wellington NB839 and two hours later was in position 6143N 0342E. He was then flying south at 1200 feet when a radar contact was made at 5 miles range. He homed to one mile when the Leigh light was switched on to illuminate the conning tower of a U-boat which was heading due south at 10 knots. Neelin lost height and attacked, releasing six Torpex DCs ahead of the conning tower at 60° to the starboard bow. He circled at six miles radius and shortly afterwards saw a Liberator make a Leigh light attack on a fully-surfaced U-boat which was firing at the aircraft. Following a second attack by the Liberator, a fairly large orange glow was seen for a minute or so. Radar contact with the U-boat was lost after thirty minutes. Five and a half hours after the attack, three light oil slicks, one a mile long, were seen. At the time it was thought by 407 Squadron that there were possibly two U-boats in company, and post-war records endorse that belief. U-1060 was sunk by Liberators Y and H of No. 311 Squadron with the FAA aircraft from HMS *Implacable*, while U-1061 was damaged by 407's Wellington although it reached a Norwegian port on the 29th.[10]

From Wick to Chivenor

No. 407 Squadron was back at Chivenor on 11 November and the following month, mindful of Christmas and perhaps Chivenor's catering standards, S/Ldr C.W. Taylor flew to Limavady to bring back some turkeys. "Cam" Taylor was no less active

operationally and was airborne on 29 December at 1644 hrs in Wellington NB855 L/407.

At 0208 hrs the following morning, he was heading due south at 900 feet when a radar contact was obtained at seven miles range. There was 2/10ths cloud, with full moonlight, some haze, and a calm sea. At position 5005N 0231W he sighted up moon a wake and then a schnorkel dead ahead at ½ mile. The schnorkel was heading north-west at 6 knots, and Taylor was too high for an attack in his first run; he turned to port and made a second run with radar contact maintained. The Leigh light was switched on at a mile but was affected by haze, although the enemy was visible in the moonlight. Five minutes after after the first radar contact, six DCs were released; the rear gunner saw all explode with Nos. 2 and 3 straddling 10-15 yards astern of the schnorkel. S/Ldr Taylor climbed to 1500 feet to transmit a report and remained in the area for an hour until PLE.

Post-war records credit his Wellington with sinking U-772 at the position reported by Taylor. U-772 had sailed from Norway on 19 November captained by KL Ewald Rademacher, who was lost with all his crew just south of Weymouth on 30 December.[11]

On writing to the author Cameron Taylor adds:

We were assigned to a creeping-line-ahead, anti-U-boat search of the Western Approaches to the English Channel. At about 1800 hrs we sighted a ship in a sinking condition down by the stern.We watched survivors getting off the ship taking the final plunge. We signalled the Navy and continued our prescribed search.

The conditions were ideal for locating a schnorkel-equipped U-boat, with a calm sea, moonlight, and little cloud. The radar was so sensitive that flotsam could be located as well as a schnorkel and as Taylor remarks, they "ignored" the radar when at 0210 hrs they picked up flotsam on the screen. Taylor continues:

> as we passed over the 'flotsam' in the bright moonlight, I could clearly see the wake of a schnorkel passing through the water so I made a circle to port lowering to 25 feet, the radar operator skilfully directed me so that I had the schnorkel in the moonstream directly in front of our light of flight. At 0212 hrs in position 4952N 0228W we paralleled the schnorkel with six 250 pound Torpex DCs set at 25 feet spacing and 25 feet depth. The rear gunner reported tons of water well above the elevation of our aircraft.

U-772 had torpedoed five ships in six days in December including on the 29th *Black Hawk* and *Arthur Sewall* in position 5028N 0228W. *Black Hawk* was beached, thus the ship seen to have been sunk by the Wellington crew was almost certainly *Arthur Sewall* of 7,176 tons. Typically of such captains, S/Ldr Taylor directs the credit for his success towards one of his fellows—F/O Myers—one of his "highly efficient" crew.[12]

No. 422 Squadron in Northern Ireland

At the beginning of 1944 No. 422 Squadron's HQ were at St. Angelo on Lough Erne. One of the first reports refers to an edition of the official *Coastal Command Review*, crediting the squadron with 100% merit in anti-submarine operations. Prince Bernhardt of the Netherlands became a guest of 422's CO when the Liberator in which the prince was returning to the UK was forced to land at St Angelo. Prince Bernhardt departed on the 13 January.

F/Sgt L.W. Guggiari gained a mention in dispatches (MiD) for his heroic efforts to save the life of a motorboat crewman who had fallen overboard in an aircraft mooring incident earlier at Bowmore in 1943.

There was a 75 mph gale on Loch Indaal, Bowmore, on 25 January. Sunderland DD831 had on board F/O Wimperis with Sgts. Metcalfe, Leach, and Duffee. The outer engines of the Sunderland were run at 1200 rpm to relieve the load on the moorings, but water entered through the nose turret, and both the APU running and additional baling were unable to cope with the inrush of water. The main pennant snapped and the Sunderland foundered as more water entered the bows. It rose on a large wave and then sank to main plane level. The aircraft had held for one hour before being torn loose from its moorings and drifting into shallows 300 yards off shore. Three of the crew abandoned the aircraft and used a dinghy, but it tore away before F/O Wimperis could reach it. He clung to the pilot head and flashed his Mae West light before being taken off by a pinnace. The Sunderland was reduced to scrap.

In February 422 Squadron moved its HQ offices from St. Angelo to Castle Archdale and on the 19th the CinC Coastal Command, ACM Sir Sholto Douglas, visited the squadron together with the AOC of No. 15 Group, AVM Sir Leonard Slatter. After an inspection of the unit, 422 Squadron aircrew were met in the crewroom at Castle Archdale. The following day one crew was on a fighter affiliation exercise in W6028; it crashed near St. Angelo at 1250 hrs. F/O A. Thomlinson and Sgt Hebenton were killed, others were injured, and taken to hospital. Sgt Bodsworth, one of the injured died in an American hospital from his injuries on 21 February.

Anti-Submarine Warfare in Coastal Command

Records of many Coastal Command Squadrons began to show a much more serious and effective approach to A/S operations in 1944, and those of 422 consider some aspects. After an examination of all reports, aircraft under Iceland, No. 18 Group and 15 Group control were assigned to patrol various areas under the control of 15 Group. All DF and radar contacts had been plotted from previous sorties, and patrols were then organised to cover the most likely areas for further U-boat contacts.

This coincided with the change of tactics of U-boats as on 7 January their groups had been dissolved and U-boats were deployed singly for attacks west of the British Isles.[13]

In January also, U-boats were operating as close as 15° West, and were thus in easy range of Coastal Command's aircraft; even in 1942, Hudsons were patrolling to 14° West from Limavady, Northern Ireland.[14]

The Sinking of U-625 by Sunderland U-422 EK591

EK591 was airborne from Castle Archdale at 1125 hrs on 3 March detailed for an A/S sweep. The captain, W/O

Frank Morton, had already completed 1500 hours flying, but this was to be his first operational trip as captain. Frank Morton gives this account:

I joined 422 on 24 December 1942 and after 433 hours with several skippers was posted to No. 4(C) OTU Alness (on Cromarty Firth) and subsequently accumulated another 1,063 hrs. It was procedure that sprog skippers fresh from OTU would have an experienced screen skipper on board for the first op. Thus on 10th March 1944 F/Lt Butler was my screen skipper. He was a very experienced and capable captain with few ops left to complete his tour.
The day was bright and sunny, the ocean calm for the Atlantic; Sid had relieved me at the wheel and I was below for a cup of tea when the alarm sounded. I returned to the 2nd pilot's seat and saw the sub, surfaced out of range and making no moves to dive.
Sid offered me the wheel; I said something to the effect: "This is a very important job, we must get Jerry; you are more experienced, you do it, I will run the intercom fire control to the crew."

Frank Morton was right; F/Lt Butler had already experienced an encounter with a U-boat and from the squadron record, it is apparent that his mind was well-prepared for this action. Morton continues:

Sid began to circle to get on the bow and the flak from the 20 mm cannon was getting closer and he started his run in with corkscrew evasive action. Suddenly all the sub crew apart from the 20 mm gunner disappeared down the conning tower and firing ceased but I could see the gunner sighting us. Our gunners were firing but with evasive action it must have been a difficult target. Sid levelled at 50 feet; Bang! The cabin filled with smoke at the same time Sid pressed the bomb release on the wheel. I asked over the intercom for injury and damage report.

The 20 mm exploding shell hit 2" to the right of the keel and in direct line for the throttle quadrant between the pilot's seats but exploded above and back of the gunner prone on the lower deck floor, having passed between his legs! Fragments of the shell pierced the tank of the WC; put out the flap indicator, the largest piece cut half-way through my rudder bar. No one was wounded. Ted Higgins the engineer said we had a 2½" hole beside the keel and dozens of holes along a seam where rivets had popped out. His solution was to stuff holes with chewing gum. We carried patching material for the shell hole.

We were miraculously lucky, another exploding shell would have taken out the throttle quadrant and we would have been in the drink and lost. We were lucky in other ways too. The attack was around mid-day and there happened to be a 423 Squadron Sunderland not far away who was homed in to take over so we could start home, hoping to get there before dark as we would have to beach her without delay at the service ramp.

The Sunderland was at 1000 feet when the U-boat was sighted at six miles on the port beam. Butler lost height to 400 feet and reduced the range to one mile as the U-boat endeavoured to keep its stern

towards the Sunderland. After ten minutes Butler seized the opportunity to make a quarter attack in a steep diving turn dropping from 400 feet levelling off to 50 feet when 400 yards from the vessel. Six Torpex DCs set at 25 feet depth and spaced at 60 feet were released. One DC was seen entering the water to starboard and three to port straddling the U-boat near the conning tower.

The U-boat circled, submerged after three minutes, and then, after another three minutes, surfaced. Almost 1½ hrs later the U-boat flashed the signal, "Fine bombish" before its crew began to abandon the vessel using a large dinghy, plus many small ones.

The Sunderland gunner who had suffered a shell between his legs was Joe Nespor who had opened his window for a better view. He recalls the two .303 Brownings in the front turret opening up together with his .5 Browning in the nose from which he fired 350 rounds.

Sid Butler typically refers to the work of others rather than himself and comments on the Sunderland crew which, although inexperienced, functioned excellently in all aspects; and of the enemy: "I have a distinct memory of a tall figure in a grey sweater who was probably the gunner responsible for the damage our aircraft sustained in the last stages of the attack, leaving his gun at the last possible moment and diving for the conning tower as we passed overhead. A brave man indeed."

The U-boat, U-625, had sailed from a French port on 29 February captained by OL Siegfried Straub; it sank in position 5235N 2019W on 10 March. While captained by KL Hans Benker it had attacked six Allied ships during 1942 and 1943. The Sunderland gunner, Joe Nespor, understood that the seventeen survivors from U-625 had perished in a storm three days after the encounter.[15]

No. 422 Squadron at Castle Archdale

After No. 201 Squadron RAF moved from Lough Erne to Pembroke Dock, 422 took over the offices at Castle Archdale which had been vacated. The two Canadian sister squadrons, 422 and 423, continued to operate from Lough Erne. On 25 April, 422's CO, W/Cmdr Frizzle, flew to Aldergrove for a conversion course on Liberators and S/Ldr W.C. Kent assumed command of 422.

No. 422's squadron badge had earlier in the year been approved by King George VI and on 7 May it was sent to London for 485 reproductions to be made. W/Cmdr Skey and S/Ldr Hunter were partly responsible for the design, which depicts the arm of a brave with a tomahawk. It appears likely, however, that the playwright, Terence Rattigan, who had served with the squadron, may have selected the motto: "This Arm Shall Do It," a quotation from Shakespeare's *Richard II*. Its aptness is apparent when a longer quote from Bolingbroke's speech is given: "And, by the glorious worth of my descent, This arm shall do it, or this life be spent."

On 25 May both RAF Sullom Voe and No. 18 Group reported that Sunderland R/422 was missing. It had been airborne from Sullom Voe at 0800 hrs on the 24th to fly a parallel track sweep north of the Shetlands and 100 miles west of the Norwegian coast. At 1419 hrs an SOS was received by Inverness which was intercepted also by Sunderland S/423 which was on the adjacent sweep. A

minute later, S/423 sighted a large puff of smoke 10-15 miles away. S/423 went to investigate where a U-boat had been sighted in position 6334N 0302E and on closing to attack the U-boat, the Sunderland crew noted some wreckage which appeared to be part of a wing 4-500 yards away from the U-boat.

Sunderland DV990, with a crew of eleven headed by Capt. G.E. Holley and with, additionally, the squadron's Gunnery Officer, F/Lt E.W. Beattie, was believed to have been shot down by the U-boat.

U-Boats in Northern Waters

For May 1944, 422 Squadron recorded that there were many sightings of U-boats which warranted the unit undertaking seventeen sorties from Sullom Voe in addition to sixteen from Castle Archdale. This is confirmed in the official naval history by Capt Roskill, who states that at that time Admiral Dönitz was reinforcing his U-boats in Norway following the thaw of ice in the Baltic. The U-boats, however, would have had only a short time to charge their batteries due to the short nights in the higher latitudes at that time of the year.[16]

Following the report of the invasion of Europe by the Allies, 422 Squadron recalled all its aircraft detached at Sullom Voe back to Castle Archdale, with all returning on 7 June with the exception of F/O Berryman's Sunderland M/422 which was unserviceable. All leave for 422 was cancelled on the 9th and anti-submarine sweeps were undertaken to the south and west of England by F/Lt Patton and F/Lt Weir.

On 422's "domestic" front, permission was received to renew publication of a Station paper. There arrived a thoroughbred spaniel, Straddle, who had been sired by the unit's former mascot Dinghy. Straddle was put in the charge of F/O Detwiller and was expected to log many flying hours, and undertaking his first op on 26 June.

With the impending departure of an American hospital in Northern Ireland which had been "of great benefit to [RAF] Station personnel," a dance was held in the Officers' Mess at Castle Archdale in appreciation. The hospital staff's move was in connection with the U.S. 8th Army Air Force.

Evacuation of French U-Boat Bases

On 4 August the Americans broke through at Avranches, and U-boats using the French ports of Brest, Lorient and St. Nazaire sailed for La Pallaice or Bordeaux, "a most hazardous undertaking" according to the German U-boat diary.[17]

The Royal Navy deployed cruisers and destroyers to counter any moves by German warships; Coastal Command's No. 19 Group laid on patrols against the U-boats sailing southwards.[18]

The Tomahawk Squadron, No. 422, was directly involved, and for 8 August records undertaking several sorties off the French coast due to "the likelihood of U-boats leaving French ports since the Brittany invasion."

T/422 NJ175 was airborne from Castle Archdale at 1223 hrs on 12 August captained by F/Lt Devine but ten minutes later an outer engine seized. With a full load of fuel and DCs the Sunderland could not maintain height on three engines. Fuel and DCs were jettisoned but it struck a small knoll two miles south of Belleek and the aircraft turned over, breaking into two. It burst into flames which enveloped the

forward section and mainplane. F/Lt Devine with F/O R.T.Wilkinson and Sgt. J. Forrest were killed instantly. Four others were seriously injured.

Non-Operational Activities

F/Lt J.A. Ferguson, 422's highly respected adjutant, was posted to the RAF Overseas HQ and on 21 September a party was held in the Officers' Mess when a silver cigarette case with £1 notes was presented to him. Air Vice-Marshal Sir Leonard Slatter visited Castle Archdale on 24 September and addressed 422's aircrew, stressing the importance of Coastal Command's role in the war and making particular reference to the flying-boat squadrons.

A diversion from duties for some personnel was to visit Irvinstown 4½ miles from base where at *Bothwell's de luxe dinery* it was possible to enjoy for 3s.6d (17½ pence) a large steak with two to four eggs and the whole covered with French fried potatoes.

F/Lt J.A. de le Paulle who had successfully ditched his Sunderland in 1943 appeared in the national news in September. He was a Frenchman with an American passport but served with the Canadian Squadron. While on a ten-day leave, he visited France and while cycling along a country road, accepted the surrender of four armed German soldiers. He later entered Paris with the American army. He had been a medical student at the Sorbonne; had been awarded the Croix de Guerre, and arrived back from his leave in time to be presented with the DFC by the King.

What might well be unique occurred on 23 October in Sunderland NZ174 U/22 which was captained by F/Lt Fallis. While on an operational patrol his F/Engineer, W/O Lepper, died of a heart attack. Base was signalled at 1220 hrs and after the Sunderland landed at 1334 hrs, the Medical Officer estimated that W/O Lepper had died one hour earlier. W/O Lepper was buried on 27th at the Church of Ireland, Irvinstown.

No. 422 Squadron Moves from Castle Archdale to Pembroke Dock

There was effectively an interchange of the squadrons with 422 scheduled for Pembroke Dock while No. 201 was transferred to Castle Archdale. No. 422 began preparations on 28 October and by 14 November the move was virtually complete with the arrival of the rear party by air at Pembroke Dock.

The change of base coincided with a change of CO for 422. A farewell party was held at Castle Archdale on 31 October for W/Cmdr Frizzle who was succeeded by W/Cmdr J.R. Sumner. At the party each officer was expected to contribute to the entertainment with such as stories, songs etc. Refreshments included, Scotch, Irish, Guinness, Coke, ginger ale, soda and coffee, buns with onions, doughnuts and hamburgers prepared "from a famous Canadian recipe."

Pembroke Dock's Station CO gave an address to personnel on 8 November commenting on the fact that Pembroke Dock was base to an RAF Squadron No. 228, No. 461 (RAAF), and No. 422 (RCAF). At that time, it was seemingly with some trepidation! Flying training began on 9 November with day and night flights for crews to familiarise themselves with local conditions.

There was an evening party held by Senior NCOs to which some officers were invited. Music was by the Station band and three musicians from 422 Squadron, with the latter providing music for a square dance. The unfamiliarity of the dancers with square dances, it was reported, was compensated by their enthusiasm.

No. 422's CO, W/Cmdr Sumner endeavoured to rent a suitable building for what was intended to be "Canada House," and tentative arrangements were made for leasing three large rooms in the Edinburgh Hotel.

On Christmas Day 1944, Service custom was followed by 422 with a designated number of officers and NCOs going to serve in the Airmen's Mess. At the Llanion barracks dinner was arranged for 1300 hrs. The Mess was decorated with holly and two large Christmas trees decked with coloured lights stood back against a wall. The Christmas menu included cream of tomato soup, poached hake with egg sauce, roast turkey and roast pork, sausage meat stuffing, roast potatoes, cauliflower, and brussels sprouts, breadsauce, Christmas pudding, rum sauce, biscuits and cheese, dessert, ales and minerals. There were two enormous Christmas cakes with almond icing decorated with flowers and leaves. It was recorded by 422's scrive as "one of the best meals served in England for the occasion." The day concluded for 422 Squadron with a WAAFs' dance in Llanion barracks which was attended by squadron personnel.

The officers and SNCOs of 422 Squadron arranged a party for corporals and airmen of the squadron and 8422 echelon on 27 December. Guests were introduced by W/Cmdr Sumner and they included the Station CO, Gp/Capt

Bolland, and the Chief Technical Officer, W/Cmdr M.J. Grennan. Through the efforts of Sgt R.M. Clements of the electrical section and a fitter, LAC S. Brydges, the first edition of a newspaper, *SHORT SLIP*, was published.

No. 423 Squadron at Lough Erne

In January 1944, two of 423's Sunderlands were armed with four fixed Browning machine guns firing forward and to be operated by the pilot. Apparently also in the nose of the aircraft, an FN5 turret was fitted with two Brownings. By 29 April, mid-upper turrets were being installed on all of 423's aircraft, in anticipation perhaps, of some intended operations over the Bay of Biscay and nearer to the enemy's bases.

F/Lt J.B. Donnett was airborne at 0300 hrs on 12 March as captain of H/423 W6008 and almost two hours later was in position 5338N 1210W when he sighted a convoy four miles away. He sent a signal to control at 1056 hrs that an engine was u/s; this was followed at 1250 hrs with another signal "May land engine trouble" when the Sunderland was then in position 5527N 1335W. A radar blip indicated there were three ships twenty miles ahead when the Sunderland was flying at 2000 feet. Three engines were failing and station was maintained with the three ships which proved to be escorts. F/Lt Donnett ditched in position 5315N 1235W. The crew was picked up by the Canadian frigate *St. Catharines*. Attempts were made to salvage the Sunderland but the swell was too great and it was sunk by gunfire after F/Lt Donnett had recovered logs, secret documents, and a camera.

U-672 Damaged by Sunderland A/423

DD862 A/423 captained by F/Lt G. Fellows was airborne from Castle Archdale at 0708 hrs on 24 April. He was flying at 2100 feet when, after $6\frac{1}{2}$ hrs, he sighted the wake of a U-boat sixteen miles away. This was confirmed using binoculars and with the vessel in position 5040N 1840W and heading south at 16 knots. Fellows maintained height for eight miles but increased speed to 140 knots and turned in preparation for an attack. At five miles the U-boat turned and opened fire but its shells fell short at 2-3 miles. At 1200 yards range the Sunderland opened fire with machine guns silencing the U-boat's gunners for the last 300 yards of the run-in; the aircraft had suffered some hits, however. Six Torpex DCs set for 25 feet and spaced at 60 feet were released from 50 feet. There was a violent explosion; later estimated to have been from the 4th depth charge, which twisted the Sunderland's frame, damaged the elevator, made the port flaps unserviceable, knocked out the rear gunner, threw another of the crew from the astro hatch position, and put all electrical circuits out of action. Fellows was able to regain control but with all the crew forward to maintain trim. Height was gained to 600 feet and as the Sunderland tracked over the area, a large oil patch was seen.

The crew considered that they had damaged the U-boat but did not claim a kill. Some post-war records credit No. 423 Squadron with sinking U-311 in position 5036N 1836W but it is now believed that F/Lt Fellows' aircraft seriously damaged U-672 which had sailed from a French port on 24 February and returned to

France on 12 May. U-311 was, however, lost on 24 April.[19]

Sunderland DD111 and U-921

On 24 May 1944 F/Lt R.H. Nesbitt was detailed for a special anti-submarine sweep and was airborne from Sullom Voe at 0330 hrs in DD111. At 0850 hrs he received a signal to home onto a Catalina "V" of 210 Squadron following the sighting of a U-boat. Nesbitt patrolled the area until at 1220 hrs he was instructed to transmit homing signals for V/210.

Two hours later an SOS was picked up and then, in position 6358N 0357E, his second pilot saw smoke or a splash on the water 10-15 miles north of the Sunderland. Nesbitt headed to the area and his front gunner then saw the wake of a U-boat sailing NNE at 12 knots. The aircraft was then at 2000 feet and closed to attack, releasing five DCs which undershot. F/T Nesbitt was later thought to have been distracted by wreckage, apparently the wing of an aircraft in position 6334N 0302E which he passed during his attack run.

A German account of what occurred on 24 May in those northern waters is given by Rainer Lang who was one of the officers on U-921:

We sailed from Bergen about 20 May and in the late afternoon of 24 May I spotted during my watch a Catalina flying-boat which obviously had seen us. I gave the order for an alarm-dive. In the meantime we received a code-message to proceed to another U-boat which was sinking and we were ordered to rescue the men who were floating in the sea. The commander gave the order to go to the surface and prepare our

anti-aircraft guns. When we came to the surface, the Catalina attacked us immediately and dropped her bombs very close to our submarine. As the aircraft flew away, it was hit and shot down by our 2cm twin-flak, and crashed into the sea about 3 nautical miles to starboard with a heavy smoke trail. We stayed on course.

Shortly after, we were attacked by a Sunderland which was flying at about 120 feet. She fired all her machine guns; our 3.7 cm flak failed and our 2 cm flak apparently missed the aircraft. The bombs (six or eight) were avoided by our captain steering very hard.

I was hit in my right arm by machine gun fire from the Sunderland and was taken below deck. Our sailors were fatally hit and died later in hospital. The captain decided, in respect of the continuing attacks by the Sunderland, to dive. Unfortunately the captain had to close the hatch from the outside so he sacrificed his life for his crew and his body went to the deep. Because of the damage caused by the attack, we were ordered to proceed to the U-boat pen in Trondheim.[20]

From No. 210's record dated 24 May 1944, Catalina V/210 with Capt F.W.L. Maxwell attacked a U-boat in position 6508N 0453E at 0719 hrs. This was U-476.[21] The official Canadian historian has considered this episode and forms the opinion that the lost aircraft was Sunderland R/422 captained by F/O G.E. Holley.[22]

F/Lt Holley had taken off from Sullom Voe at 0800 hrs for a sweep parallel to Nesbitt's 100 miles west of the Norwegian coast, and an SOS was received from "R" by Group HQ at 1419 hrs. Sunderland

R/422 with a total of twelve on board failed to return.

D-Day for No. 423 Squadron at Castle Archdale

On 6 June 1944 No. 423 Squadron heard broadcasts giving enemy reports of paratroops landing in France and 423 awaited BBC reports at 1300 hrs for confirmation. From the AOC in Chief, Coastal Command, ACM Sir Sholto Douglas, came a special order of the day: "The great day we have all been waiting for has arrived. The invasion of the continent of Europe has started. In this operation Coastal Command has a vital role to play. Our job is to 'hold the ring,' this is to prevent the enemy from interfering with our invasion convoys and so to ensure the safe passage to the continent of our troops and their supplies."

During the first half of June, 423 Squadron carried out thirty A/S sweeps, mostly in the northern area of the Bay of Biscay and in the South-Western approaches. There were also six sorties from Sullom Voe over the Norwegian waters and three of the Sunderlands were detailed for special patrols.

By 16 June all of 423's aircraft were being equipped with 1.7" flare chutes in anticipation of making night attacks on U-boats. By the end of the month eight of the Sunderlands had been fitted with the navigational device GEE and one with a radio altimeter. All this equipment was indicative of intended sorties eastwards for night attacks rather than westwards to the Atlantic.

Sweeps over the Atlantic were still being undertaken, however; thus F/O P.B.C. Pepper on 8 June in Sunderland DV978 sighted in position 5257N 1702W

oil patches and air bubbles which were increasing. He remained in the area for thirty minutes and then released two depth charges. F/Lt H.C. Jackson who flew later to the same area in Sunderland DW853 sighted yellow-coloured planks and a barrel. All those signs were indicative of a U-boat in that area.

No. 423 Squadron's Emblem

F/Sgt C.H.E. Cook thought of having an emblem on Sunderland W6000 A/423, the unit's first aircraft at Oban and passed the idea to LAC Garnier, an artist in the armament section. LAC Garnier pencilled a drawing of a white eagle flying out of the sun onto a U-boat. This was shown to the CO, W/Cmdr Rump, who was delighted and thought it would make a good squadron badge.

A colour version was painted using the pale yellow and red from the Macmillan tartan. A letter was sent to Overseas HQ in London and there was further correspondence with the College of Arms. The emblem was to represent a Canadian reconnaissance squadron formed in Scotland. The bird became a Canadian bald-headed eagle poised to strike but the U-boat was ruled out by heraldic conventions. An attached motto *Quarimus et Petimus* lent simple dignity to, *We Search and Strike*.

The emblem was approved by King George VI and the Chief of Air Staff and went into production with colours to the London printing firm Messrs. Sellwoods & Micklewright. Formal handing over of the badge had taken place with the Acting AOC in Chief, AVM W.A. Curtis and with 423's CO at that time (8 June 1943), W/Cmdr Rump. The original, which would have borne the King's signature, came to be hung in Lincoln's Inn, the RCAF Overseas HQ. Subsequently, Mrs. Rump presented a framed copy to the RAF Club in London.

On 12 July F/O C.M. Ulrich was airborne at 0508 hrs in DV978 for a sweep westwards and at 0832 hrs sighted the wake of a periscope four miles away. He was then flying at 1200 feet in position 5758N 1150W. The periscope was 4-5 feet above the water giving a wake 8 feet long. Ulrich attacked from 50 feet releasing eight depth charges set for 25 feet depth and spaced at 60 feet. Half an hour later, two torpedo-shaped objects 12-15 feet long were seen. F/Lt R.M. Johnson, who had taken off for a sweep shortly after Ulrich, witnessed this attack from sixteen miles away and headed for the area. If the U-boat had been damaged, it was apparently not enough require it to sail for a port.

Medical officers and nursing sisters from Necarne American Hospital were invited to a dance in the Officers' Mess on 16 July. About thirty young ladies from Enniskillen Hospitality League were also guests and, as the squadron scribe records: "supplied the necessary sparkle and feminine charm to deter the inclination for a booze up."

No. 423's CO, W/Cmdr Archambault, was posted to HQ No. 15 Group, and on 16 July a farewell party was held in the evening to which guests from Station HQ and No. 422 Squadron were invited. There was a formal handing over of command of 423 Squadron at a parade the following day to W/Cmdr P.J. Grant.

Restrictions had been imposed on leave and travel for service personnel prior to the invasion of Europe, but on 23 August these were lifted and such as 423 Squadron personnel were permitted to travel to England and Eire. This news coincided with the liberation of Paris by Allied forces.

Sinkings, Sightings, and Losses

F/O J.K. Campbell was airborne in NJ183 at 0700 hrs on 3 September. This was for an A/S sweep and, from Capt Roskill's account, part of an intensive search for U-482 which had sunk three ships up to that date; the one on the 3rd being Fjordheim of 4,115 tons lost in position 5555N 0928W.[23]

At 0800 hrs Campbell sighted a schnorkel in position 5543N 0915W. It was heading south at 4 knots three miles away. Campbell closed the range and as he went into attack from 50 feet, the schnorkel was still about 2 feet above the surface. But, his DCs failed to release, and the U-boat disappeared before another attack could be made. He contacted an escort group by R/T and control by W/T while circling the area and homing in escort vessels with whom he co-operated. F/O Campbell sighted four lifeboats and a raft, with one of the lifeboats apparently occupied and perhaps from the ill-fated ship Fjordheim. The commander of U-482, KL Graf von Matuschka, was to prove extremely successful in making full use of his schnorkel-equipped U-boat, but was sunk on 16 January 1945 by an Escort Group.[24]

There was engine failure at 0930 hrs on 6 September for Sunderland B423 ML823 which crashed north-west of Donegal Bay. There was a total of ten in the crew captained by F/O E.F. McCann. The following day, the Royal Navy picked up WO2 R.H. Voyce, the sole survivor; he was uninjured, but had spent twenty-one hours in a dinghy. Two weeks later, the body of F/Lt G.F. Cornwell was recovered from the sea by HMS *Braithwaite* in position 5511N 0835W. It was prepared for burial and committed to the sea.

F/O J.N. Farren was airborne on 11 September at 0530 hrs as captain of ML825, detailed for an A/S sweep. While flying at 1200 feet 4½ hrs later, he sighted whitish vapour or steam nine miles away on the surface in position 5651N 0804W. Height was lost while he closed the range, and the vapour disappeared as if cut off, but a slight wake was seen extending 100 feet indicating a U-boat heading 195°. Farren attacked at 1003 hrs from 50 feet altitude aiming 700 feet ahead of the apex of the wake, releasing eight DCs set at 25 feet, and spaced at 70 feet, but only four DC's from the port side fell.

Reports were transmitted and three escort vessels were homed to the scene, with them beginning attacks on the U-boat contact. Farren remained in the area for over six hours until PLE was reached and it was essential for him to return to base. The naval historian, Capt Roskill, credits the Canadian frigate *Dunver* and corvette *Hespeler* with sinking U-484 with no mention of the Sunderland.[25] An American list includes 423 Squadron's part, and with U-484 sunk in position 5630N 0740W.[26] The captain of U-484 at that time, KK Heinrich Schafer, was credited with sinking four ships while commanding U-183.[27]

Counter-measures against Schnorkel-fitted U-Boats

Beginning on 18 September, Sunderlands from 423 Squadron were detailed each night on flare-dropping in the area to the north where U-boats were thought to be operating. Flares were released from a height of 1500 feet every four minutes from 2000 hrs until 0630 hrs the following morning.

In October an intensive training program was instituted which was to be completed by December. Two submarines from the Royal Navy, HMS *Upshot* and HMS *Vulpine*, were involved in the exercises every day at specified hours and were intended to increase the efficiency of radar operators in detecting U-boats at schnorkel depth. November provided a lull in anti-U-boat operations, and the opportunity was used to undertake further training in night operations with homing by radar; bombing, using the Mark III low-level bomb-sight and the 1.7" flares to illuminate targets. ASR launches fitted with radar reflectors were used on Lough Neagh as targets in addition to Innismurray Island in Donegal Bay. Radio altimeters were being fitted to the Sunderlands. A type 70 radar trainer was available at Castle Archdale with the scanner in a tank of water which would reduce the signal from a miniature island at the bottom of the tank. This trainer was to be used in conjunction with the Link trainer; thus making it a joint exercise for pilot and radar operator.

An attack was made on a U-boat which was schnorkelling on 19 November by Sunderland NJ187 which was airborne from Castle Archdale at 0704 hrs. seven-and-a-half hrs later while flying at 2000 feet the captain, F/Lt Whitney sighted a whitish disturbance on the sea six miles away. As Bruce Whitney writes in retrospect: "We did a violent 180° turn to investigate a false sighting; the turn apparently frightened a sub a couple of miles off beam. His crash dive created a disturbance which we bombed without result.

According to squadron record, the U-boat was heading north-west at 14 knots using its schnorkel and the Sunderland attacked with only two depth charges from 75 feet and set for 25 feet depth. Three hours later a radar contact was made in position 5603N 0922W but which disappeared. Two escort vessels which had arrived on the scene were informed by R/T.

No. 423 Squadron's record includes an extract from the official Coastal Command Review for October 1944 which considered that the last of the U-boats leaving French ports had arrived in Norway and pointing out that the lack of U-boat sightings and low shipping losses was indicative of Coastal Command's success in conjunction with surface vessels. The review added that due to schnorkelling, the ball had been passed to the asdic operators in the escort vessels. The German U-boat diary for the period October 1944 to January 1945 has two headings: "The Schnorkel Proves Its Worth" and "Disadvantages Accruing From the Loss of the Biscay Bases." The length of the trip for U-boats to operational areas was increased by 600-1000 miles and U-boats were inactive for twice their previous times.[28]

The RAF's counter measure against submerged U-boats became "High Tea" and No. 423 Squadron had training on this system intensified by the end of 1944. It involved releasing a pattern of sonobuoys which would pick up sound waves from a U-boat and transmit a signal to the aircraft by electromagnetic means.

Attack on a Schnorkel U-Boat

One of 423's last attacks in 1944 was by F/Lt J.N. Farren. He captained Sunderland E/423 on 28 December and at 1054 hrs had reached position 5339N 1026W when F/O Strobl in the 2nd pilot's seat sighted a whitish cloud ten miles away on the surface and then later a second cloud of vapour at 14 miles. Both were moving on a southerly course. Both vapour clouds disappeared as the Sunderland approached but a periscope was seen heading south-west at 2 knots. F/Sgt Goebel in the nose turret saw it turning gradually, apparently searching for the aircraft. Farren swooped to attack and tracked over the periscope at 150 knots.

Eight Torpex DCs were released from 25-50 feet and so aimed that the first DC would enter the water 100 feet short of the periscope. They all exploded and heavy oil was seen bubbling to the surface forming a patch 300 yards in diameter. W/T and R/T signals were made together with homing transmissions. The Navy's 2nd Escort Group was fifty-five miles away but four escort vessels arrived on the scene at 1648 hrs when details were sent to the SNO.

The squadron's CO, W/Cmdr Grant, considered that the U-boat was "certainly damaged," and the highly experienced Station Commander, G/Capt Oulton, remarked: "It certainly looks as though damage was inflicted on the U-boat."

References to Chapter 7
1. GüH plans 73 & 74
2. GüH App.III p.110; USSL p.166; CCWR p.10
3. CCWR p.12; USSL p.168; GüH App.III p.115
4. GüH App.III p.116
5. Ibid; CCWR p.18; USSL p.168
6. SWR III/2 p.56
7. GüH para. 449 and para.450

8. GüH para.452
9. GüH para.458
10. CCWR pp.11 and 16; USSL p.170; GüH App.III p.117
11. CCWR p.13; USSL p.171; HH p.292; GüH App.III p.115
12. JR p.188
13. GüH para.396
14. GüH para.399
15. GüH App.III p.114; USSL p.167; JR p.303
16. SWR III/1 p.260
17. GüH para.449 and para.450; SWR III/2 p.130
18. SWR III/2 p.130
19. USSL p.167; GüH App.III pp.111 & 114
20. Letter to J.Stewart
21. AH FC p.28
22. RCAF III p.409
23. SWR III/2 p.181
24. USSL p.171
25. SWR III/2 p.181
26. USSL p.170
27. JR p.313
28. JuH para.466

Chapter 8

The Strike Squadrons: January– December 1944

The weather at RAF Wick on 14 January 1944 was "fair" when a shipping strike was laid on to the Naze, Southern Norway with nine Beaufighters from 404 Squadron and seven from 144 Squadron escorting eight Torbeaus from 144. W/Cmdr Willis, CO of 404 in L LZ446, led the anti-flak formation from 144. Off Lister an enemy convoy of three merchant ships with two escort vessels was sighted, while astern was a second convoy.

All the aircraft attacked and RP and cannon hits were scored on the leading escort while F/O Thomsett in M LZ451 and F/O Keefe in H NE355, gained RP hits on a 4000-ton merchant vessel. No. 144 Squadron aircraft which also attacked this vessel saw explosions.

F/Sgt Hunt's aircraft, JLZ179 was seen emitting black smoke while he was diving to attack and not seen again. WLZ173 with F/O Wilkie lost height when 120 miles from base and ditched. F/O Hodson circled but saw no survivors. The second convoy was attacked by W/Cmdr Willis and W/O McGrath who had lost contact with the main formation at Lister.

Six of 404's aircraft returned safely to base; a seventh, had slight damage to the starboard wing. No. 144 Squadron lost two

of their aircraft. The Coastal Command record lists *Wittekind* (4029 tons) and *Entre Rios* (5,179 tons) both sunk, and *Maurita* (1,569 tons) as damaged in this strike.[1]

S/Ldr Gatward in RNE198 led six of 404's aircraft for a Rover patrol on 20 January accompanied by an anti-flak escort from 144 Squadron. Landfall was made at Bremanger from where they turned north. In position 6207N 0505E an enemy convoy of a 5000 ton merchant ship with four escort vessels was sighted also heading north, while further ahead was another convoy. All the aircraft attacked the first convoy. The anti-flak formation dealt with the four escort vessels while 404 Squadron attacked the merchant ship from landward, scoring thirty hits with rocket projectiles. There was some AA fire and three aircraft were slightly damaged. There were a large number of explosions on the ship, which was left on fire enveloped in smoke and steam. This would have been *Emsland* of 5,170 tons which was sunk.

There was a lot of black smoke from one of the escorts which had been attacked by S/Ldr Gatward, and it was considered damaged with the enemy reporting a number of casualties among its crews. The formation set course for base from Stadtlandet, landing safely with no casualties. It was rightly considered a most successful raid.[2]

On 26 January, from 404's record, more ships were probably damaged, but not so recorded by Coastal Command. Six of their Beaufighters were escorted by six from 144 Squadron but en route, F/O Fair had to turn back with engine trouble. Landfall on the Norge coast was made at position 6229N 0556E from where the formation headed southwards along the coast. At 1131 hrs at Stadtlandet, a convoy of three merchant ships with four escorts was sighted heading north. F/O Shulemson and F/O Keefe attacked the escort to seaward with F/O Keefe scoring four hits with RPs; Shulemson then attacked a merchant ship scoring two rocket hits. W/O Hallatt and W/O French fired rockets at the escort astern with Hallatt gaining four hits. One escort was left on fire (probably due to F/O Keefe), and a merchant ship and another escort were left enveloped in smoke. There was accurate flak and rockets from the convoy and flak from the shore, and Shulemson's and Keefe's aircraft were damaged. F/O A.C. Dixon in GNE328 attacked the leading merchant ship with rockets, probably scoring hits, but was then himself attacked by three ME109s and shot down in flames.

Shulemson had set course for base but then saw M/144 attacked by an ME109 and turned back to engage the enemy, who then followed Shulemson out to sea. M/144 broke clear and Shulemson gained cloud cover. W/O French landed at Sumburgh, the others at base and with no casualties. Writing to the author about this operation, Shulemson's English navigator, Peter Bassett, comments:

The award of the DSO to Sydney was the result of our raid on 26 January when we were jumped upon by some ME109s after we attacked a small convoy off Stadtlandet. One of our crews had returned to base half-way over and committed the ultimate sin of climbing and chattering in morse, so the enemy simply had to plot his reciprocal course to calculate our exact landfall in Norway. We were leading the formation of twelve aircraft so, the leading navy, I had to take regular drifts to make sure that landfall would be correct, getting a little assistance by Aldis lamp from other squadron navigators in order to give my pilot several course alterations en route. Sydney, seeing one of our aircraft shot down, decided to turn on one of the ME109Gs seen attacking another of our aircraft which managed to escape as the German naturally turned upon us.
We were able to outwit it with tight turns in and out of cloud before it had to return to base—fortunately several hours of fighter affiliation had been carried out at Wick just previously so we knew how close an aircraft could be allowed to approach before taking action!

Both Shulemson and Bassett before finishing their service were awarded the DFC.

At Wick on 1 February 1944 the weather was reported as dull with low cloud but nine of 404's Beaufighters were detailed for a Rover patrol to Stadtlandet with five aircraft from 144 Squadron. The formation was led by S/Ldr Ken Gatward,

DFC, who, finding the weather too bad at Stadtlandet, headed north where a convoy of one merchant ship with three escort vessels was sighted. Of this strike, Chuck Page, one of the Beaufighter pilots writes:

> The weather was so bad on this trip that we had to use our formation lights to keep together and I never did see the MV that was reported burning. I was number two to the formation leader, S/Ldr Gatward as he attacked the leading E/V with a salvo of eight HE rockets. I fired my SAP rockets just as there was a bloody great flash from Gatward's hit. My rockets were wasted because he had destroyed the 500 ton E/V.

This was truly so; Coastal Command gives the escort vessel KUJ.16 [Aux.UJ1702] of 500 tons being sunk in this strike together with the merchant ship *Valencia* of 3,096 tons.[3]

In addition to these two vessels sunk, all the others (from 404's record), were left burning and damaged. It was the eighth successful strike led by Ken Gatward.

The work of the squadron was acknowledged in the next few days with the BBC recording unit visiting 404 Squadron, the award of the DSO to F/O Sydney Shulemson, DFCs to F/Lt K.S. Miller and P/O J. Young and a mention for S/Ldr Gatward. A group of Toronto businessmen headed by Mr. R. Pearce of the *Northern Miner Press* offered to adopt the squadron—the offer was accepted.

Chuck Page recalls being part of an escort to the Home Fleet which included HMS *King George V* and the French battleship *Richelieu,* together with two aircraft carriers and cruisers heading for Trondheim. At that time large convoys were sailing to Russia and the German battleship *Tirpitz* still posed a threat. Of the Russian convoys, Page comments that it took him twenty minutes to fly round one of forty-two ships.

On 18 March S/Ldr Gatward led a large exercise which involved seventy-two aircraft including thirteen from 404 Squadron. Returning from leave, Chuck Page:

> Got a shock. The airfield was overloaded with Beaufighters and the Mess so crowded that some aircrew officers were sleeping on the ante-room floor. All seven Coastal Beaufighter Squadrons were assembled for a possible strike against *Tirpitz* which was rumoured about to make a dash from its lair. The rumour proved false and our visitors returned to their bases. Huge sighs of relief—the *Tirpitz* with a heavy escort would not have been an easy target.

The Troopship Monte Rosa

In March 1944 a No. 333 (Norge) Squadron Mosquito had reported the movements of a ship of 14,000 tons thought to be taking German technicians back to Germany after working on the battleship *Tirpitz* following damage caused by the Royal Navy. On 30 March the weather was good and a strike was laid on by 404's CO, W/Cmdr Willis. His force comprised nine RP armed Beaufighters from 404 and, from 144 Squadron, five Torbeaus and four Beaufighters armed with cannon. One of 404's pilots, John Symons recalls:

> After briefing we headed for the Flight office for our flying gear; there was a little more tension than usual due to waiting and from briefing we expected to encounter fighters. Our

ground crew were just a little more solicitous on this occasion; as usual they knew as much about it as us. I always found the routine of getting underway to be rather pleasant. It was such a familiar procedure. The engines were started, run up and tested. We moved off and joined the parade around the perimeter track. Off-duty aircrew gave us thumbs up. Once airborne we swung to port and headed east over a perfectly calm North Sea. Our Squadron was made up of two Vics and we were to starboard of the CO's group. No. 144 Squadron flew a short distance behind on the port side.

Overall, we were eighteen aircraft flying at 500 feet in loose formation. I was amazed at the calmness of sea and air. I trimmed the aircraft. It flew hands off for two minutes without varying its direction or height. Under these pleasant circumstances it was hard to believe we were on a mission of destruction. I remember looking over at the other aircraft and wondered whether we would all get back from this one. At that moment the whole exercise seemed quite unnecessary. As we flew on, with the sun setting behind us our shadow streaked across the mirror calm sea before us.

About halfway to Norway we dropped down to fifty feet above the sea. This was our usual practice to stay under the German radar for as long as possible. It was not long when I noticed a bump on the horizon looking like a fence post but Len voiced it, "That will be smoke from the *Monte Rosa* Johnny." We started to see small specks circling the

column of smoke, some high, some low down. It would be the fighter escort circling *Monte Rosa* and her sea escorts. Just ahead of us appeared a string of low-lying rocky islands.

For the time being they blocked our view of *Monte Rosa* and the coastline. Chuck Willis came on the air confirming that our target was dead ahead and he was opening up to full throttle. We followed suit.

This was an exhilarating moment. As we approached the low islands our CO announced that we were about to climb to our attacking height of 1200 ft, ending with "Climbing now!" We all rose together and there before and ahead of us was a panorama in the foreground of which was the *Monte Rosa*, painted all white and the largest ship we had ever seen. Behind her was a large destroyer looking more like a cruiser than otherwise. There was a scattering of trawler size flak ships around *Monte Rosa* mostly to seaward. In the background was the low-lying coastline. Northward there were the mountains. The fighters continued to circle in a seemingly playful mood, some very low to the water as if showing off to the passengers on the ship. We appeared not to have been seen. Our leader was immediately on the air with instructions. Our section was to attack the destroyer. He also gave orders to the 144 Squadron aircraft. He sounded enthusiastic and told us in effect to get stuck in and do a good job. To line up our target we had to slip over to port by which time it was necessary to start our 20 degree dive at the destroyer.

I opened up with cannons and machine guns. From this distance the splashes surrounded the vessel appearing as a small rainstorm. Something to starboard caught my eye. It was a FW190, a formidable German fighter. It was close beside us and climbing at about 45 degrees. It had been a split second glance. An equally swift thought—that fighter would be sitting directly above us when we came out of this dive and turned to port.

But it was back to directing our firepower at the destroyer. This became concentrated on the ship itself. I pressed the button for the rockets. We felt the surge of an extra 10 knots by the rockets leaving their rails. I ceased firing and started a pull-out and steep climbing turn and with rudder added some skidding motion one way and then the other.

After almost a 180 degree turn and climbing slightly, an ME110 fighter passed ahead of us and going north. I turned after it but Len yelled to go to port—fighters astern. I went to port and fast. From then on Len and I yelled back and forth he giving me detailed information about where the fighters were and whence would the first one attack. At first there were five after us but only two made passes. Twice we did a violent corkscrew manoeuvre after which they gave up the chase. The adrenalin had flowed in abundance. We never had time to experience fear we were too busy. Jimmy Keefe caught up with us. At least half of his tail had been shot away and he referred to other damage. He asked us to escort him back to Wick where he asked for and

gained immediate permission to land (made without brakes or flaps). We had heard that Chuck Willis had been seen to ditch as did two other aircraft.

No. 404's record confirms Symons' account. Landfall was made at Utsira when almost immediately the troopship was sighted escorted by three vessels, including a destroyer.

Waiting for the Beaufighters to begin their strike was the Luftwaffe near Haugesund with about nine single-engined fighters—ME109s and FW190s with five ME110s, two Arados, and one B&V138. W/Cmdr Willis had his force in two flights with the second led by F/Lt Robinson. He had sighted the enemy fighters and gave exact instructions to each member of the formation as to the form of attack. He ordered the attack and then dived for the main target—the troopship, F/O Young and F/O Fair probably obtained underwater hits with RPs and cannon; F/O Keefe, F/O Smith, and F/O Symons concentrated their RPs and cannon fire on the destroyer just astern of the troopship, all claiming hits despite its avoiding action, and it was left enveloped in clouds of steam. F/O Rancourt attacked another escort leaving it emitting smoke and flames. There was intense AA from both the shore batteries and the convoy and four of 404's aircraft suffered considerable damage.

F/O Rancourt had an encounter with an ME110 and shot it down in flames. He then pursued another ME110 but was driven off by a FW190. P/O Mallalieu also engaged an ME110 but inconclusively.

Two aircraft from 404 failed to return; the two leaders, W/Cmdr Willis and F/Lt Robinson. W/Cmdr Willis in LZ297 was seen to ditch and he and his navigator climb into a dinghy; F/Lt V. Robinson and his navigator F/O W.D. Levine were lost in LZ314.

The torpedoes released by No.144's Torbeaus had been set to run too low and this strike was credited with damaging *Monte Rosa* of 13,882 tons, but 404's record concludes with: "This was a brilliant and successful attack smothering the escort vessels and allowing the torpedo aircraft to attack the main target. Much credit is due to the squadron commander in 'A' [LZ297] for his able leadership"[4]

Of this strike, G/Capt Charles Willis, writing to the author from Vancouver in 1993 comments: "This was the most sizeable target I was involved with, and in leading that attack, I was shot down then picked out of the sea by a Blohm & Voss flying-boat and taken POW."

No. 404 Squadron's last successful strike before the lead-up to D-Day was on 7 April. The weather was reported good, and eight aircraft from 404 acted as anti-flak for four 144 Squadron Torbeaus on a Rover patrol. They were all airborne about 0930 hrs and when off Stadtlandet sighted three merchant ships with six escort vessels which were southbound. The Beaufighters led by F/O Keefe in NE355 concentrated on three escorts sailing in line abreast to seaward of the rear merchant ship and smothered the escort screen, allowing Torbeaus to close on the merchant ships. P/O Mallalieu, F/O Symons, and F/O Taylor attacked the middle ship and F/O Rancourt attacked the rear escort.

There was moderate flak from both the convoy and shore batteries. No. 144 Squadron claimed a torpedo hit but only the MV *Cornouaille* of 3,324 tons is recorded as being damaged in this strike.[5]

Chuck Page, who took part in this strike adds: "For the rest of April we got in only two Rovers, our time being used on bombing training...this was not a popular idea with us." The training was related to using 500 pound bombs designed to burst in the air but the aircraft were without bombsights. Such a method was certainly used by at least one Coastal Command Squadron—No. 524, but with Wellingtons, a bomb sight and 250 lb bombs released from a great height so that the aircraft itself would not be blown up.

No. 404 Squadron at Davidstow Moor

On 8 May 1944 No. 404 Squadron prepared to move from Wick down to Davidstow Moor. Their record states that they'd miss the comforts of Wick, one of the best-equipped stations the squadron had experienced, but, that the move would be a welcome change for some of the ground staff who had been in Scotland since 1941. Two days later the main party of both 144 and 404 Squadron personnel left by train under F/Lt Stevens. Those who were flying left an hour later under W/Cmdr Gatward.

The main party arrived at Davidstow Moor the following afternoon to find the station widely dispersed and that 404 was to be located on a hill with accommodation incomplete, poorly equipped, and some distance from hangars. By 13 May they had enough tables and chairs to open offices. Bicycles which had been issued to aircrew were withdrawn for ground staff, who had to travel three miles from their billets. Transport was laid on at the Mess centre to take personnel to work.

On 17 May there was night flying with six crews on a homing exercise with No. 524 Squadron Wellingtons. The following day they received news from the Air

Ministry that W/Cmdr Willis had been captured on 30 March and was a POW. Apparently he had been picked up by a German ASR flying-boat.

To date, No. 404 Squadron had been the only unit to successfully attack shipping with RPs and without an escort, which prompted Coastal Command to send public relations officers to 404 for photographs to be taken and a write-up to be made.

From Davidstow Moor they would now be operating over what the Australian Sunderland Squadron No. 10 called "Tiger country"—The Bay of Biscay—although from German records the enemy had a healthy respect for both Sunderlands and Coastal Command's Beaufighters.[6] However, on 19 May a formation led by W/Cmdr Gatward had an escort of twenty-eight Spitfires. Ten of 404's Beaufighters were armed with 60 pound RPs and were supported by thirteen aircraft from 144 as anti-flak escort. They sighted a destroyer, four M-class minesweepers, and a torpedo boat. All the ships were attacked, and it was claimed that they had all been hit and left damaged. One aircraft from 144 Squadron failed to return, and a number of others were damaged by AA fire.

D-Day

On 6 June 1944, 404 Squadron heard, not only of the D-Day landings, but had also a report of three Narvik-type destroyers steaming up the English Channel to interfere with the invasion forces. They were briefed at 1400 hrs and fourteen aircraft from 404 armed with 25 pound RPs with seventeen aircraft from 144 as anti-flak, took off at 1830 hrs. They were escorted by eight Mosquitoes from 248 Squadron. Landfall was made at Ushant before flying south-east to sight the target near Belle Isle. W/Cmdr Lumsden led 144 Squadron; F/O S. Shulemson, DSO, led 404's attacking force. Initially three minesweepers were seen and mistaken for the target, and a surfaced U-boat; the latter was attacked by 248 Squadron. It was Sydney Shulemson of 404 who correctly identified the three Narvik destroyers. He deployed his sub-leaders—F/O Hodson and F/O Dwornik—to starboard to take the end and front ships respectively. Four of 404's aircraft attacked the leading destroyer with RPs and cannon with many underwater hits claimed. Its superstructure was damaged by cannon fire, and large columns of smoke were emitted. Nine other Beaufighters attacked the centre destroyer, many holding fire until at point blank range so that they could not miss.

The large number of attacks on the centre destroyer was due to it having increased speed, placing itself in the centre. F/O Taylor in NE744, finding the centre so crowded, skirted to attack the last destroyer, scoring hits between the funnels with cannon fire after releasing a salvo of RPs. While en route to base, Q/144 ditched and F/O Wainman remained on the scene to give instructions and saw the crew get into their dinghy. After reporting the position, he returned to base low on fuel. During the strike, No. 48 Squadron shot down a JU88 of which 404 had been quite unaware.

Five aircraft were refuelled and took off at 0027 hrs on 7 June for a further strike. They flew singly but on the same track. En route a U-boat was sighted and flak was seen from the direction of Ushant. Their target, the three Narvik destroyers, were located and there was smoke still rising from the centre ship due to the earlier attack. F/O Ridge in NE426 attacked with RPs in pairs, the last released from 200 yards range. He claimed at least two direct hits and two underwater strikes. While pulling away his tail wheel was hit by a bullet and his navigator's cupola was shattered. F/Lt Christison released a salvo from 400 yards against the first destroyer, and the American, Lt F.F. Guyott in LZ295, claimed four direct and four underwater hits on the last ship. As he pulled away, he was aware of an explosion on the second or third destroyer lighting up the first one. There was a red glow and then a burst of flame 200 feet high with the vessel on fire from stem to stern in the interior. The squadron record gives: "Although this attacking force was made up of practically new crews, their performance was the work of hardened veterans."

The terse Coastal Command record confirms that destroyers Z32 and Z24 of 3,664 tons each and ZH.1 of 3000 tons were damaged by 144 and 404 Squadrons on the night of 6-7 June.[7]

On 9 June W/Cmdr Gatward led a further attack by twelve Beaufighters from 404, twelve from 144, with a fighter cover of twenty-four Spitfires. They found one of the destroyers had been beached and report: "one DR destroyed."

While still based at Davidstow Moor, 404 Squadron achieved another successful strike against the Kriegsmarine. Twelve of their Beaufighters led by W/Cmdr Gatward in NE425 were airborne just before 1300 hrs on 30 June and with an escort of Mosquitoes from 248 Squadron. They spotted an enemy convoy which was stationary, of two M-class minesweepers, a merchant vessel of 2-3000 tons, and a tanker of 6-800 tons.

They attacked with 60 pound and 25 pound RPs. There was smoke from both the tanker and the merchant vessel. W/Cmdr Gatward shot up with his cannon a gunpit on the land. One of the escorting Mosquitoes ditched and was seen to float for about three minutes but no survivors appeared. F/O Shulemson and F/O Johnson returned with engine trouble but all the others were able to attack. Coastal Command's record credits 404 with 248 and 235 Squadrons in sinking the naval auxiliary vessel UJ.1408 of 530 tons.[8]

No. 404 Squadron at Strubby, Lincolnshire

Of 404 Squadron's next deployment, one of their pilots, Chuck Page recalls:

On 5 July we moved to Strubby on the Lincolnshire coast. We had barely settled in when the next day we were off to Langham (on the Norfolk coast), to join their Wing and the North Coates wing for a big strike in the Heligoland Bight.

About fifty Beaus took part and we attacked a convoy of nineteen ships including ten escort vessels. This was the biggest show I was ever on and I got the biggest scare of my tour on this one. Our beau was boxed in by flak. The 88 mm shells were bursting so close I could hear them over the sound of our engines and Blackie was yelling to me "get weaving" because he had tracers, probably 20 mm, zipping just over his head. Obviously I got out of this hot spot and to attack a 4-5000 ton MV.

No. 404 Squadron's ten Beaufighters had taken off from Langham within five minutes from 1920 hrs on 6 July. Leading the Wing, which included aircraft from 489 and 144, was 455 Squadron. The convoy was seen to comprise eight to ten merchant vessels in two columns with escorts on both quarters and ahead and when attacked was in position 5403N 0714E Several of the ships were flying balloons. But for two which had engine trouble, F/O Rossiter and F/O Angus, all of 404 attacked the aft end of the convoy. Apart from F/Lt Hodson in NE687 who landed at Langham, all of 404 returned to Strubby. Sunk in the raid was the merchant vessel *Stadt Riga* (3,002 tons), and damaged was *Ernst Brocklemann* of 1900 tons.[9]

Two days later the squadron was on another successful strike when four Beaufighters from 404 led by W/Cmdr Gatward in NE825 after being airborne from Strubby at 0427 hrs, were able to rendezvous with 144 Squadron Torbeaus from North Coates plus aircraft from 236 and 254.

When in position 5403N 0745E a convoy of sixteen ships—six MV's and ten escorts were sighted. All the aircraft attacked from landward and down sun. Many RP and cannon strikes were noted plus several torpedo hits. A number of ships were left with smoke rising from them.

Coastal Command lists five ships sunk in this raid: *Tannhauser* (3200 tons); *Miranda* (736 tons); *Sif* (1;437 tons); M.264, a minesweeper (750 tons); and ASR boat No. 555 (58 tons).[10]

Strikes off the Frisian Islands

While still at Strubby and operating over the North Sea, 404 Squadron undertook two more successful strikes in July. On the 18th ships were attacked off

the Frisian Islands in conjunction with 144, 236, and 254 Squadrons. At least four ships were left on fire and R-139 of 90 tons was sunk.[11]

S/Ldr Schoales led the Beaufighters from 404 on 21st in LZ451 and this strike was again off the Frisians, an area in World War II to be respected because of the German heavy defences against bombers heading for Germany. A convoy of twenty to twenty-five ships was sighted, including about ten merchant vessels. They were attacked with RPs and cannon despite heavy and light flak and even a flame thrower, which was attached to the mast of one ship. Schoales' Beaufighter was on fire during his attack and his navigator suffered some burns in putting it out. Three other aircraft from 404 were also hit. The results were much better than could be deduced from 404's record, with two ships credited as being sunk by Beaufighters from 144, 404, 455, and 459 Squadrons. They were a merchant vessel, *Orient* (4,160 tons) and a minesweeper M307 (750 tons).[12]

Detachment to Davidstow Moor

On 5 August 1944, 404 Squadron was instructed that all available crews and aircraft should proceed from Strubby to Davidstow Moor, Cornwall, and with sufficient ground crew and equipment. That same day the ground staff were flown by Dakotas. By 8 August eighteen of their aircraft with twenty-four aircrews were detached to Davidstow Moor. Two of 404's Beaufighters flown by W/Cmdr Gatward and Lt Guyett had made a recce of St. Helier, Jersey, on the 7th. They were fired upon but after recognition signals the firing ceased. Lt Guyett returned to base but W/Cmdr Gatward landed at Cherbourg, the first Coastal Command aircraft to land in France since the invasion, according to 404's record.

The following afternoon W/Cmdr Gatward led fifteen aircraft from 404 with eight from 236 Squadron on an anti-shipping Rover patrol from Ushant to Noirmoutier. Three M-class minesweepers and one smaller minesweeper were attacked in a bay just off Noirmoutier. There was AA fire from the ships and the shore and Beaufighter F/404 was seen to dive steeply into the water. This was NE354, flown by F/O R.S. Forestell with navigator F/O I.C. Robbie, who failed to return to base. All four minesweepers were however sunk in this strike.[13]

At about 1100 hrs on 12 August nine of 404's Beaufighters armed with cannon and 25 pound RPs and cannon. No. 404 was led by S/Ldr Schoales acting as anti-flak. They patrolled between Ushant and Isle de Re and it was off La Pallice and Isle de Re that a 4000-ton merchantman was sighted with its escort vessel. Both ships were attacked, with the escort "practically blown out of the water" and with both ships left "smoking and enveloped in red flames." No. 404 informed the Navy for them to complete the destruction. A large splash in the water was seen during the attack and one of 404's crews failed to return. That crew comprised W/O Heavner and P/O Baker. The Command's record conflicts with 404's by crediting No. 236 Squadron with Mosquitoes from Nos. 235 and 248 with sinking four ships on this date.[14]

On 13 August 1944 the weather at Strubby and Davidstow Moor was good. At 0650 hrs at Davidstow Moor twelve of 404's aircraft were airborne under S/Ldr Hanway to form part of a wing led by No. 236 Squadron. A shipping recce was made

from Ushant to the Gironde river mouth. While en route a signal was received to attack three U-boats and four escort vessels at the Gironde. These were, however, not sighted but two ships described as *sperrbrechers* were sighted stationary near Royan. Each squadron attacked a ship, 404 selecting the right-hand one and attacking from the direction of the land. There was much AA fire from both ships and shore with a number of aircraft hit and damaged. One ship was seen enveloped in flames and from which the AA ceased. It was then believed that one ship had been sunk and the other left on fire. In fact the two ships, *Scwannheim* and *Magdeburg*, are recorded as sunk. Two aircraft failed to return; one from 236 and "Z" of 404 Squadron.[15]

No. 404 Squadron's CO, W/Cmdr Ken Gatward, DSO, DFC, undertook his last op with the unit on 14 August, to Verdun at the mouth of the Gironde. He led seven of his Beaufighters armed with 25 pound RPs and cannon together with seven from 236 Squadron. They were airborne by 1830 hrs from Davidstow Moor, and at 2112 hrs in position 4528N 0102W sighted a 2000-ton depot ship, six trawlers, and two tugs. All the ships were attacked and twenty-six hits with RPs were claimed on the depot ship with additional possible underwater hits. There was a sheet of flame from it followed by black smoke.

P/O Hallatt's aircraft was hit in the port engine, and W/Cmdr Gatward, while breaking away after his attack, had serious damage to his Beaufighter NE800. It was hit in the port engine, port aileron, and starboard wing such that the aircraft was difficult to control. His navigator, Red McGrath, GM, went forward to assist until Gatward jammed a crash hatchet into the controls. He returned safely, but three aircraft landed at Predannack.

Ken Gatward had finished his tour and in the 404 Squadron record appears: "We have lost a wonderful leader." Writing to the author about his time with 404, G/Capt Ken Gatward comments: "I have very fond memories of my Canadians both as a Flight Commander and as CO. They, and their British navigators, were the finest bunch of buddies I ever had the honour to fly with."

As a Flight Lieutenant with No. 236 Squadron, Ken Gatward had the distinction of taking the French tricolour to German-occupied Paris in 1942. Fighter Command had no suitable aircraft and the Air Ministry gave the task to Coastal Command whose C-in-C personally briefed Gatward at Northwood HQ. He made the flight on 12 June and after dropping the tricolour, shot up the Hotel de Crillon which was occupied by the Kriegsmarine.[16]

The Gironde River

For much of the war the Gironde estuary had been used by German U-boats and Italian submarines as well as by the destroyers and auxiliary vessels which still remained. No. 404 Squadron made a further recce to the Gironde on 24 August, led by S/Ldr Tacon. Ten of their aircraft armed with RPs were airborne from Davidstow Moor by 1625 hrs. F/Lt Chuck Page, who piloted NT916 recalls:

It was a strike against two destroyers in the Gironde estuary with 236 Squadron. Both ships were probably sunk. The diciest part of this trip was when we got back to Portreath where the cloud base was 100 ft.

[Davidstow was socked in] This of course provided some hairy moments but thanks to the expert flying control staff we got down safely."

He landed with almost no fuel left. From the squadron record, the destroyers had been stationary but got under way when attacked. Despite heavy flak, hits on one blew off the superstructure and it was left on fire.[17]

F/Lt Christison in NV291 had one engine hit by flak; he feathered the prop and landed at Vannes with a 236 Squadron aircraft which was also damaged. Christison and his navigator were ferried back to base by 236 Squadron. One of 236 Squadron's aircraft was seen to ditch; F/O Wallace in NE425 while in the circuit was out of fuel and, despite the low cloud base, made a good crash-landing. F/O Johnson's elevator on NE426 jammed after he landed.

S/Ldr J.A. Hanway, AFC, with navigator F/O M.F. Payne led a recce in NV191 on 26 August along the Brittany coast and to the Gironde. There were six aircraft from 404 armed with RPs and cannon together with others from 236 Squadron. Southwest of Île de Sein three small coastal vessels were attacked and left damaged and smoking. No targets were seen at the mouth of the Gironde and Hanway decided to attack a 2000-ton, merchant vessel in Royan harbour from the town side with RPs and cannon. There was some heavy flak from the town and intense light flak from two auxiliary vessels north-west of the harbour. Hits were scored on the 2000-ton vessel and explosions were seen with it enveloped in smoke. The leader of No. 236 Squadron had some trouble and headed for Vannes where he crash-landed. S/Ldr Hanway had been heard to reply to all messages until ten minutes after the attack—he failed to return to base. Two other aircraft had minor flak damage. No. 404 Squadron rated seven of their strikes in August 1944 as being successful in addition to other sorties.

No. 404 Squadron Moves to Banff

On 1 September 404 Squadron was at Strubby in Lincolnshire but preparing to leave for Banff in Scotland with an advance party leaving that day. By this time the new CO, W/Cmdr E.W. Pierce, had assumed command. With the arrival of W/Cmdr Gatward to spend a few days with them, W/Cmdr Pierce made a short speech and called upon Jimmy Hawkins to say a few words.

At this gathering, Ken Gatward received an ovation which was as the squadron scribe reports: "a fitting tribute to our former boss." The AOC No. 16 Group RAF came to say goodbye to the aircrew and from the RCAF Overseas Branch HQ came a war artist, F/O Don Anderson, to be attached to the squadron and record its activities.

The main party left for Banff on 3 September by train with the station CO, G/Capt Ward, DFC, seeing them off. The air party left the same day. F/Lt W.R. Christison, described as a "red-headed lad from Lennoxville, Quebec," was awarded the DFC on account of his accomplishment on 24 August. He was appointed deputy Flight Commander of B Flight. The main party arrived at Banff on 4 September and the following day the train was being unloaded.

The base was found to be less dispersed than some others but bicycles were still required. The scribe records: "everyone settling in, never have we had such splendid meals served to all ranks.

The current topic is 'Wasn't that a great meal we had at noon, I wonder what is for supper?' " They found the station well-equipped and commented on the foresight and patience of one who had planted a garden of flowers in front of SHQ.

The Biscay and Channel Ports

Following the invasion of Europe by the Allies on Operation "Overlord" in June, the prime needs were to supply the armies with petrol and food. Ports were required in addition to the "Mulberry" harbour at Arromanches.[18]

Cherbourg was captured on 25 June and in July, Cherbourg and Arromanches were required to supply the Allied armies.

On 18 August, Hitler ordered the evacuation of south and west France except for the ports of Brest, Lorient, St. Nazaire, La Pallice, and Bordeax, but Brest, which was required to supply the Americans, was captured on 18 September following the assault which began on 25 August.[19]

It had been anticipated by the Admiralty that U-boats and some ships would be evacuated from French ports which were threatened by the Allies and there was a move south in August of U-boats from Brest, Lorient, and St. Nazaire to La Pallice and Bordeaux. There was a further move of U-boats to Norway beginning on 16 August, with thirty-one ultimately arriving in Norway.[20]

Canadian troops had suffered serious losses in an assault on Dieppe in 1942 but troops from the 1st Canadian Army commanded by General Crerar were able to take that port on 1 September for ships to enter on the 5th. They had the additional task of clearing ports from

LeHavre northwards and by 9 September had reached Bruges. The German garrison in Le Havre surrendered on 12 September.[21]

The aim of General Montgomery was to capture Antwerp, but although his 2nd Army was able to enter on 4 September, both banks of the Scheldt were covered by the enemy, and it was to be 28 November before an Allied convoy sailed up the 70-80 miles stretch of water to Antwerp. Boulogne was taken on 22 September and a "Pluto" pipeline to it was completed on 26 October.[22]

As the situation changed on the land, so were there maritime movements by both the enemy and the Allies. For Coastal Command, its squadrons were required to support our naval forces and to report on and attack enemy shipping. For the Canadian Squadrons within Coastal Command their deployment is seen to fluctuated between Nos. 16, 18, and 19 Groups RAF, perhaps at a day's notice.

At Banff on the Moray Firth, No. 404 came under 18 Group RAF but the Canadian character of the unit was not suppressed. The bar in the mess was found to be too small and by 9 September a new one was "taking shape" built from oddments found on the camp. They deplored not being entertained by a Canadian group, The Blackouts and there was the wish that "Someday we hope to see a show with Canadian girls in it."

Armed Recces to Norway

A major operation was laid on for 9 September with take-off at 1430 hrs. This was to be an armed recce from Stavanger southwards to Christiansand with eleven aircraft from 404, and fifteen from 244, including six Torbeaus, and escorted by 235 Squadron Mosquitoes.

No. 144 Squadron's CO, W/Cmdr Gadd, DFC, led the formation, while W/Cmdr Pierce flew as No. 2 to F/Lt Christison, who led 404. En route there was an occasional rain storm but on reaching the Norge coast they encountered very heavy rain and low clouds. The leaders decided to abandon the mission and return to base. They were visited by the CinC Coastal Command, ACM Sir Sholto Douglas, and the AOC No. 18 Group, AVM S.P. Simpson.

The new bar was officially opened by Sir Sholto and all drinks were on the Station CO, C/Capt the Hon. Max Aitken. As the 404 Squadron scribe adds: "everyone took full advantage of his generosity." The unit had had three Squadron and wing moves in four months for which, no doubt, the CinC allowed.

The following afternoon another Rover recce was laid on for the Wing, this time from Kristiansund then south to Stavanger. It was preceeded by a 333 (Norge) Squadron Mosquito recce aircraft but no report was received from it. W/Cmdr Gadd led the formation; S/Ldr Schoales led 404 who were disappointed at encountering no enemy aircraft although there was heavy flak from Helvig. Two ASR Walruses were sighted "waiting to pick up the pieces" as 404 reported.

The official artist, Don Anderson, had drawn a series of portraits of various squadron members each in a little over 30 minutes but on 11 September departed for London to design Victory loan posters.

S/Ldr Schoales led the Banff wing on 14 September to patrol from Egero to Kristiansund. In addition to twelve 404 Squadron Beaufighters, there were aircraft from Nos. 235, 248, and 144, making a total of forty-three. They flew at sea level but on sighting the Norge coast climbed to 2000 ft.

A small convoy of ships was sighted off the Naze, but all were apparently neutral Swedish, and the Wing re-formed. There was heavy flak from Kristiansund but none of the aircraft was hit. The patrol was continued to Hombersund and as they turned to set course for base, an enemy convoy was seen. It comprised three merchant ships with three escort vessels. F/Lt Taylor, F/O Ridge and F/O Long attacked the leading escort vessel with RPs and cannon—it blew up. This would have been the auxiliary VP1608 *Sulldorf* of 264 tons credited as sunk in this strike.

S/Ldr Schoales, F/O Mallalieu, F/O Baribeau and F/Lt Wainman attacked a large merchant ship and claimed twenty-two RP hits and this vessel was left smoking and in flames. It was probably the 3,323 ton *Iris* which was credited as damaged by the strike wing. Six hits with RPs were claimed by F/Lt Hallat on another merchant ship while F/O Dworick scored four hits on a smaller merchantman.[23]

The leading escort vessel was seen to be sinking while all the others were emitting flames and smoke. Although there was not a lot of flak it was accurate and three of 404's aircraft were seriously damaged.

F/O A. Menual's machine was hit in the starboard propeller and the windscreen was completely shattered. Menual was stunned and wounded in the right arm, shoulder, and chest by flying perspex and glass. His face had pieces of perspex embedded in it, and his navigator, F/O J. Thomas, assisted him in controlling the aircraft and gave first aid. They were a new crew but managed to bring the Beaufighter back safely, and Menual

landed although unable to see through the windscreen; a "wonderful display of courage and devotion to duty" records 404's scribe. Beaufighter O/404 flown by F/O Baribeau had ditched but only one was seen to enter the aircraft's dinghy. It was Baribeau, who became a POW.

S/Ldr Schoales suffered damage to his starboard engine; the propeller was feathered, and for the third time he brought back a damaged aircraft from a Norge sortie but this time to land at Crimond which was still under construction for the Navy.

He was met by a watchman, a visiting sailor and a policeman. He was taken to Frazerburgh, and the Station CO, G/Capt Aitken, sent his car to pick up the crew. For F/O Dwornick and P/O French with their navigators it was their twelfth strike and they were recorded as "outstanding in their keenness and fortitude" This was the first strike by the Banff wing, but it was marred for 404 by the loss of a crew.

Five days later, on 19 September the weather was good and 333 (Norge) Squadron aircraft had reported two merchantmen with one escort vessel. The Wing was led by 144 Squadron's CO, W/Cmdr Gadd, but with S/Ldr Schoales leading 404's eleven aircraft; No. 235 Squadron provided fighter cover, and the patrol was to be from Utvaer to Bremanger. En route they flew above cloud and through fog but it cleared at the Norge coast. Near Askvoll a convoy of three—a merchantman, a passenger ship, and an escort vessel—were sighted, while to the south there were five small ships ahead of a merchant vessel. All the ships were attacked and one escort was seen to blow up, a merchant vessel was left burning and aground, and a number of hits were claimed by 404 on a large merchant ship. Coastal Command's record gives two ships being sunk in this strike: *Lynx* (1,367 tons) and *Tyrifjord* (3,080 tons).[24]

Three small ships were sunk on 21 September when S/Ldr Rodgers of 144 Squadron led about forty aircraft, including eleven headed by S/Ldr Christison from 404. This was on a patrol from Christiansand to the Naze but the ill-fated ships were sighted off Lister. All the aircaft returned to base but F/O Lee in NE626 landed with one engine at Crimond.

Aircraft Losses

No. 404 Squadron lost two aircraft in an accident on 2 October. As eleven Beaufighters from 404 were about to form up for a strike to Sogne fjord, two collided. They were crewed by P/O E.R. Davey with F/O L.E.E. Robinson, and F/O G.A. Long with F/O F.M. Stickel. They crashed a short distance from Banff and there was no time for them to bail out.

There was a happier event the following day; the weather was considered unsuitable for flying and the crews were released. Some were able to visit Aberdeen while P/O C.F. Page was married to a young lady from Wick. The USAAF pilot, Lt F.F. Guyett, flew the best man, P/O French, to the wedding.

With good flying weather forecast for 9 October, crews were briefed early at 0300 hrs for a recce to Utsira. W/Cmdr Gadd led the formation from 144, 235, and 404 with W/Cmdr Pierce heading No. 404's seven crews in HV291. 404's aircraft were all airborne by 0529 hrs and they set course individually. At 0627 hrs flares were sighted in position 5918N 0433E which had been dropped by a 281 Squadron Warwick. The strike force

formed on the outer flares before heading south. At 0730 hrs in position 5840N 0527E an enemy convoy of ten ships comprising five merchantmen, a coaster, and four escorts was sighted.

All of 404's aircraft attacked with RPs and cannon from 500-400 feet altitude at ranges for RPs from 700 down to 450 yards. No. 404's record claims two torpedo hits on one MV, and one torpedo hit on a second MV. From Norwegian sources No. 404 Squadron understood at the time that two merchantmen and a trawler were sunk while the coaster was seriously damaged. Coastal Command has recorded only *Rudolf Ooldendorff* (1,116 tons) and *Sarp* (1,116 tons) as being sunk in this strike.[25]

A Sortie to Denmark

S/Ldr Christison from 404 led the Wing on 15 October to what was new terrain for many crews. It was a patrol from Skaw, Denmark, to Hombersund and the Naze for thirty-eight aircraft representing 144, 235, and 248 Squadrons together with twelve from 404. South of Kristiansund two small ships were attacked with RPs and cannon.

One, a tanker, blew up the *Inger Johanne* of 1,202 tons, while an auxiliary *Mosel* VP1605 of 426 tons was left burning and in a sinking condition. All the aircraft returned safely although W/O Jackson's Beaufighter had damage to the tailplane caused by flying debris as he attacked the exploding tanker.[26]

S/Ldr Maurice of 248 Squadron led the Banff Wing with crews from 144, 235, 248, and 333 and twelve aircraft from 404 Squadron on 21 October. This was an armed recce to Askevold where, on finding no target, the Wing split into two formations. F/O John Symons led some of

404 north to Stadtlandet but with no sighting, returned to base. S/Ldr Christison led the remainder of 404 Squadron south to Haugesund harbour and attacked two merchant vessels with RPs and cannon. Both ships were left on fire. There was considerable flak and S/Ldr Christison's Beaufighter LZ451 suffered a large hole in the tailplane, but all the aircraft returned safely to base. This was the last operational sortie for F/O John Symons and his English navigator, F/O Len Barcham. Credited to the Wing as sunk were two merchant ships, *Eckenheim* (1,923 tons), and *Vestra* (1,422 tons).[27]

No. 404 Squadron at Dallachy

No. 404 Squadron was now scheduled to move from Banff to Dallachy, and the station CO could gain no reprieve. The move began at 0900 hrs on 22 October and with the aircraft leaving at 1415 hrs. Dallachy had been a satellite of Banff and had suffered "considerable robbery" from the parent station. The Squadron found the usual shortage of transport and there was not even enough blankets and mattresses for the airmen.

The record states "considerable chaos" and a "hopeless mess." For 404, which was the following February to suffer losses of 54% in one shipping strike, it was hardly a pleasant beginning.

Two days later, the cry was still the lack of chairs, tables, telephones, transport, bicycles, and at one site, for the service echelon, no water. This writer was on detachment there in 1945 when conditions seemed little better. No. 404 was unlucky enough, apparently, to be the first Squadron to operate from Dallachy.

The American pilot, Lt F.F. "Freddy" Guyott of the USAAF had completed his tour of operations with the Canadians by the end of October and was posted to the 70th replacement control depot AAF station 594. On occasion he had led the Squadron aircraft in strikes and 404's record describes him as being "a very popular member."

The weather was unsuitable for flying on 7 November and the Squadron was released and granted a liberty run in to Elgin, about 12 miles west of Dallachy. The following day operations were resumed with a Rover patrol laid on from Utvaer to Stadtlandet and including aircraft from 144 and 455 Squadrons. The six aircraft from 404 were led by F/O Boileau, and landfall was made at 6051N 0439E. The whole formation of Beaufighters remained outside the islands while two Mosquitoes from 333 Squadron searched leads and anchorages. In Midgulen fjord five ships were sighted: two merchantmen, two coasters, and an escort vessel. Exceptionally, one vessel was identified at the time as *Helga Ferdinand* and claimed as sunk by three of 404's aircraft flown by F/O Boileau, F/Lt Taylor, and F/O Lee.

All the ships were attacked with RPs and cannon; initially they were claimed as severely damaged but later reports stated that the two merchantmen were sunk. From the Command's record, they were *Aquila* (3,530 tons) and *Helga Ferdinand* (2,566 tons). Also damaged was *Framnaes* (307 tons).[28] A box barrage was suffered during the aircrafts' approach but the flak was spasmodic after the strike commenced and all the aircraft returned safely.

Two ground staff, LAC J.W. Dean and LAC J.V. Routley, left for repatriation to Canada on 9 November, and two days later the RCAF Overseas HQ informed the squadron that five more ground staff, fitters and riggers who had been away from home for almost three years, were to be repatriated.

A Strike From Wick

On 27 November following a report of a large merchant ship in Sula fjord, a strike was laid on with four aircraft from 489 and six from 404 Squadron, to be led by F/Lt Shulemson, DSO, in Z/404 NV177. They were airborne from Wick by 1141 hrs and landfall was made at Svinoy light but no target was seen and they returned to position 6225N 0603E for a strike against a convoy seen earlier steaming at 7 knots on a course of 170°. It comprised one merchantman of 5000 tons, one of 3500 tons, and three escorts.

F/O Jones scored cannon hits on the large merchant ship but his RPs overshot. F/Lt Wainman and F/O Coyne attacked the second MV and Coyne claimed eight hits with RPs; Shulemson claimed eight RP hits on the leading escort vessel which caught fire and was low in the water. The 5000 tonner was left smoking. Beaufighters flown by F/Lt Wainman and F/Lt Shulemson were both hit by flak and one of the latter's engines failed. Wainman's navigator, F/Lt Stoddart, had his flying suit and parachute ripped by flak. From post-war records the two MVs, namely *Fidelitas* of 5,740 tons and *Jersbek* of 2,804 tons, were damaged.[29]

Another of 404's ground staff, Sgt.M. Godin was repatriated after serviing overseas for almost five years. Meanwhile, at Dallachy in December 1944, plans were made for Canada House which was to be at one end of a dining room that had not been in use. There was co-operation from Capt Horn of the Canadian Forestry Corps unit near Dallachy and material was salvaged for the end of the dining hall to be partitioned off. Two men from the Forestry Corps volunteered to do the work in their own time. They were Corporal Guay and private Gavin, who finished the partition by 3 December ready for the Canadian Legion to furnish it.

Canada House was opened on 6 December furnished with chairs, chesterfields, writing tables and was provided with stationery, magazines, Canadian newspapers, radio, and a small billiards table and a table tennis table. The walls were decorated with pictures of Canadian scenes and the coats of arms of the Canadian provinces. Chocolates, soft drinks, etc. were available at a counter staffed by ladies from the local community and supervised by Flying Officer and Mrs. Henderson.

The last successful strike in 1944 for 404 Squadron, albeit tragic, took place on 9 December. F/Lt Wainman led nine Beaufighters accompanied by aircraft from Nos. 144 and 455 and with Mustangs from 315 Squadron. They were airborne by 12 noon for a strike to Utvaer and in position 6116N 0456E, sighted an unescorted ship. In the attack thirty hits with RPs were claimed and the vessel was left ablaze from bridge to stern following two explosions. Thirty minutes later it was reported beached but burning fiercely.

X/404 NV173, flown by F/O A.K. Cooper with navigator W/O C.F. Smith, was believed to have struck the mast of the ship as the port wing came off; the Beaufighter turned over onto its back, fell into the water and exploded; no survivors were seen. This had been the second operation for the crew and Cooper and Smith had been with 404 for less than a month. The ship was *Havda* of 678 tons.[30]

From 20 December 1944 there were some lighter moments for No. 404 Squadron; Canadians in the UK whether with an RCAF or RAF Squadron received parcels from home and in the case of those in 404, chocolate, sweets, etc. were provided for Christmas parcels given to about seventy-five children of Spey Bay School to be distributed at their Christmas party.

On 20 December the marriage took place of P/O J. Perry, DFC, to a Scottish lass from the Falkirk area. On Christmas Day the Squadron was released from 1100 hrs until 2359 hrs. There were two sittings for the traditional dinner served by the officers to other ranks.

In the afternoon most Canadians on the station visited Canada House, where they received a free issue of bars of chocolate, sweets and cigarettes. Later in the day many ground and aircrew gathered in the Flights' crew room for a few hours.

By the end of 1944, No. 404 Squadron was equipped with seventeen Beaufighters and had 599 personnel.

Albacore Operations

At the beginning of 1944, No. 415 Squadron still suffered the disadvantages of being divided into two flights, one of those with out-dated aircraft. This is reflected in the unit's operational records, which lack the cohesion and thoroughness this writer associates with RCAF records.

From the Albacore detachment at Manston on 20 January 1944, F/O D.C. Thomson was airborne at 2320 hrs in L/415 for a patrol to the Boulogne area. While flying off the French coast he sighted two ships five miles from Le Tourquet. They were steaming south-west and thought to be German destroyers.

Thomson released six 250 pound bombs against the leading vessel and three of them were seen to explode with large flashes, causing a fire. There was inaccurate flak with a heavy barrage from the second destroyer.

Fire and flames were seen emitted from the leading vessel for a considerable distance. F/O Thomson was subsequently awarded the DFC.

F/O Norman Chadwick with his navigator W/O A. Bernel were airborne from Docking at 0100 hrs in an Albacore on 22 February and an hour later were flying over enemy vessels at 3000 feet off Boulogne. He was unable to see any target but was homed to the ships by his navigator using ASV. Six bombs were released from 800 feet on the rear vessel and there was a huge yellow explosion resulting from a direct hit. The vessel was claimed as destroyed.

Wellington Operations

One of 415's Wellingtons was captained by S/Ldr M.V. Gibson who was airborne at 1759 hrs on 8 February from North Coates. This was for a "Gilbey" operation which would have been to illuminate an enemy convoy by releasing a series of flares; the strike aircraft would then attack.

In this case, the strike aircraft were Beaufighters. By 2017 hrs no sighting report had been received from S/Ldr Gibson and at 2230 hrs RAF station Coltishall reported the sighting of a dinghy. At 2250 hrs the Wellington was reported to have ditched in position 5250N 0209E which is just off the Norfolk coast. F/O G.S.L. Anderson was airborne from Docking at 2153 hrs on 14 February for a "Deadly patrol B." This was an anti-E-boat operation in co-operation with the Navy. For the Navy, German E-boats represented an adversary worthy of respect. They were built of metal, had a low profile, were powered by diesel engines, and were extremely fast. At night they were able to leave continental ports and harass Allied shipping off the east coast. The Royal Navy's MTBs compared unfavourably with the E-boats, having wooden hulls, and petrol as fuel and were many knots slower.[31]

Wellingtons could be used to locate and then indicate the position of the enemy by dropping flares. Wellingtons also worked independently of the Navy by releasing bombs from, say, 6000 ft. The bombs were designed to detonate in mid-air to provide a large shrapnel effect.

At 2258 hrs F/O Anderson located E-boats which were engaged by the Navy. Three or four E-boats were damaged by the Allies, whose casualties were reported as "light."

In February, Ken Ashfield, an aircraft captain with 415 Squadron was detached to North Coates with his Wellington crew and a ground crew to work with the Beaufighter strike Wing for another "Gilbey" operation. As Capt. Ashfield now adds:

The Wellington left an hour to two hours before the Beaufighters depending on the area to be radar searched, and the nine to twelve Beaufighters came out to a waiting line which they flew at 500 feet stepped altitudes. Directly we picked up a target, we called them into our position and gave them a time we would drop our first stick of twelve flares. We would then climb to 4000 feet and position ourselves between the land and the convoy allowing the Beaufighters to attack from seaward along the flare path.
We carried two sticks of twelve in the bomb bay and a further twelve in 3 feet high cardboard cylinders in the fuselage. Invariably, we had to make two runs for the late arrival, and sometimes three, which involved the sweating gunners in stripping open the containers and pushing the flares down the chute as quickly as possible. These detachments lasted two weeks to a month and we did several of them. After returning to Bircham Newton we resumed our anti-shipping patrols with bombs along the coast.

On 1 March 1944 visibility was reported as excellent, with moonlight and a moderate sea. P/O Ashfield was airborne from North Coates in Wellington HZ653 armed with 500 pound bombs. At 2210 hrs he was in position 5257N 0436E where a 5000-ton vessel was stationary having been attacked earlier that day. Ashfield released three 500 pound bombs from 3500 feet spaced at 80 feet. They had instant fuses and three explosions were seen with a direct hit by the third bomb on the ship, causing a huge fire and leaving the ship listing. This vessel must have been *Maasburg* of 6,415 tons which sank off Borkum, north-west of Texel and was credited to the 415 Squadron Wellington with Beaufighters from Nos. 143, 236, and 254 Squadrons.[32]

F/O R.H.Watt shared the credit in a "Gilbey operation" on 3 March with 254 Squadron Torbeaus. He was airborne from North Coates with thirty-six recce flares and at 2142 hrs located a merchant vessel escorted by three minesweepers. He signalled to base and when all the Torbeaus reported contact, F/O Watt released twenty-four flares. There was light and heavy flak but the Wellington returned to Docking. The merchantman *Diana* of 1,878 tons was sunk in this strike.[33]

No. 415's Albacore Flight at Manston

In March 1944, No. 415's Albacore flight was still operating from Manston. Norman Chadwick, who was flying M/415 with F/O Bartlett as navigator, gives this account of a sortie on the 16th:

Our normal procedure was to be controlled by radar from Dover, where they had a sea-sweeping scope, and an air-sweeping scope, and by plotting, could direct us to our target by instructing over VHF radio. We normally operated in total darkness, not in the moon period. If the vessels were moving, one could see the wakes from fluorescence in the water. On this particular occasion, we were directed to what was apparently several vessels, but they were stationary, and we could not see anything. Our on-board ASV radar was next to useless. We were near the limits of our patrol area, and running short of gas, so control decided we should not bring back our six 250 lb bombs with air-burst detonators, but jettison the bombs live on instructions, when by the plot, they thought we would be over vessels. We dropped the bombs as instructed, they exploded above the water, and the vessels started shooting at random. We missed by about half a mile, not too bad considering the distance from Dover, using two radars and a manual plotting table.

On the 23rd D/O D.C. Thomson, DFC, was airborne at 0028 hrs to be vectored by control to west of Berck. He sighted nine or ten vessels estimated at about 175 feet long and possibly minesweeper-trawlers with three smaller vessels. He attacked from 900 feet using six general-purpose 250 pound bombs. One direct hit was seen and the ship caught fire and continued burning for a few minutes. Flares were dropped but nothing more was seen.

The following night F/Lt R. Armstrong, RAF, was airborne at 0052 hrs but had to return with an engine unserviceable. He was airborne again from Manston 1½ hrs later and, while flying between Calais and Dunkirk, received a signal from base of an enemy convoy in the area. Later the convoy opened fire on the Albacore, and he sighted a large merchantman or tanker heavily escorted. It was attacked by diving the Albacore from 4000 to 1000 feet and releasing six 250 pound bombs. Two direct hits were claimed. The ship was the *Atlanta* of 4,404 tons which was credited as damaged by 415 Squadron off Gravelines.[34]

Another Albacore which was airborne that night to attack the same convoy suffered the loss of its navigator. P/O L.W.F. Rivers captained D/415 with navigator F/O A.F.G. Hughes.

The convoy was located and Rivers attacked two vessels which were only 40 yards apart by diving to 1200 feet and releasing six bombs. His aircraft was hit by flak and Hughes was seriously wounded. They returned to Manston but F/O Hughes died that day.

Patrols off the Dutch and French Coasts.

From North Coates on 20 April, Wellington L415 HZ653 was airborne on an armed recce. Captained by P/O Ken Ashfield, it was to patrol the convoy route off the Dutch coast. Ashfield sighted an enemy convoy of five merchantmen with three escort vessels steaming SSW at 8 knots. The ships fired green, yellow, red, and white parachute flares which lasted for five minutes. Five 500 pound bombs were released at 60 feet spacing. From Ken Ashfield's own modest account, one ship was severely damaged and left burning, while another was damaged. In fact, from the Command's record, a *sperrbrecher* No. 102 *Condor* of 889 tons was sunk, and a merchant vessel of 924 tons *Storfors* was damaged. P/O Ashfield was diverted on returning to Acklington touching down at 0430 hrs.[35]

On 6 May, Ashfield, while flying near the Dutch coast, had one engine on his Wellington HZ756 fail. He headed for home to Docking losing height all the way. As he continues:

> Over the Wash we picked up the DREM system of lights of Langham and proceeded around the circuit. On short final with the undercarriage down and a bit of flap, the other engine cut and we plopped down into a ploughed field with anti-invasion poles in it. By some miracle we didn't hit one, the undercarriage took the shock and came out of the top of the engine nacelles, nobody was hurt.

One of 415's Albacore pilots, F/O W.G. Brasnett, flew a successful sortie from Thorney Island on 24 May to the French coast. He was airborne at 0140 hrs and when north of Port En Bassen sighted some ships. He attacked from 2000 feet releasing five 250 pound bombs spaced at 40 feet. One bomb was seen exploding on what was believed to be a minesweeper. There was a large glow from the target seven minutes after the attack and the ship was claimed as either sunk or severely damaged. Brasnett's Albacore suffered considerable flak but was undamaged and he returned to Thorney Island. The vessel was a torpedo boat of 800 tons, *Grief*, which was sunk in Seine Bay.[36]

Final Operations for No. 415 Squadron with Coastal Command.

The operational procedure for 415's Albacores, according to Norman Chadwick, "was either to be on standby alert and scramble when instructed, or else to be on a mid-channel patrol, and hope something would venture out, and we would be on the spot, so to speak, to make an attack." On the night of 12 June,

> It was very dark, control was very busy, and we think they were routinely vectoring us back and forth without really checking on their radar. Time was approaching dawn, and I looked below and discovered we were flying over farmland.
> We immediately set course for base, and on later calculation, found that we had gradually been drifting overland for some time, and over some pretty heavily defended coastline! We came back over the sea close to Dunkerque, and had we flown directly over the port, there was a strong likelihood that we would have run into heavy flak while flying at low altitude and not very fast at 90-100 knots.

On 24 June F/O Chadwick with his navigator P/O Bernel were on a strike in Albacore L/415 off Calais. Seven to nine small vessels, probably German "E" or "R" boats were sighted in a V formation. Chadwick released six 250 pound bombs in a stick along one arm of the V formation and claimed as sunk two of the craft. Although small vessels, they remained a serious menace to shipping right up to the end of hostilities.

One of the last of 415's Wellington sorties in Coastal Command was flown by Ken Ashfield, who remarks:

On 7 June 1944 we started anti-E-boat patrols continually off Dieppe, Le Havre and Ostend. It was interesting as the Buzz bomb [V.1s] had started. On 4 July flying HZ635 we carried out a cross-over patrol off Dieppe, encountering Buzz bombs, also night fighters which we shook off, and later attacked seven E-boats, destroying one and damaging others.

Transfer of No. 415 Squadron to Bomber Command

The unit was informed that effective 12 July 1944 it was to be transferred from Coastal to Bomber Command, as was No. 8415 Servicing Echelon. From its current establishment of fifteen Albacores and ten Wellington XIIIs, it was to be re-equipped with twenty Halifax IIIs. The Albacore flight was renamed No. 119 Squadron and, from Norman Chadwick's log book, that was on 12 July.

The final Coastal Command operations for the unit were flown on 20 July with such as Albacore Y on smoke-laying but that aircraft was recalled. Wellingtons O, K, and N were flown on the same date by F/O Ashfield, F/O D.M.

Brotherhood, and F/O G.S.L. Anderson. They were on armed recces from north of Borkum to Dunkirk. Their armament included six 500 pound bombs and fourteen flares.

An entry in the operational record of what was 415 Squadron, dated 31 July, is from Eastmoor, Sutton-on-Forest, Yorkshire. There is a résumé by the Squadron commander J.G. McNeill of:

taking over an ex-Coastal Command Squadron on 15th I found myself in the unusual position of having on my strength three types of crews—Halifax, Wellington and Albacore—with the operations of the Halifax on Bomber, and the Coastal Command work of the Wellington and Albacore, overlapping. As Squadron Commander I also found myself having the ex Squadron Commander still on my strength.

References to Chapter 8
1. CCWR p.25
2. Ibid
3. Ibid
4. Ibid
5. Ibid
6. GüH para. 296
7. CCWR p.28
8. Ibid
9. CCWR p.22
10. Ibid
11. Ibid
12. Ibid
13. CCWR p.29
14. Ibid
15. Ibid
16. PJ p.178
17. CCWR p.29
18. WSC VI p.166
19. SWR III/2 p.131
20. SWR III/2 pp.129 and 131
21. WSC VI p.168
22. SWR III/2 p.137
23. CCWR p.26

24. CCWR p.25
25. Ibid
26. Ibid
26. Ibid
27. Ibid
28. Ibid
29. Ibid
30. CCWR p.26
31. From conversation with the Royal Navy's
    MTB crews, Felixstowe, May 1945
32. CCWR p.21
33. Ibid
34. Ibid
35. Ibid
36. Ibid

Chapter 9

Strikes Over Norway: January– May 1945

No. 404 Squadron at Dallachy

In January 1945 although it was obviously a matter of time before Germany would be defeated, Coastal Command aircraft operating over the North Sea off the Norwegian and Dutch coasts could expect to encounter serious opposition from both shore batteries, shipping and enemy fighters.

Even with fighter cover with such as Mustangs from 315 Squadron, sorties to Norway remained hazardous, and for formations of strike aircraft there was the natural hazard of rocks if flying at low level, and the mountains surrounding the fjords at higher altitudes. Many aircrew stated, nevertheless, that the weather was the worst enemy.

On 6 January 1945 the weather at Dallachy was mild but cloudy. Six aircraft from 404 were led by an American, F/Lt S.B. "Tex" Rossiter, on a Norge patrol accompanied by twenty aircraft from 144, 455, 315 and as ASR, a Warwick from No. 279 Squadron. Snow squalls precluded attacks on large ships which were sighted, but they were able to sink a lighter of 300 tons—MW151. On returning to base the weather had deteriorated and two aircraft landed at Milltown, another at Lossiemouth.[1]

Two days later, although there was hail and snow with a high wind, S/Ldr Christison led a formation of twenty-one aircraft including six from No. 404 Squadron on a Norge patrol. They sighted what was described as two merchantmen with a tug towing a large barge. There was fairly heavy and accurate flak, but two ships, the *Fusa* of 172 tons and *Trygg* of 28 tons, were sunk.[2]

S/Ldr Christison again led a formation of the Dallachy Wing on 10 January with aircraft from 144, 489, and 455 with eight from 404. He had also two Mosquito outriders from 333 Squadron ex-Banff, and two ASR Warwicks from 279 ex Frazerburgh. Fighter cover was provided by ten 315 Squadron Mustangs from Peterhead. Landfall was made at Lepso Island and Christison was advised of a target by a 333 Squadron outrider. A trawler was attacked but most of the strike Wing followed Christison against a merchant ship moving into a jetty at Haramoy Island. Both vessels were set on fire and the smaller one exploded. Two aircraft failed to return; one from 455, and one from 144 Squadron.

The following afternoon a strike was laid on to attack ships reported in Flekke fjord. They were supported by ten Mosquitoes from the Banff Wing as AA cover plus three more as strike aircraft. ASR aircraft were two Warwicks. When the formation was about to make landfall at Lister they were attacked by about nine enemy fighters, largely ME109s. No. 404's aircraft stayed in close formation and turned out to sea while the Mosquito fighters dealt with the enemy. Some of the enemy fighters attempted to attack the 404 formation but all returned to base. In the affray, 144 Squadron lost a Beaufighter, and one Mosquito from Banff was lost. A Warwick was last seen attempting to drop a lifeboat near the crashed Mosquito. The fighter escort had claimed three ME109s destroyed, one FW190 probable, and one ME109 damaged. These were apparently from an airfield at Lister.

The winter of 1944-1945 was cold, with snow certainly from East Anglia up to the Moray Firth in this writer's experience. No. 404 Squadron was released from operations on 17 January and F/O J.M. Cook who had returned from a course on Loran navigation gave a lecture to aircrew on that subject. At Spey Bay Hall in the evening there was a party for the Squadron and echelon personnel to which some senior Dallachy officers and the COs of 144, 455, and 489 Squadrons were invited. A small band provided music for dancing, and refreshments included turkey sandwiches, a rarity under wartime conditions. F/Lt Jackson, aided by Sgt.J.E. Maloney, was responsible for the general arrangements.

A strong east wind brought occasional snow, with enough for 2-3 inches to be on the ground, and 404 was released until 2359 hrs. A further 2-3 inches of snow fell during the night of the 20th, and the following day, 160 officers and men from 404 worked in three shifts clearing snow

from 1600 hrs. By 2300 hrs, with the aid of a snow-plough, half of the runway at Dallachy was clear. On 22 January the first shift began at 0900 hrs and finished clearing the main runway by noon. By the following day it was possible for three crews to take off on practice flights.

F/Lt H.L. "Howie" Wainman with his navigator, F/Lt J.R.E. "Uncle John" Stoddart, RAF, completed their first tour of operations in which they had flown forty-nine sorties including thirteen strikes. In January, 1944 they had spent forty-six hours in a dinghy after a successful ditching after their aircraft had been hit by flak and Stoddart's parachute had been pierced by fragments.

"The Airscrews," an RCAF concert party, boarded the wrong section of a train on 26 January and instead of performing in the hall at RAF Dallachy, found themselves at Elgin railway station rather than the nearest one to Dallachy—Spey Bay. The following evening after playing to a packed house at Dallachy, the concert party was invited to Canada House.

Snow continued to prevail along the east coast of Britain in the winter of 1944-45, and fuel supplies to RAF stations comprising coke of doubtful quality were limited. There was the anomaly for some aircrew to find it more comfortable in an aircraft than in one's billet! By 29 January No. 404 Squadron received enough fuel to light fires in the offices; it was another cold day and the weather was such that a formation of thirty-nine aircraft, with F/O Savard leading nine from 404, had to return to base.

In a summary for January 1945 the Squadron gives the daily average of 17.7 aircraft on charge with 12.6 serviceability. Strikes on the 6th, 8th, and 9th were considered successful. "Canada's Weekly" of 5 January had published an article, "Canadians in Coastal Command" which included a photograph of one of 404's English navigators, F/Lt C. Clayton Corder, CGM, Croix de Guerre, from Grays, Essex.

Black Friday

At Dallachy on 9 February 1945, the day was clear and warm and the Wing was ordered to patrol between Sandoy and Bremanger.[3] The force of forty-six aircraft was led by W/Cmdr C.G. Milson, DSO, DFC*, the CO of No. 455 (RAAF) Squadron. The wing comprised eleven Beaufighters from 455, nine from 144, one from 489 (RNZAF), eleven from 404, twelve 65 Squadron Mustangs and two ASR Warwicks from Frazerburgh. Leading those from 404 was S/Ldr Christison in U-NE339.

F/Lt Pat Flynn, DFC, now one of the few current survivors from that mission, in writing to the author gives this account:

I was flying "T" NE686 leading the port "vic" behind S/Ldr Christison. My No. 2 (port) was Roger Savard, who subsequently was shot down. He survived as a POW. Bill Jackson was on my starboard side. He too, was shot down that day. We crossed the coast south of the Norde fjord with orders to await the report of the two outriders.

They had been sent to scout the anchorages and the targets of the enemy and to report back to the strike wing. Mistakenly, they reported no targets in the expected anchorages.

The basic plan of the strike wing was to commence the attack from the land to seaward, but as the main force proceeded over Norde fjord, there was flak from ships, and shore batteries opened fire. This resulted in a change of plans. The main force had to make a large "S" turn to reposition for the attack. This prolonged manoeuvre, between the steep sides of the fjord, resulted in a very ineffective strike. The results were disastrous!

The extra time required to reorganise into position, gave the German fighters from Bergen (less than forty miles away from the attack), sufficient time to join the affray, and in fact, they were amidst the attacking force. The effective German fighters and the well-prepared flak sites were to blame for most of the casualties. The Germans had previously set ashore, in good positions, anti-aircraft guns. This gave them an added advantage.

My navigator, F/O "Mike" Michael, during a steep turn on the attack into the fjord, shouted that my No. 2 Rog. Savard had slipped underneath our aircraft. His flying position was due to the steepness of the fjord. I straightened out the airplane and observed Roger going down in smoke before hitting the ice. He and his navigator "Middy" were pulled out of the water by a German flak crew. F/O Middleton reached shore but did not live. Roger, although wounded, became a POW for the remainder of the war with Germany.

After straightening out my aircraft to avoid Savard, the only target available was a Z-33 destroyer which was tied up to the shore. I attacked with my cannons and explosions were seen on the bridge, and although from near bow-on, two of my rockets did strike and I was credited with two hits.

Climbing up the side of the fjord, I saw two FW190s attacking a Beaufighter. I fired at the nearest FW190 which then broke off and headed downward. I then turned my guns on the other and opened fire but with inconclusive results. By then I had reached the top of the north shore of the fjord; I broke downward and flew out to sea. I observed several encounters between German fighters and Beaus in the distance. Five of the eleven Beaufighters of 404 Squadron returned to base at Dallachy.

The disastrous results of "Black Friday" were, in my opinion, a direct result of the outriders' report. Stating that no ships were in the target area resulted in the planes flying the extra circuit. Any surprise we may have had was lost and gave time for the enemy fighters to join the affray. If the attack had gone as planned, i.e. taking off, flying out below radar, crossing the coast and climbing, then attacking seaward, we could have completed our mission and been on our way back to base leaving the German fighters insufficient time to muster and join the action.

No. 404's official record confirms much of what Pat Flynn has written; of the nine Kriegsmarine vessels, only three were anchored away from the sides of the fjord, thus six ships would have presented very difficult targets even without the shore batteries and the arrival of enemy fighters; the steep sides of the fjord alone provided excellent protection.

Nevertheless, Christison, F/Lt Stewart, and F/O Nelson attacked a heavily armed escort vessel claiming a total of seven hits with RPs. Those in 404 Squadron had been unaware of the ships on the other side of the fjord or the batteries on a hill, and flew through an intense box barrage.

Ten or twelve FW190s were reported, and the Beaufighter "rescued" by Flynn must have been NE825 flown by F/Lt Stewart, one of those to return but severely damaged. F/O Nelson in NT916 also saw two FW190s on the tail of a Beaufighter; he attacked and shot one FW190 down.

The second FW190 turned towards Nelson but his navigator scored hits with his machine gun on the enemy which broke off the engagement. S/Ldr Christison was also pursued but got away from the three FW190s. The Mustang fighters claimed two FW190s destroyed and one damaged. No. 404 Squadron believed that at least four of the ships were damaged. Of the aircraft failing to return, most crashed in the mountains, one made a belly landing on the ice, and another ditched.

I happened to be on detachment at Dallachy on 9 February and was on the airfield near our Wellington when the surviving Beaufighters flew back from Norway. They landed like a flight of wounded ducks; a number just pancaking. The scene was like a Hollywood film set—but this was real. Later in the Mess I saw some of the Beaufighter aircrew with their clothing truly in ribbons. As was the way in Coastal Command, one always saw aircrew with a task worse than one's own. In the Mess about that time, I heard broadcast Elgar's "Chanson de Matin," music ever to recall in my mind 404 Squadron's "Black Friday." In studying many operational records, I have seen only one other squadron to suffer such a loss of 54%; again, it was a Canadian squadron, No. 407 and on a shipping strike.

No. 144 Squadron lost one Beaufighter; 455, two; and No. 65 Squadron, one Mustang. Exceptionally, there is now a memorial in Norway with the names of those aircrew who were lost in this strike and one at Bogmoor in Scotland commemorating the Squadrons of the Dallachy Wing. The latter is on the Fochabers to Spey road where once was the main gate to RAF Dallachy. It is built of stone, including some from Australia, Canada, New Zealand, and Ireland and was unveiled in July 1992.

Rover Patrols

On 26 February three of 404's Beaufighters were airborne just after 1800 hrs for lone Rover patrols. F/O Wallace in NV291 made his landfall at Mandal before flying to position 5813N 0832E and then heading on reciprocal. On his VHF radio he was given the position of an enemy convoy by F/O Coyne and sighted a merchant ship with three escorts in position 5800N 0720E. There was intense flak but he attacked with RPs. He then escorted L/455 which was in distress to base. F/O Moe, who had made landfall near the Naze, and F/O Coyne also attacked the same convoy, the latter claiming four hits above the waterline between the stack and stern of the merchantman. The Command's record credits No. 404 Squadron with damaging *Rogn*, a merchant ship of 835 tons.[4]

For No. 404 Squadron the 8th March was mild but cloudy when nine of their Beaufighters were on a strike with forty other aircraft against six ships reported to be in Vindapol, Midgulen. Eight of 404's

aircraft led by S/Ldr Schoales in NE669 were armed with RPs while O/404 with cannon acted as an outrider. Landfall was made at Sandoy from where they flew inland directed by outriders. The six ships were located and included two merchantmen and a car ferry. Six hits with eight possibles using RPs were claimed by five from 404 on the ferry; two more of their Beaufighters claimed four hits on one of the naval vessels with four possible hits below the waterline. Credited to the Wing as sunk in this strike were *Phoenicia* (4,124 tons) and *Heimdal* (978 tons).[5]

L/404 NV427 flown by F/O R.C. Ridge with his RAF navigator P/O P. McCartney was believed to have attacked the larger merchant ship and was seen flying up the fjord with an engine on fire. L/404 failed to return to base, as also one from 455 Squadron. The escorting Mustangs reported sighting aircraft wreckage and two dinghies partly inflated but with no aircrew.

The Dallachy Wing made another successful strike on 24 March. This was to Egersund harbour with ten aircraft from 144, eight from 455, four from 489, and six of 404's Beaufighters. They were escorted by fourteen Mustangs from No. 65 Squadron and two 269 Squadron ASR Warwicks. The attack was made in sequence with 404 leading from SSW to north against three merchantmen and three escort vessels. F/O Flynn who was in NV177 recalls:

I was flying the Beaufighter Z/404. My position as No. 2 (port), deputy leader to S/Ldr Christison. Jack Coyne was flying as No. 3 (starboard). We attacked from the sea and the leading "vic" was hit by the radar-controlled flak. S/Ldr Christison was shot down. Jack Coyne lost his starboard engine and S/Ldr Christison turned the attack over to me. I called the attack and proceeded to fire on the escort vessel with cannons and rockets. The vessel sank! I called for a port break and observed that Chris was ditching his aircraft. S/Ldr Christison had previously reported that his navigator F/Lt Toon was wounded. Chris did a perfect ditching; I watched and saw only one person escape from the Beaufighter and then saw him in a rubber dinghy. I circled in company with a Mustang aircraft and called on my radio for an ASR Warwick to drop an airborne lifeboat.

My navigator dropped a smoke float and we circled for about five to ten minutes. My starboard engine was losing oil pressure and I informed the Mustang of my problem which remained circling as I headed for base. I later shut down my starboard engine and returned to base on one engine.

This was a classic thirty-first trip for S/Ldr Christison. He had been recommended to be "tour-expired" by F/Lt Beacok, the medical officer. F/Lt Beacock did not greet the returning crews of fighters. This was the first and only time he did not do so in two and a half years of Squadron duty.

This was the last strike of 404 Squadron on Beaufighters as we subsequently converted to Mosquitoes. We lost one Beaufighter from 144 Squadron, one from 455(RAAF) Squadron and two from 404, S/Ldr Christison, DFC* and F/O Algoe.

In R/404 NV428 with Christison was navigator F/Lt F.J. Toon, DFC; in U/404 NE339 with F/O R. Aljoe was navigator F/Sgt C.E. Orser. Recorded as sunk by the Beaufighters of the Dallachy wing were *Thetis* (2,788 tons) and *Sarp* (1,116 tons).[6]

No. 404 Squadron Converts to Mosquito Aircraft

The unit commenced a move from Dallachy to Banff on 3 April with three civil lorries being loaded at 0830 hrs and all available station motor transport (MT) assisting. By 2300 hrs there were still two loads to be moved. By the 6th the rear party had arrived at 404's new base but some echelon personnel remained at Dallachy to service Beaufighters which had not been reallocated.

Nine new Mosquito aircraft arrived at Banff on the afternoon of 9 April which proved to be a fine sunny day, and 404's scribe adds: "If this is spring, we shall not mind spending a summer in NE Scotland."

The following day S/Ldr L.H. Jenkins from the Historical section of the RCAF Overseas HQ visited 404 Squadron to discuss the preparation of Forms 540 and 541 (operational records) with the Intelligence Officer and adjutant. A party was laid on by the aircrews who acted as hosts to some of the ground staff in the aircrew canteen. This was in appreciation of the serviceability record maintained for the aircraft.

By the 18th of April conversion to Mosquito aircraft was almost completed and was achieved three days later despite the lack of dual-control machines.

No. 404 Squadron's First Mosquito Operation

This distinction was achieved by F/O D.A. Catrane with navigator F/Lt A.E. Foord on 22 April in a Mark VI H/404 RF851. It was armed with cannon and machine guns and was airborne at 0926 hrs. F/O Catrane had been detailed for a Norge shipping recce and made landfall at Utsire. He crossed inland and covered all anchorages to the Naze before continuing easterly to Christiansand harbour and the airbase at Ksevik. Anchored about 200 feet offshore at Ksevik were a B&V138 and a HE115. The B&V138 was attacked and emitted smoke 500 feet high, the flying-boat being destroyed. They set course for base from Okso lighthouse. During April, the squadron's daily average was twelve Mosquito aircraft with a serviceability of eight.

On 2 May about eighty U-boat commanders were handed instructions under operation *Regenbogen* at Flensburg. The code-word *Regenbogen* related to the scuttling of U-boats, but those able to dive were to sail to Norway.[7]

On that same day S/Ldr H.W. Jones led four of 404's Mosquito aircraft as part of the fighter cover in the Banff strike wing against U-boats moving northwards through the Kattagat. The strike force comprised thirty-five Mosquitoes, twenty-four Mustangs, and two ASR Warwicks.

According to the U-boat diary, such aircraft were able to hunt over the whole of the Kattagat and into bays and harbours, destroying twenty-one U-boats between the 2nd and 6th of May.[8]

One of those ill-fated U-boats was U-2359 which was sunk by the Banff Wing, together with a minesweeper M293 of 750 tons; damaged was a type XXIII U-boat.[9]

The official naval historian Capt Roskill pays one of his welcome tributes to Coastal Command and writes of the danger of being shot down by German fighters on Norge sorties.[10] Losses of aircraft from all Commands during January to May 1945 against enemy shipping at sea were 131 set against 129 vessels sunk and 41 damaged.[11]

No. 404 Squadron's final success was on 4 May when the CO, W/Cmdr Pierce, led seven of their aircraft, two serving as fighter cover and five as part of the strike force with thirty-four Mosquitoes of the Banff wing supported by eighteen Mustangs and three ASR Warwicks to the Kiel area of the Kattagat. At position 5645N 1055E an escort vessel steaming at 10 knots was attacked by two of 404's aircraft, scoring twelve hits with RPs above the waterline. The Wing headed south to 5619N 1120E where a convoy of seven ships in line astern were all attacked. Six were considered to have been severely damaged but smoke prevented a detailed report. The Command's record credits it with sinking the 3,750 ton *Wolfgang* L.M. Russ and damaging two other merchantmen of 998 tons and 3,540 tons respectively—*Gunther Russ* and *Angemos*.[12]

V.E. Day— Victory in Europe

For No. 404 Squadron at RAF Banff, the skies were cloudy with rain. A church parade was held at 0900 hrs in No. 2 hangar after which the Squadron was released for the day, although there were varied celebrations throughout the station.

On 10 May, 404 Squadron launched "HMCS Buffalo," their "repat ship" in a tank near Station HQ and it was christened by W/Cmdr Pierce. A bonfire was lit by the Station CO, G/Capt the Hon. Max Aitken, DSO, DFC. Effigies of Hitler and Goering were burned. Verey pistols were fired and the night concluded with the toasting of G/Capt Max Aitken into the water tank.

F/O Coyne, DFC, on 12 May led five of 404's Mosquitoes as escort to a naval force taking VIPs. This might have been ships including HMS *Devonshire* which was taking the Crown Prince Olav of Norway with the Norwegian Government from Rosyth to Oslo.[13]

F/O Savard phoned the Squadron from Bournemouth the following day. He had been shot down on 9 February and became a POW. On 18 May he returned together with their former CO, W/Cmdr Charles "Chuck" Willis, DFC. The latter, also an ex-POW had been shot down in LZ297 on 30 March 1944. There was a station party the following day during which W/Cmdr Willis was presented with a large cup engraved with the signatures of the aircrews.

On 22 May an early Met. Flight was undertaken by F/O Bundy to check if conditions were suitable for two Norge Squadron Spitfires to take off from Dyce, Aberdeen, for Stavanger. The Spitfires were subsequently led by S/Ldr Schoales, DFC with a 333 Squadron Mosquito. After refuelling at Sloa, Stavanger, they took off for Gardeermoen near Oslo, and S/Ldr Scoales returned to base two days later.

No. 404 Squadron was officially disbanded on 25 May 1945 when all personnel were technically posted to RAF station, Banff. Documents etc which they record as being shipped were: two Squadron scrap books, the original Squadron badge, two rolls of honour, a scroll of awards, and copies of forms Nos. 540, and 541 (operational records).

No. 404 was the only RCAF Squadron with which I came in contact during the war; first at RAF Dyce in 1942 when it

was equipped with Blenheims, and again in February 1945 with its "Black Friday" at Dallachy, although I was aware of many Canadians serving in RAF Squadrons.

References to Chapter 9

1. CCWR p.26
2. Ibid
3. JH p.382
4. CCWR p.26
5. CCWR p.27
6. Ibid
7. GüH para.485
8. Ibid
9. CCWR pp 11,16, 27
10. SWR III/2 p.280
11. Ibid
12. CCWR p.28
13. SWR III/2 p.263

Chapter 10

The Flying-Boat Squadrons:1945

No. 422 Squadron at Pembroke Dock

During the night of 18 January and the following morning there were gales and a rough sea. 422's aircraft survived the conditions but four Sunderlands were lost from the other two Squadrons at Pembroke Dock. Two sank at their moorings and the other two broke loose from their moorings and were driven ashore. Gusts of up to 90 mph were reported.

There was snow on 24 January and a snowball fight between No. 461 (RAAF) Squadron and 422 Squadron personnel. The following day a snowball fight was led by two of the squadron commanders, W/Cmdr Lywood and W/Cmdr Hampshire from 228 and 461, respectively. A severe blizzard followed the next afternoon and there was a shortage of fuel on the station. The winter of 1944-45 proved to be bad over much of Britain.

On 1 February F/Lt R. Haines, DFC, of 422 Squadron was married to a nurse, Doris M. Murphy, a Canadian girl who was with Queen Alexandra's Nursing Service, the ceremony taking place at St. John's church.

The 422 Squadron Canadians introduced their custom of square dances and a "regular hoe down was held featuring square dances, reels etc for an entire evening." The first of such events was held at St. Patrick's church hall on 2 February and attended by about fifty couples. Band instruments had been acquired and it was hoped that 422 would form its own band. This was prompted by 422's pianist, Sgt Leckie of the armament section.

On 22 February, 422's first full-time padre arrived from Canada. He was Padre Braine who, in October 1989, as the Rev. Dr. Braine, gave a short address to the 422 Squadron Association at the RCAF memorial in Stanley Park, British Columbia. No. 422's publication, *Short Slip*, came out on the 16th and was sold at 1d (0.002) per copy, but the issue cost £2 ($4) and there were 550 on 422's strength.

Canada House was opened at Pembroke Dock on 5 March with tea served from 1430-1800 hrs. No. 422's CO had ten airmen who worked voluntarily for four weeks redecorating rooms, and they were hosts to local civilian supporters and a few of the senior station officers and ladies, in all, about fifty in number.

Canada House was located in the rear portion of Trinity Church in Meyrick street and was formerly known as Trinity Hall. An all-ranks dance was held on

March 7 in the Llanion gymnasium, which was decorated with a large coloured map of Canada showing nine provinces and the positions of the principal cities illuminated by small electric lights. Flags, balloons, and coloured lights were also used. Guests included the Station Commander, G/Capt Boland and Mrs. Boland, W/Cmdr and Mrs. Grennan. Bouquets were presented to those ladies and corsages to all the other ladies. The CO's of the Squadrons then at Pembroke Dock, Nos. 228, 422, and 461, also attended. Refreshments were served in several sittings. Dancing was from 1930 to 2300 hrs and the event was considered to be one of the most successful of those organised by 422 Squadron.

Anti-U-Boat Successes

News came of the award of the DFC to a Flight Commander, S/Ldr J.W. Langmuir, following attacks on U-boats while operating with Eastern Air Command. This, coupled with a series of sightings by 422 in the United Kingdom, "raised Squadron morale to a high point." The AOC-in-C, Coastal Command, Air Chief Marshal Sir Sholto Douglas visited Pembroke Dock on 12 March with the AOC of 19 Group to consider not only aircraft and operations but also the billeting of personnel.

No. 422's Intelligence Officer, F/Lt Creeper, became responsible for bringing the Squadron's *Line Book* up-to-date and for further entries. A committe of station officers arranged an all-ranks dance to be held in the Llanion gymnasium with proceeds from the dance to be put in a fund to provide a stained-glass window commemorating the various squadrons which operated from Pembroke Dock.

Post-war, circa 1994, the stained glass window was transferred to the RAF Museum at Hendon, to the consternation of many former aircrew.

Following news of the posting of Pembroke Dock's Station Commander, G/Capt Boland, a party was arranged in his honour on 30 March. He was presented with a framed copy of 422's Squadron badge. G/Capt Boland responded with reference to his initial misgivings on having RAF, RAAF, and RCAF Squadrons on his station but stated that it had proved a success. A further presentation to G/Capt Boland was an autographed portrait of 422's mascot, the spaniel Straddle from F/Lt Detwiller.

Loran Exercise

F/O Denroche was airborne from Pembroke Dock at 1348 hrs in Sunderland ML884 Z/422 for what was intended as a routine Loran navigational exercise. At 1536 hrs he was flying at 1000 feet in position 5412N 0505W when white smoke was sighted three miles away. Denroche headed towards it but at one mile the smoke ceased. The Sunderland circled the area and a sonobuoy was dropped which gave a positive signal. A report to control was transmitted and a pattern of sonobuoys was completed which indicated the presence of a U-boat with engine revs of 90 rpm. The smoke, which would have been from a schnorkel, reappeared and on course 125°. Denroche headed for an attack but the smoke disappeared.

At 1735 hrs a periscope was sighted in position 5409N 0505W and Denroche attempted an attack, but his DCs hung up. Half an hour later three destroyers commenced a search and a DC was dropped by the Sunderland to indicate the

U-boat's former position. After another ten minutes the schnorkel and periscope were sighted ½ mile from the destroyers. Denroche again attempted an attack at 2149 hrs and, later, the Sunderland was ordered back to base.

Three days later, F/Lt Cook captained NJ173 W/422 and after being airborne for nine hours, his front gunner reported a partly submerged conning tower. Cook dived down from 1000 feet but the U-boat had submerged. The Sunderland circled and dropped a pattern of sonobuoys in position 5248N 0515W. Signals were received; one ordering the Sunderland back to base, another from escort vessels asking for details of the situation, and the position of the U-boat when it submerged was given to the escorts.

On March, two more Sunderlands from 422 Squadron had similar experiences to Cook and Denroche. They were flown by F/Lt Giles and F/Lt Fallis. F/Lt Giles made an attack in position 5404N 0451W but his DCs overshot. F/Lt Fallis co-operated with escort vessels and witnessed them attacking with hedgehogs. Post-war records give U-1302 as having been sunk in this area on 7 March by the frigates HMCS *La Hulloise*, *Strathadam*, and *Thetford Mines*. Exceptionally, the frigates were able to identify the U-boat from the log books which formed part of the debris which surfaced after their attacks.[1]

On 8 March F/Lt Berryman was on a Loran exercise in Sunderland ML884 when at 1408 hrs smoke was sighted on the surface in position 5535N 0637W five miles away. An attack was made releasing two DCs. A pattern of sonobuoys was dropped and contact with the U-boat maintained, but the Sunderlands were ordered back to Mount Batten.

Social Activities at Pembroke Dock

G/Capt W.H. Hutton succeeded G/Capt Boland as Station Commander of Pembroke Dock on 3 April. He had earlier served at the Air Ministry and with No. 210 Squadron. On the 4th, an RCAF show played to capacity and the cast was later received in the Aircrew Mess for what they considered to be the best meal they had enjoyed since coming from Canada. Subsequently the cast was entertained in the Senior NCOs' Mess.

An impromptu musical evening was arranged in the Officers' Mess with F/O Barry Moore at the piano. F/O Alex Platsko, cornet; F/Lt Detwiller, saxophone; F/Lt Jim Nesbitt, guitar; F/Lt Doc Stewart, viola. 422's CO, W/Cmdr Sumner, with Capt Hervieux led the singing.

A bugle band was in process of formation under F/O Platsko with nine bugles, ten side drums, one tenor, and one bass drum already acquired.

The ball season was opened by G/Capt Hutton pitching and W/Cmdr Sumner batting the first ball. The RCAF Bournemouth band provided music in advance of the game, while the Salvation Army auxiliary service sold Pepsi Cola and peanuts during the game.

No. 422 Squadron Receives Mark V Sunderlands

When the Squadron received its first Mark Vs on 7 April, W/Cmdr Sumner and S/Ldr Langmuir made test flights. Their report was "the boat is really a swell job and are most enthusiastic of the performance."

The complete change to Mark Vs was expected to be complete within two months.

S/Ldr Langmuir was detailed for a special recce on 5 April. After being airborne at 0255 hrs in NJ173 he contacted Fore 27 of the Royal Navy. This was at 0745 hrs in position 4548N 0151W. A half hour later he was off Point de la Coubre and flying at 1200 ft. There was AA fire from shore batteries which proved to be inaccurate. At 1100 hrs the Sunderland was off La Pallice which had been used as a U-boat base. Langmuir flew close to the shore and took photographs from 1500 feet despite heavy flak from both shore batteries and guard ships. The Sunderland returned fire on the ships but itself suffered no damage.

On 6 May, plans were being made for V-Day after an announcement by the BBC that the Prime Minister would be speaking to the nation on the 10th, although before that time, V-Day was to be announced. No. 422's record for 7 May stated that the Prime Minister would speak to the nation at 1500 hrs and the King at 2100 hrs. VE-Day was to be the 8 May.

VE-Day at Pembroke Dock

A voluntary thanksgiving service was held in the Station church which was well attended. In the afternoon 422 played against a team from HMCS *Ville de Quebec*. In the evening there were two large all-ranks dances held in Llanion barracks, one in the gymnasium, the other in the Airmen's Mess. Both were filled to capacity. F/Lt Detwiller, F/Lt Nesbitt, F/O Platsko, and F/O Moore provided the music in the Airmen's Mess when it was found that no others were available. They were thanked by the Station Commander.

W/O2 Frederick, No. 422's discipline Officer, wrote the poem, "The Saga of 422 Squadron," which gives a true reflection of the unit's service under three commanders.

There was a fatal accident on 12 May. A flight engineer, F/O N.C. Hunt, was on duty at the slipway watching aircraft when a lorry on reconstruction work backed into him, knocking him down and running over his legs and lower body. F/O Hunt was taken to the RAF Hospital at Haverfordwest but died of shock from his injuries the following morning.

There were two thanksgiving services supported by 422 Squadron which were held on 13 May at Pembroke Castle and in the square at Pembroke Dock. All three fighting services were represented in addition to civilian organisations.

No. 422 Squadron's Anniversary

Although not the true date, 422 elected to celebrate its anniversary on 24 May. The unit assembled at Llanion barracks before the salute was taken by Air Marshal Johnson in the square at Pembroke Dock. It was attended by the Mayor and Town Clerk with the Town Council. In the afternoon a baseball game was opened by Air Marshal Johnson pitching, W/Cmdr Sumner catching, and G/Capt Hutton, the Station Commander, batting. The other team was provided by 423 Squadron from Castle Archdale. A dance was held in the evening at Llanion barracks with music by the RCAF Streamliners.

On 31 May there was a meeting for all Canadian personnel at Pembroke Dock in the Station church. W/Cmdr Sumner informed them that effective 1 June 1945 No. 422 Squadron would cease to be in Coastal Command but would be with

Transport Command. Plans were announced for personnel to be relieved from some duties for them to attend classes in a variety of subjects. The Squadron had been formed in April 1942; the "anniversary celebrations" were effectively a farewell to Coastal Command.

The last operational sortie in Coastal Command for the Squadron was flown by F/Lt Stevens in Z/422 ML884 on 30 May for a convoy escort and an eleven-hour flight. He met the convoy at position 4813N 0720W.

The 3 June marked the first official week-end off for personnel at Pembroke Dock and some took the opportunity of visiting surrounding areas. On the 5th all aircraft were grounded following the transfer of 422 to Transport Command. A party from Transport Command headed by G/Capt Franklin conferred with 422 Squadron although no definite policy had been decided. A stag party for the three Squadrons at Pembroke Dock, 228, 422, and 461 was held in the Officers' Mess which just preceded the postings of some from 228 and 461 on 12 June. They flew to their new bases at Castle Archdale and Mount Batten respectively three days later. There were some problems with billeting when personnel from 201 Squadron returned to Pembroke Dock.

No. 422 had some engineers posted to No. 426 Squadron while some officers and NCOs were posted to Torquay pending repatriation prior to service in the Pacific or European theatres. By now, 422 recorded:

PD is but a ghost of its former self. Empty halls and ante-rooms where one's footsteps echo back...as we pass through rooms looking for remaining bodies. A few Sunderlands tug gently at their moorings impatient to be on

their way again. The remaining Squadron, 422 wanders about the camp,...trying to keep busy.

No. 422's sister Squadron, No. 423, was to serve its final months with Coastal Command in Northern Ireland and continued in 1945 with anti-submarine warfare.

Attacks on U-Boats by No. 423 Squadron

F/O A.R. Pinder was airborne from Castle Archdale in Sunderland ML746 on 11 January and, after flying for six hours, his front gunner sighted smoke at sea level. As Pinder approached, the smoke disappeared to leave a patch of foam. An attack was attempted, but the bomb aimer was unable to locate the patch of foam. The Sunderland turned to port and using the low-level bomb-sight, two 250 pound depth charges were released from 200 feet and spaced at 80 feet. The crew was later reproved for not releasing all their DCs. Perhaps also they reflected on the delay which resulted from using the bombsight instead of the captain releasing the DCs in a diving attack.

Four days later H/423 was airborne at 0708 hrs captained by F/O R.M. Bartlett. When in position 5318N 0510W at 1612 hrs, a swirl was sighted. Bartlett was then flying at 1700 feet and reduced height in a spiral dive to 200 feet when the low level bomb sight was used to release six Torpex DCs spaced at 55 feet. Only a large patch on the sea, 200 feet by 300 feet, was seen, apparently of oil.

Sunderland NJ183 crashed at 1230 hrs on 12 February and the entire crew of five officers and six NCOs was killed. This was near Dromore road, three miles east of Irvinstown. The funeral of the crew was held four days later at Irvinstown parish church. It was attended by station personnel from Castle Archdale and also local citizens in addition to those from 423 Squadron. A number of local businesses closed as a mark of respect.

Events at Castle Archdale

At the beginning of March 1945, G/Capt Gordon succeeded G/Capt Oulton as Station Commander, and in No. 423 Squadron, W/Cmdr S.R. McMilland succeeded W/Cmdr P.J. Grant who was posted to the Canadian Overseas HQ. No. 201 Squadron, RAF, also based at Castle Archdale, challenged the Canadian Squadron to an evening of games; there was some doubt as to who won. In April, 423 held a party in Kesh, with some going by cycling, others by walking. There was dancing with partners from the WAAF and from civilian life. The adjutant queries in his report, who, if any one, called for the Service Police (Sps) to the party.

At the beginning of May, the Orderly Room and discip. staff were entertained in Irvinstown at McKenna's Bar and "Ma" Bothwell's dining room; the hosts being various leaders and the Squadron adjutant.

Following VE-Day, No. 423 Squadron, like other units, carried on with patrols and escort missions, and on 13 May, three of 423's Sunderlands undertook operational sorties. One of these, captained by J.F. Magor, took photographs of surrendered U-boats. By the end of May, 423 still had seven Mark III Sunderlands on charge and a total personnel of 416. They were warned of an intended move to Transport Command which ultimately came into effect on 6 June 1945. The Squadron had completed a total of 1,392 operational

sorties during its service with Coastal Command.

During 423's final days at Castle Archdale there were a number of parties, including a farewell one for G/Capt Gordon who was posted to the Azores and to welcome his successor as Station Commander, G/Capt Burgess. Sporting events included games against the US Marines and the US Navy.

On 17 July a party of officers, NCOs and airmen took part in the lining of the route followed by the King and Queen with Princess Elizabeth who were visiting Londonderry.

Repatriation and Postings to Bassingbourn

Redundant aircrew from 423 Squadron, seventy-five officers and thirty-five NCOs, left on 25 July for RAF Snaith pending repatriation, and an advance party of forty-eight other ranks with F/Lt J.D. Matheson and W/O Hamilton left for Bassingbourn. The main party for Bassingbourn, and thus Transport Command, followed on 5 August. Their journey was via Irvinstown, Larne, and Stranraer with an overnight stop at a transit camp in Larne.

At Bassingbourn on 15 August 1945 at 0001 hrs, the station Tannoy announced the end of the Japanese phase of World War II. Duties for personnel still prevailed; many would be required in transporting ex-POWs and others from various parts of the world. For just such a task, 423's first Liberator (surely a most apt name), was airborne on 21 August with S/Ldr R.F. Milne, S/Ldr Sattler, and F/O Longly for the proverbial "circuits and bumps." On 28 August, aircrew who intended flying were given the choice of Liberators or

Dakotas but at the end of the month they were informed that 423 Squadron was to be disbanded on 3 and 4 September. Those remaining with Transport Command went to Down Ampney or Snaith and ground crew to Aldermaston.

The Canso Squadron

The year 1945 began for No. 162 Squadron at Reykjavik with four aircraft on operations, but on the social side, officers paid courtesy visits to the NCOs' Mess and in the evening some officers visited the Royal Navy. Later there was a formal dance at Camp Maple Leaf with music provided by an American orchestra. Despite winds of up to 97 mph none of the Cansos was damaged. On 20 January the temperature at Reykjavik dropped to 1° F. Pipes were frozen and there was a breakdown of the generator. Another problem was a difference of opinion between flying control and aircraft captains.

On 6 February Liberators Nos. 571 and 572 arrived with nearly two tons of mail, the first for 162 Squadron since 22 December. On 16 February eighteen ground crew who had spent a year in Iceland took off in Liberator 3704 for Canada, leave, and repatriation. In the following days there was much snow with high winds, and many personnel spent their time digging out their huts. There was drifting and some roads were blocked and the runways were unserviceable. By the end of the month, the sky cleared and eleven aircraft were airborne on operations, training, or testing.

During March, the Squadron achieved 1600 hrs flying, and when cloud base was apparently down to the deck, F/Lt D.J. Orr's aircraft sent a signal "taxying home."

He landed at sea and taxied for an hour to reach Reykjavik.

F/O L.O. Martin with his crew of eight was airborne in Canso 11066 at 0545 hrs on 3 April. Weather over his patrol area, north-east of the Faeroes, was considered good with a ceiling of 1000 to 1500 feet. F/O Martin failed to return. The only signal from Canso 11066 was five minutes after take-off. A thorough search was made but no wreckage or dinghies were sighted.

Later it was thought that the Canso had been shot down by a German Met. Aircraft from Norway, which were known to operate in that area. On 5 May a ship recovered the bodies of F/O C.G. Solmundson and F/Lt A.G. Thomson, confirmed by their identity discs. This was west of north, eighteen miles from Enars Rock, Westmann Isles. They were subsequently committed to the sea.

On 20 April a signal from Goose Bay reported that Canso 11076 flown by P/O B. Lahey was missing. Two days later it was reported that all nine of the Canso crew were alive but two were badly burned; they were P/O Lahey and P/O W.R. Baggett.

No. 162's engineer officer's report for 1 April mentions the one problem which occurred with P&W Wasp engines, i.e., ignition associated with sparking plugs and harness. Additionally 162 reports magneto trouble with "carboning of points and burning."

The Squadron heard on 7 May that all U-boats had been recalled to bases by Admiral Dönitz and that the BBC had reported that peace terms were being signed at General Eisenhower's headquarters. W/Cmdr Sully announced that all Squadron personnel would be confined to camp for 48 hours to prevent any actions which would result in breaches of discipline. The following day there was a muster parade in the station theatre when nominal rolls were called. Winston Churchill's address to the nation was relayed and this was followed by a short Squadron service conducted by 162's padre. On the 9th, 162 was again confined to barracks following a report of some damage having been caused in Reykjavik and there was a wish for the RCAF to be free from criticism.

F/O Clarje while on patrol on 11 May sighted a 740-ton U-boat which was fully-surfaced. Signals were exchanged in a mixture of German, French, and English. The following day F/Lt J.K. Guttormson located a ditched Sunderland flying-boat about 65 miles south of the Faeroes. It was from No. 330 (Norge) Squadron then based at Sullom Voe. Guttormson circled and guided a fishing vessel from the Faeroes which was able to rescue all of the Sunderland crew.

A thanksgiving service was held in the state cathedral, Reykjavik, on 13 May for all British troops in Iceland. No. 162 Squadron was represented by about forty personnel headed by their padre, S/Ldr F.A. Lawrence. On 26 May a signal was received from Coastal Command HQ that, with effect from 1 June, No. 162 Squadron RCAF was to be withdrawn from the line and that arrangements for the unit's return to Canada would be through the RCAF Overseas HQ.

No. 162 Squadron Moves from Reykjavik to RCAF Sydney, Nova Scotia

The Squadron continued with anti-submarine patrols, convoy escorts, and a full training programme until 7 June. The first of the unit's aircraft to take off

for Goose Bay was Canso 11023 captained by S/Ldr J.C. Wade who was airborne from Reykjavik at 0001 hrs on 7 June. He touched down again after a flight of 11 hrs 40 mins. The following day he flew from Goose Bay to Sydney, taking 4 hrs. 25 mins. In addition to a crew of nine, there were three ground crew as passengers. The last aircraft recorded for this transit flight was Canso 11074 captained by F/O R.J. Mills who was airborne shortly after S/Ldr Wade from Reykjavik. A notable exception was Canso 11081 captained by F/O G.J. Davis with navigator F/O Ron Wales and W/AG P/O D. Johnson which flew via Prestwick down to Northolt, in the London area, en route to the Azores.

No. 162 Squadron had undertaken 2100 operational sorties totalling 22,856 flying hours. They had lost six aircraft on operations with thirty-four aircrew. They had sunk five U-boats, shared the sinking of one other U-boat, and damaged a seventh. The many awards won by 162 Squadron personnel included a VC.

In a Station and Squadron Commanders' Conference held at Coastal Command HQ on 20 December 1944 the following was stated (apparently from a No. 18 Group report):

> Wick with 162 which was a Squadron of Canadian Cansos from Iceland did exceptional work. They had a magnificent system of training and still more training... every pilot went through a syllabus...and then back to operations again. At one time, if we had good operational intelligence, we said: "Go on, we'll put 162 right in the middle."

No. 162 Squadron was disbanded at Sydney, Nova Scotia, on 7 August 1945.

Chapter 10 References

1. JS p.292

APPENDIX A

U-Boats Sunk or Damaged in Attacks Involving Canadian Squadrons in Coastal Command

Date	U-Boat	Captain	Sqdrn	Aircraft	Pilot	Position	Remarks
13.5.43	U-456	KL A.Teichert	423	Sun.W6008	F/Lt J.Musgrave	48°37'N 22°39'W	S C/E HX237 2XDCs & HM Ships
4.8.43	U-489	OL Schandt	423	Sun.DD859	F/O A.Bishop	61°11'N 14°38'W	S 6xDCs Sun. shot down
7.9.43	U-669	OL Köhl	407	Wel.HF115	P/O E.O'Donnell	45°36'N 10°13'W	S 5xDCs
19.9.43	U-341	OL D.Epp	10	Lib.587	F/Lt R.Fisher	58°40'N 25°30'W	S C/E ONS 18 6xDCs
8.10.43	U-610	KL V.Freyburg	423	Sun.DD863	F/Lt A.Russell	55°45'N 24°33'W	S C/E SC143 4xDCs
17.10.43	U-470	unknown	422	Sun.JM712	F/Lt P.Sargent	59°50'N 30°30'W	D C/E ON206 2xDCs Sun. shot down
22.12.43	U-1062	OL K .Albrecht	404	Bfr.NE198	P/O K.Miller	57°59'N 06°52'E	D RPs & cannon
11.2.44	U-283	OL G.Ney	407	Wel.MP578	F/O P.Heron	60°45'N 12°50'W	S 6xDCs
10.3.44	U-625	OL S.Straub	422	Sun.EK591	F/Lt S. Butler	52°35'N 20°19'W	S 6xDCs
17.4.44	U-342	OL Hossenfelder	162	Can.9767	F/O Cooke	60°23'N 29°20'W	S 3xDCs
24.4.44	U-672	unknown	423	Sun.DD862	F/Lt F.Fellows	50°36'N 18°36'W	D 6xDCs
4.5.44	U-846	OL E.Hashagen	407	Wel.HF134	F/O L.Bateman	46°04'N 09°20'W	S 6xDCs
24.5.44	U-921	OL A.Werner	423	Sun.DD111	F/Lt R. Nesbitt	63°34'N 03°02'W	D 5xDCs
3.6.44	U-477	OL K.Jensen	162	Can.	F/Lt McBride	63°59'N 01°37'E	S 4xDCs
7.6.44	U-989	KL H. von Roitberg	407	Wel.HF149	S/L W.Farrell	*************	D +224 sqdrn Well.F.T.
11.6.44	U-980	KL H.Dahms	162	Can.9842	F/Lt Sherman	63°07'N 00°26'E	S 4xDCs
13.6.44	U-715	KL H.Röttger	162	Can.9846	W/C Chapman	62°45'N 02°59'W	S 4xDCs Canso shot down
20.6.44	U-971	OL W.Zeplien	407	Wel.HF134	F/O F.Foster	*************	D 6xDCs
24.6.44	U-1225	OL Sauerberg	162	Can.9754	F/L D.Hornell	63°00'N 00°50'W	S Canso shot down
30.6.44	U-478	OL R.Rademacher	162	Can.9841	F/Lt McBride	63°27'N 00°50'W	S +86 sqdrn
4.8.44	U-300	OL F. Hein	162	Can.9841	F/O Marshall	62°25'N 14°30'W	D
30.10.44	U-1061	OL O. Hinrichs	407	Wel. NB839	F/O J.Neelin	61°43'N 03°42'E	D 6xDCs
30.12.44	U-772	KL E.Rademacher	407	Wel.NB855	S/L C.Taylor	50°05'N 02°31'W	S 6xDCs schnorkel U-boat
2.5.45	U-2359	Bischoff	404	Mos.	*************	57°29'N 11°24'E	S with Banff Wing
2.5.45	U-?	unknown	404	Mos.	*************	*************	D with Banff Wing

APPENDIX B

Ships Sunk or Damaged in Strikes Involving Canadian Squadrons in Coastal Command

Date	Ship	Tonnage	Sunk or Damaged	Sqdrn	Aircraft	Postion	Leader or Pilot
13.10.41	*Hamm* 109-dredger	100	S	407	Hudson	Terschelling	S/Ldr Lynham
1.11.41	*Braheholm* MV	5676	D	407	Hudson	Borkum	S/Ldr Lewis
11.11.41	*Vios* IV Aux. 1JM96	190	S	407	Hudson	Ijmuiden	W/Cmdr Styles
19.11.41	*Mars* MV	699	D	404	Blenheim	Norway	S/Ldr McHardy
9.12.41	*Madrid* MV	8777	S	407	Hudson +217 Bfrs.	Ijmuiden	W/Cmdr Styles
5.1.42	*Cornelia Maersk* MV	1892	S	407	Hudson	Ijmuiden	S/Ldr Anderson
4.5.42	*Sizilien* MV	4647	S	407	Hudson	Terschelling	W/Cmdr Brown
8.5.42	*Ruth* MV	3726	S	407	Hudson	Texel	W/Cmdr Brown
8.5.42	*Burgundia* MV	1668	D	407	Hudson	Emden	W/Cmdr Brown
8.5.42	*Namdo* MV	2860	D	407	Hudson	Texel	W/Cmdr Brown
15.5.42	*Selje* MV	6698	S	407	Hudson	Terschelling	F/Lt Christie
16.5.42	*Madeleine Louise* VP2002	464	S	407	Hudson	Terschelling	F/Lt Christie
26.5.42	*Uranus* MV	935	D	404	Blenheim	Christiansand	S/Ldr McHardy
29.5.42	*Niels R. Finsen* MV	1850	S	407	Hudson	Ameland	F/Lt R.M.Christie
30.5.42	*Varmdo* MV	2956	S	407	Hudson	Ameland	P/O O'Connell & F/S Howe
12.6.42	*Senta* MV	1497	S	407	Hudson	53°55'N 07°34'E	P/O Taylor
18.1.43	*Algeria* MV	1619	S	407	Hudson +321	Terschelling	F/Lt de le Haye
14.4.43	*Tom* MV	2092	D	415	Hampden	Borkum	P/O K.G. Walthen ?
15.4.43	*Borga* MV	4821	S	415	Hampden	Ameland	F/O P.N. Harris
18.5.43	*Ernst V.Briesen* VP1106	408	S	415	Hampden	Ameland	unknown
18.5.43	M.345 M/sweeper	750	S	415	Hampden	Ameland	Sgt W.G. Pilkington?
17.7.43	F.D.61 UJl705	548	S	404	Bfr +235	60°45'N 04°40'E	S/Ldr Gatward
30.9.43	*Sanet Swithun* MV	1376	S	404	Bfr	62°11'N 04°11'E	W/Cmdr Willis

Date	Ship	Tonnage	Sunk or Damaged	Sqdrn	Aircraft	Postion	Leader or Pilot
14.1.44	*Wittekind*	4029	S	404	Bfr +144	Naze	W/Cmdr Willis
14.1.44	*Entre Rios* MV	5179	S	404	Bfr +144	Naze	F/O Thomsett, F/O O'Keefe
14.1.44	*Maurita*	1569	D	404	Bfr +144	Naze	F/O Thomsett, F/O O'Keefe
20.1.44	*Emsland* MV	5170	S	404	Bfr +144	62°07'N 05°50'E	S/Ldr Gatward
1.2.44	KUJ16 UJ1702	500	S	404	Bfr +144	N. of Stadtlandet	S/Ldr Gatward
1.2.44	*Valentia* MV	3096	S	404	Bfr +144	N. of Stadtlandet	S/Ldr Gatward
1.3.44	*Maasburg* MV	6415	S	415	Well. +Bfrs 143,254,236	52°57'N 04°36'E	P/O Ashfield
5.3.44	*Diana* MV	1878	S	415	Well. +Bfrs 254	off Gravelines	F/O R.H.Watt
23.3.44	*Atlanta* MV	4404	D	415	Albacore	Gravelines	F/Lt Armstrong
30.3.44	*Monte Rosa* liner	13882	D	404	Bfrs +144	Utsire	W/Cmdr Willis
7.4.44	*Cornouaille* MV	3324	D	404	Bfrs +144	Stadtlandet	F/O O'Keefe
20.4.44	*Condor* Sperr.102	889	S	415	Wellington	Dutch coast	P/O Ashfield
20.4.44	*Storfors* MV	924	D	415	Well.H2653	Dutch coast	
24.4.44	*Grief* t.b.	800	S	415	Albacore	Seine Bay	F/O W.G. Brasnett
6.6.44	Z-32 destroyer	3664	D	404	Bfrs +144 +248 Mos.	Belle Isle	F/O S.Shulemson
6.6.44	Z-24 destroyer	3664	D	404	Bfrs +144 +248 Mos.	Belle Isle	
6.6.44	ZH-1 destroyer	3000	D	404	Bfrs +144 +248 Mos.	Belle Isle	
30.6.44	FV 439 UJ1408	530	S	404	Bfrs+235 +248 Mos.	Biscay	W/Cmdr Gatward
6.7.44	*Ernst Brocklemann*	1900	D	404	Brs +144,455	53°04'N 07°14'E	Led by 455 sqdrn
6.7.44	*Stadt Riga*	3002	S	404	Bfrs+144,455	53°04'N 07°14'E	
8.7.44	*Tannhauser*	3200	S	404	Bfrs +144,236,254	53°03'N 07°45'E	W/Cmdr Gatward

Date	Ship	Tonnage	Sunk or Damaged	Sqdrn	Aircraft	Postion	Leader or Pilot
8.7.44	*Sif*	1437	S	404	Bfrs +144,236,254	53°03'N 07°45'E	
8.7.44	*Miranda*	736	S	404	Bfrs +144,236,254	53°03'N 07°45'E	
8.7.44	M.264	750	S	404	Bfrs +144,236,254	53°03'N 07°45'E	
8.7.44	ASR boat 555	58	S	404	Bfrs +144,236,254	53°03'N 07°45'E	W/Cmdr Gatward
18.7.44	R.139	90	S	404	Bfrs +144	Frisian Is.	S/Ldr J.A. Hanway
21.7.44	*Orient* MV	4160	S	404	Bfrs +144	Frisian Is.	S/Ldr Schoales
8.8.44	M.366 minesweeper	750	S	404	Bfrs +236	Noirmoutier	W/Cmdr Gatward
8.8.44	M.367 minesweeper	750	S	404	Bfrs +236	Noirmoutier	
8.8.44	M428 minesweeper	750	S	404	Bfrs +236	Noirmoutier	
8.8.44	M438 minesweeper	750	S	404	Bfrs +236	Noirmoutier	
12.8.44	*Saveland* Sperrbecher	7087	S	404	Bfrs+236, Mos.248,235	Ile de Re & La Pallice	S/Ldr Schoales led 404
12.8.44	*Germania* VP410	427	S	404	Bfrs+236, Mos.248,235	Ile de Re & La Pallice	
12.8.44	M.370 minesweepers	750	S	404	Bfrs+236, Mos.248,235	Ile de Re & La Pallice	
12.8.44	*Marie Therese* M.4204	288	S	404	Bfrs+236, Mos.248,235	Ile de Re & La Pallice	
13.8.44	*Schwannheim* sperrbecher	5339	S	404	Bfrs +236	Royan	S/Ldr Hanway led 404
13.8.44	*Magdeburg* sperrbecher	6128	S	404	Bfrs +236	Royan	
14.8.44	*Schwerzes Meer* MV	3371	S	404	Bfrs +236	Verdon	W/Cmdr Gatward
14.8.44	*Le Leroux*	50	S	404	Bfrs +236	45°28'N 01°02'W	
20.8.44	*August Bosch*	401	S	404	Bfrs +236,254	Biscay	unknown
20.8.44	*Jean Marthe* M.4214	156	S	404	Bfrs +236,254	Biscay	

194

Date	Ship	Tonnage	Sunk or Damaged	Sqdrn	Aircraft	Postion	Leader or Pilot
24.8.44	Z24 destroyer	3664	S	404	Bfrs +236	Gironde estuary	S/Ldr Tacon
24.8.44	T24 destroyer	1780	S	404	Bfrs +236	Gironde estuary	
14.9.44	*Sulldorf* VP1608	264	S	404	Bfrs +144	Hombersund	S/Ldr Schoales
14.9.44	*Iris* MV	3323	D	404	+Mos 235,248	Hombersund	
19.9.44	*Lynx* MV	1367	S	404	Bfrs +144	Askvoll	W/Cmdr Gadd Led Wing
19.9.44	*Tyrifjord* MV	3080	S	404	+Mos 235	Askvoll	S/Ldr Schoales Led 404
21.9.44	*Vangsness* MV	191	S	404	Bfrs +235 Mos	Lister	S/Ldr Rodgers (144)
21.9.44	*Hygia* MV	104	S	404	Bfrs +144 Mos	Lister	S/Ldr Schoales (404)
21.9.44	fishing vessel	75	S	404	Bfrs +144	Lister	
9.10.44	*Rudolf Ooldendorff* MV	1953	S	404	Bfrs +144	58°40'N 05°27'E	W/Cmdr Pierce
9.10.44	*Sarp* MV	1116	S	404	Bfrs +144	58°40'N 05°27'E	
15.10.44	*Inga Johanne* MV	1202	S	404	Bfrs +144	Christiansand	S/Ldr Christison
15.10.44	*Mosel* VP1605	426	S	404	Bfrs +144 +Mos. 235,248	Christiansand	S/Ldr Maurice (248)
21.10.44	*Eckenheim* MV	1923	S	404	Bfrs +144,455	Haugesund Hbr	F/O Boileau (404)
21.10.44	*Vestra*	1422	S	404	+Mos. 235,248	Haugesund Hbr	
8.11.44	*Aquila* MV	3530	S	404	Bfrs +144,455 +Mos. 333	Midgulenfjord	
8.11.44	*Helga Ferdinand* MV	2356	S	404	Bfrs +144,455 +Mos. 333	Midgulenfjord	
8.11.44	*Framnaes*	307	D	404	Bfrs +144,455 +Mos. 333	Midgulenfjord	
27.11.44	*Jersbek* MV	2804	D	404	Bfrs +489	62°25'N 06°03'E	F/Lt Shulemson
27.11.44	*Fidelitas*	5740	D	404	Bfrs +489	62°25'N 06°03'E	
9.12.44	*Havda* MV	678	S	404	Bfrs +144,455	61°16'N 04°56'E	F/Lt Wainman

Appendix

Date	Ship	Tonnage	Sunk or Damaged	Sqdrn	Aircraft	Postion	Leader or Pilot
6.1.45	MW151 lighter	300	S	404	Bfrs +455	Norway	F/Lt S.B. Rossiter
8.1.45	*Fuse* MV	172	S	404	Bfrs +455,144	Norway	S/Ldr Christison
8.1.45	*Trygg* fishing vessel	28	S	404	Bfrs +455,144	Norway	
26.2.45	*Rogn* MV	835	D	404	Bfrs	58°00'N 07°30'E	F/O Koyne
8.3.45	*Phoenicia* MV	4124	D	404	Bfrs + 144,455,489	Vindapol	S/Ldr Schoales
8.3.45	*Heimdal* MV	978	D	404	Bfrs + 144,455,489	Vindapol	
24.3.45	*Thetis* MV	2788	S	404	Bfrs + 144,455,489	Egersund Hbr	S/Ldr Christison
24.3.45	*Sarp* MV	1116	S	404	Bfrs + 144,455,489		
2.5.45	M.293 minesweeper	750	S	404	Mos. +143,235	Kattagat	S/Ldr H.W. Jones
4.5.45	*Wolfgang L.M. Russ* MV	3750	S	404	Mos.+143, 235,248,333	Kattagat	
4.5.45	*Gunther Russ* MV	998	D	404	Mos.+143, 235,248,333		
4.5.45	*Angamos* MV	3540	D	404	Mos.+143, 235,248,333		

N.B. The following variations are given by Kim Abbott in "Gathering of Demons":

30.11.41 *Ester* 1250 tons sunk and *Svolder* 3243 tons damaged by 407 Sqdrn rather than by 86 Sqdrn off Borkum.

9.12.41 A ship taking survivors from *Madrid* was probably damaged by P/O Cooper of 407 sqdrn; *Madrid* presumed hit by 217 sqdrn.

10.1.42 *Turbiegen* probably by P/O Cooper off Den Helder.

APPENDIX C

Representative Data of Aircraft Operated by Canadian Squadrons in Coastal Command

Aircraft	Mark	Engines	Wing Span	Length	Height	Wing Area	Wing Loading	Weight Empty	Weight Loaded	Speed Max.	Speed Cruising	Endurance
Albacore	I	Taurus 1085 hp or 1130 hp	50'	39'9½"	15'3"	623 sq.ft	17lb/sq.ft	7200 lb	10,365 lb	159 mph	113 mph	
Beaufighter	X	2x Hercules 1670 hp	57'10"	41'8"	15'10"	503 sq. ft.	50lb/sq.ft	15600 lb	25,200 lb	303 mph	180 kts	4½ hrs
Blenheim	IV	2x Mercury 920 hp	56'4"	42'7"	9'10"	569 sq.ft.	31lb/sq.ft		14,400 lb	256 mph	150 kts	6 hrs
Canso		2xWasp 1200 hp	104'	63'10"	20'2"	1400 sq.ft	24lb/sq.ft	20900 lb	33,970 lb	179 mph	100 kts	14 hrs
Hampden		2x Pegasus 1000 hp	69'2"	53'7"	14'11"	668 sq.ft	28 lb/sq.ft	11,780 lb	18,765 lb	254 mph	142 kts	
Hudson	V	2xWasp 1200 hp	65'6"	44'4"	11'10½"	551 sq.ft	34lb/sq.ft	12,810 lb	18,500 lb	260 mph	130 kts	6 hrs
Liberator	VI	4xWasp 1200 hp	110'	67'1"	17'11"	1048 sq.ft	59lb/sq.ft	37,000 lb	62,000 lb	270 mph	125 kts (Mk V)	15½ hrs
Sunderland	III	4x Pegasus 1030 hp	112'9"	85'4"	32'10½"	1487 sq.ft	39lb/sq.ft	33,000lb	58,000 lb	205 mph	125 kts	11.9 hrs
Wellington	XIV	2x Hercules	86'2"	64'7"	17'5"	840 sq.ft	35lb/sq.ft	18,556 lb	29,000 lb	255 mph	140 kts	10 hrs

References: RAF Ip.412; RAF IIp.375; RAF IIIp.408; OT (RAF aircraft) pp.134,140,168,295,390,453; CFS (Hudson profile)p.176; OT (FAA aircraft)p.153

APPENDIX D

Squadron Codes

No. 10 PB (1939-42); UK (1942)

No. 162 GK (1942); DZ (allotted)

No. 404 EE (1941); "2" (1944); EO (1944)

No. 407 RR (1941-43); "1"; C1 (1943-45)

No. 413 QL (1941-42)

No. 415 GX (1941); NH (1943-44)

No. 422 DG; "2"

No. 432 AB (1942);"3"; YI (1944-45)

Bibliography

Abbott, Kim. *Gathering of Demons*. Inkerman House: Perth, Ont., 1987.

Air Historical Section. *RCAF Logbook, Silver Jubilee of the RCAF*. Ottawa, 1949.

Boeschoten, L/Col G.Van. *Swordfish: The Story of 415 Squadron*. Greenwood N.S.,1982.

Bowyer, M.J.F., and J.D.R. Rawlings. *Squadron Codes 1937-56* Cambridge: Patrick Stephens, 1979.

Churchill, Winston S. *The Second World War*. Vols 1-6. London: Cassell, 1948-54.

Craven, W.F., and J.L. Cate. *Europe: Torch to Pointblank,* Washington: University of Chicago Press, 1983.

Cremer, L/Cmdr Peter. *U-333*. London: Bodley Head, 1984.

Crowther, J.G., and R.Whiddington. *Science at War*. HMSO, 1947.

Cunningham, Adml of the Fleet, Viscount of Hyndhope. *A Sailor's Odyssey*. London: Hutchinson, 1951.

Douglas, W.A.B. *The Official History of the R.C.A.F.* Vol. 2. Toronto: University of Toronto Press, 1986.

Greenhous, Brereton, S.J. Harris, W.C. Johnson and W.G.P. Rawling. *The Official History of the R.C.A.F.* Vol.3. Toronto: University of Toronto Press, 1994.

Halley, James J. *The Squadrons of the RAF and Commonwealth, 1918-1988*. Air Britain, 1988.

Hendrie, Andrew. *Seek and Strike: The Lockheed Hudson Aircraft in WWII*. London: William Kimber, 1983.

_____. *Flying Cats: The Consolidated Catalina Aircraft in WWII*. Shrewsbury: Airlife Publishing Ltd, 1988.

_____. *Short Sunderland Aircraft in World War II*. Shrewsbury: Airlife Publishing Ltd., 1994.

Herlin, Hans. *Verdamter Atlantik*. München:Wilhelm Heyne Verlag, 1985.

Herrington, John. *Air War Against Germany and Italy 1939-1943*. Canberra:Australian War Memorial, 1954.

_____. *Air Power Over Europe, 1944-1945*. Canberra: Australian War Memorial, 1963.

Hessler, Günter. *The U-boat War in the Atlantic*. London: H.M.S.O., 1992.

Jones, H.A. *The War in the Air*. Vol. 2. Oxford: Oxford University Press, 1934.

Joubert, ACM Sir Philip. *Birds & Fishes: The Story of Coastal Command*. London: Hutchinson, 1960.

Keegan, John. *The Times Atlas of the Second World War*. London, The Times 1989.

Kostenuk S., and J. Griffin. *R.C.A.F. Squadrons and Aircraft.* Toronto: A.H. Hakkert Ltd., 1977.

Midlebrook, Martin. *Convoy: The Battle for Convoys SC122 and HX229.* London: A. Lane, 1976.

Morison, Samuel E. *The Battle of the Atlantic, Sept.1939-May 1943.* Boston: Little, Brown, 1975.

_____. *The Atlantic Battle Won, May 1943-May 1945.* Boston: Little, Brown, 1984.

Peyton-Ward, Capt D.V. *Coastal Command's War Record, 1939-1945.* London, 1957.

Raleigh, Walter. *The War in the Air.* Oxford: Oxford University Press, 1922

Rawlings, John D.R. *Coastal Support and Special Squadrons.* London: Jane's, 1982.

Richards, Denis. *The Fight Against Odds* (RAF Vol.1). London: H.M.S.O., 1953.

Richards, Denis, and Hilary St.J. Saunders. *The Fight Avails* (RAF Vol.2). London: H.M.S.O., 1954.

Roskill, Capt S.W. RN. *The War at Sea.* Vols 1-3. London: H.M.S.O., 1954-1961.

Rohwer, Jurgen. *Axis Submarine Successes, 1939-1945.* Annapolis: US Naval Institute Press, 1983.

Saunders, Hilary St.J. *The Fight is Won* (RAF Vol.3). London: H.M.S.O., 1954.

Schull, Joseph. *The Far Distant Ships.* Annapolis: US Naval Institute Press, 1987.

Shores, Christopher F. *Lockheed Hudson Marks I-VI.* Leatherhead Profile Publications, 1973.

Thetford, Owen. *Aircraft of the RAF since 1918.* London: Putnam, 1979.

_____. *British Naval Aircraft since 1912.* London: Putnam, 1991.

Washington Naval History Division. *United States Submarine Losses in WW2.* Washington: Naval History Division, Office of the Chief of Naval Operations, 1963.

Operational Records On Microfilm:

No.162 Squadron Reels C12259 and C12260

No.404 Squadron Reel C12269

No.407 Squadron Reels C12273 and C12274

No.413 Squadron Reel C12283

No.415 Squadron Reel C12285

No.422 Squadron Reel C12295

No.423 Squadron Reel C12296

Glossary and Abbreviations

AA	Anti-aircraft	F/O	Flying Officer
ABC	Andrew B. Cunningham, Admiral of the Fleet, Viscount Hyndhope	F/Sgt	Flight Sergeant
		FTR	Failed to Return (of aircraft)
A/Cmdre	Air Commodore	GEE	Code name for a navigational system using electromagnetic wave pulses from ground stations giving blips on a CRT which were used in conjunction with a special chart.
ACHQ	Area Combined Headquaters		
ACM	Air Chief Marshal		
A/F/Lt	Acting Flight Lieutenant		
AH	Andrew Hendrie		
AHQ	Area Headquarters	GOC-in-C	General Officer Commanding-in-Chief
AHS	Air Historical Section (Canadian)	GR	General Reconnaissance
Aldis lamp	A lamp used to transmit messages in Morse code by operating a mirror and sighting through a fixed telescopic sight.	GüH	Gunter Hessler
		HAJ	H.A. Jones
		HE	High Explosive
AM	Air Marshal	Hedgehog	Anti-submarine device used by the Royal Navy
AOC	Air Officer Commanding		
APU	Auxiliary Power Unit	HH	Hans Herlin (German historian)
A/S	Anti-submarine	HMS	His Majesty's Ship
ASR	Air-Sea-Rescue	HMAS	His Majesty's Australian Ship
ASV	Aircraft-to-Surface-Vessel Equipment which transmitted electromagnetic waves which would be reflected back by vessels to produced a "blip" on the screen of a cathode ray tube(CRT).	HMCS	His Majesty's Canadian Ship
		HS	Hilary St. George Saunders (RAF historian)
		IFF	Identification Friend or Foe. An automatic transmitter in aircraft for its identification which could also be used for homing others.
ATA	Air Transport Auxiliary		
AWM	Australian War Memorial		
C&C	Craven & Cate (American historians)	JH	John Herrington (Australian historian)
		JK	John Keegan (British historian)
CCWR	Coastal Command's War Record 1939-1945	JR	Jurgen Rohwer (German historian)
		JS	Joseph Schull (Canadian historian)
CFS	Christopher S. Shores	KA	Kim Abbott
C-in-C	Commander-in-Chief	KIA	Killed in Action
CLA	Creeping Line Ahead. A navigational search method.	LCT	Landing Craft-Tank
		LORAN	Long-Range-Navigation. A system using signals from four ground stations
CO	Commanding Officer		
Cross-Over-Patrol	A navigational search method.	Mae West	A life-jacket which could be inflated by mouth or by a CO2 bottle
CRT	Cathode Ray Tube	MID	Mention In Dispatches
DC	Depth Charge	ML	Motor launch
D/F	Direction Finding	MM	Martin Middlebrook
DFC	Distinguished Flying Cross	MTB	Motor Torpedo Boat
DR	Dead Reckoning (navigation)	MU	Maintenance Unit
E/A	Enemy Aircraft	MV	Merchant Vessel
ENSA	Entertainments National Service Association	OL	*Oberleutnant zur See*
		OPS	Operational Sorties
ETA	Estimated Time of Arrival	OT	Owen Thetford
FAA	Fleet Air Arm	OTU	Operational Training Unit
FC	*Flying Cats*	PC	Peter Cremer, L/Cmdr (Capt of U-333)
F/Cmdr	Flight Commander	PJ	ACM Sir Philip Joubert de la Ferté
FK	*Fregattenkapitan* (Commander)	PLE	Prudent Limit of Endurance
F/Lt	Flight Lieutenant	P/O	Pilot Officer

PRU	Photo-Reconnaissance-Unit
RAAF	Royal Australian Air Force
Radar	American term applied to equipment such as the British ASV
RAF	Royal Air Force
RCAF	Royal Canadian Air Force
RNAF	Royal Norwegian Air Force
RNethNAS	Royal Netherlands Naval Air Service
RNZAF	Royal New Zealand Air Force
RP	Rocket projectile
R/T	Radio Telephony
SAP	Semi-armour-piercing
Schnorkel	Tubes extending above the surface from a U-boat enabling it to run on Diesel engines while submerged.
SEM	Samuel Eliot Morison (American naval historian)
Sgt	Sergeant
S/Ldr	Squadron Leader
Sonobuoy	A device released from aircraft which converted sound waves to an electromagnetic signal received in aircraft to detect U-boats.
Sperrbrecher	A German-controlled ship which was heavily armed against aircraft
S&S	*Seek and Strike*
SS	*Short Sunderland Aircraft in World War II*
Sqdrn	Squadron
ss	Steamship
SWR	S.W. Roskill, Capt RN (official naval historian)
u/s	unserviceable
USN	United States Navy
USSL	United States Submarine Losses in WWII
W/Cmdr	Wing Commander
W/O	Warrant Officer
W/op	Wireless Operator
Wop/AG	Wireless operator/Air Gunner
WR	Walter Raleigh (British historian)
WSC	Sir Winston Spencer Churchill
W/T	Wireless Telegraphy

Index